The Run-Up to the

PUNCH BOWL

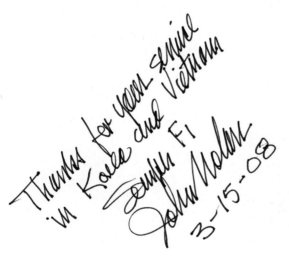

Thanks for your service
in Korea and Vietnam

Semper Fi
John Molan
3-15-08

ACCLAIM FOR

THE RUN-UP TO THE PUNCH BOWL

"Great book! John Nolan has written a magnificent account of the Marines in action during the Korean War. It is a story about the Marine spirit and ethos. Every American should read this with pride in the Corps of Marines."

General Anthony C. Zinni, USMC (Ret.)

"It's a wonderful book. The writing is superb; it flows, it's moving, highly descriptive and strikes just the right tone—neither laconic nor emotional. Every Marine should read it."

Haynes Johnson, Journalist, Author

"This is a book about Marines, ordinary Americans who under unimaginable pressures do the extraordinary day after day. You will laugh. You will cry. And after reading John Nolan's memoir, you will have a far more profound understanding of the barbarity of war."

Mark Shields, Columnist; Commentator, *The NewsHour*

"John Nolan's timeless story of men in battle during the heavy fighting in Korea, 1951, bears all the marks of a classic—good men, hard men, decent men in brutal, near—constant combat. What they accomplished in those battles would be reflected later in their lives—those who kept them—as many would become highly successful in the Marine Corps and in other careers."

Colonel John W. Ripley, USMC (Ret.) (*The Bridge at Dong Ha*)

The Run-Up to the
PUNCH BOWL

A Memoir of the Korean War, 1951

JOHN NOLAN

To order additional copies of this book, contact:
Xlibris Corporation
1-888-795-4274
www.Xlibris.com
Orders@Xlibris.com
30448

For Joan

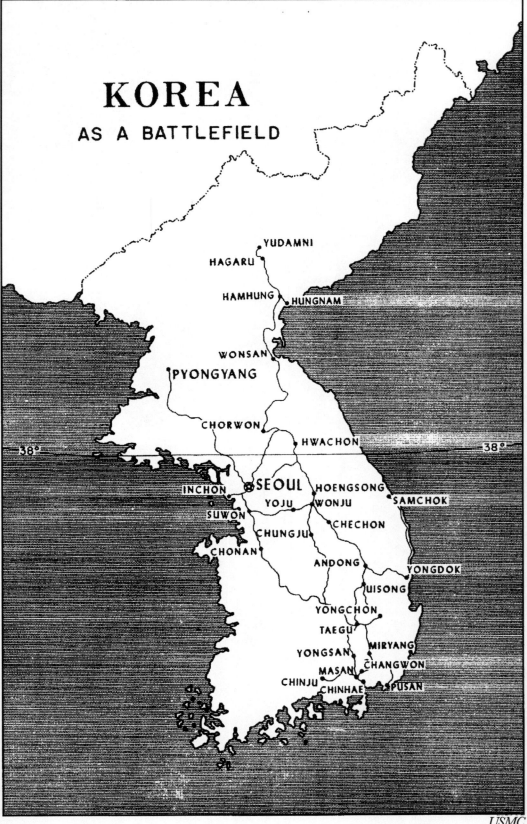

KOREA
AS A BATTLEFIELD

YUDAMNI

HAGARU

HAMHUNG   HUNGNAM

WONSAN

PYONGYANG

CHORWON

38°   HWACHON   38°

INCHON   SEOUL   HOENGSONG
YOJU   WONJU   SAMCHOK
SUWON
CHUNGJU   CHECHON
CHONAN
ANDONG   YONGDOK
UISONG
YONGCHON
TAEGU
MIRYANG
YONGSAN   CHANGWON
MASAN
CHINJU   CHINHAE   PUSAN

USMC

Contents

Preface

During 1951, the second year of the war in Korea, I served there as a rifle platoon leader in the First Marine Division. For about six and a half months, I was in Baker Company, First Battalion, First Marines, and I had Baker Company's first platoon for most of that time. Then I was briefly the S-2 (intelligence officer) of the First Battalion before being rotated back to the States early in 1952.

Clearly, my role in the Korean War was minor. And I was not even there for the memorable and storied events of the war: the Pusan perimeter, the landing at Inchon, and the Marines' heroic breakout from the Chosin Reservoir. But when I got to Korea, we were still in the attack, moving north from Wonju in something called Operation Killer, and well into the fall of 1951 there was hard fighting on combat patrols as well as in the attack. The peace talks had started during that summer, and the front stabilized along lines that both sides held until the armistice, two years later, in the summer of 1953.

Korea is sometimes referred to as the forgotten war, and because it happened more than a half century ago, it would be fair to ask, "Why write about it now?" The answer in my case requires a little explanation.

The first part of the answer is that for me Korea was a formative experience, memorable perhaps because at the time it was the only thing I'd done other than go to school. To this day, I remember some of my experiences in Korea so vividly that I think of them, often in the face of threat or uncertainty. The advantage in thinking of them at times like that is that they can usually make the present look like a piece of cake.

Another part of the answer is that it has taken me a very long time to distill the experience and really to understand it. So I like the thoughtful observation of another Marine that to understand "the changes that war has made in a man requires the passage of time and the establishment of distance from the remembered self." Even more, I like his further thought that "it isn't surprising that most war memoirs come late in life, that memory dawdles and delays." I have dawdled and delayed, but if I hadn't, I'm not sure I'd have gotten to these recollections with the perspective I now have.

That perspective includes the view that war experiences are significant because, unfortunately, wars have been much more prevalent than we might think, more the rule than the exception. Will Durant, in looking back over all of recorded history, is supposed to have found that there were only twenty-nine years when there was not a war going on someplace in the world. The twentieth century, of course, was bloody, indeed. Including Korea, America fought four major wars in the twentieth century. And the twenty-first has not started out much better. There are wars all over the world today, and in Iraq, we may be seeing a new development, the war beyond the war. World history confirms that wars have been almost continuous and that they have been often considered and written about years after the fact. Tom Brokaw isn't the only one concerned with the war experiences of an earlier generation.

I might say a few words about pulling these recollections together. During the time I was in Korea, I thought I might someday write about the experience. A diary or journal would have helped for that purpose, but it seemed to me not to be a good idea generally. At any rate, I didn't keep one. But what I did do was write letters home regularly—sometimes daily—and in the letters, I tried to keep track of where we were and what we had done. Because those letters were to my family who kept them at my request, they constituted together an almost daily record of the time I spent in Korea. They provided the structure, a dated chronology that I have found useful in this writing. Because I've written from the letters—often updating them—this is not a journal. But it is the functional equivalent of a journal, and much of it may be read like one.

After my return from Korea, I put the letters aside. There was too much else going on. I did write a few magazine articles about Korea, and from time to time, I'd talk about the war, usually with other Marines. But for many years, I was too busy to get back to writing about it.

When I looked at the letters recently, and when I thought of writing about the experience, I recalled a number of questions I'd had earlier, questions that I'd never answered. There was more I wanted to know about Korea itself, how it had fit into the Cold War, how we happened to be there, and what impact the conflict there had had on the present. Fortunately, there is now a lot of material available on these subjects, and I've been able to tap into it. In sum, the result of that reading can be found, mostly in the first chapter of this book.

More difficult were my efforts to get in touch with Marines I'd served with in Korea. Although we were all young then, fifty years is a long time to look back. Many of those who survived Korea are gone now, and others are hard to reach, or even hard to find. There have been a couple of recent reunions of the Seventh Basic Class I was in at Quantico. And at Eagle River, Wisconsin, in 1986, there was a reunion of Baker Company, First Battalion, First Marines, the rifle company I served in. Contacts at those gatherings helped to fill in some of the gaps.

For getting in touch with those who served in the first platoon of Baker Company, I've had the invaluable assistance of Vic Heins, a sergeant who was our platoon guide in 1951. He now lives outside Seattle, and he's done an extraordinary job of staying in touch with the other Marines of our platoon. With his help, I've managed to talk with many of them, I believe almost all who are still available. Those conversations have contributed significantly to this story and to my feeling that I've got it as close to right as I can get it.

I've also been able to talk at length with six others from the Seventh Basic Class, who went out to Korea when I did, right after we finished at Quantico. They served there as rifle platoon leaders around the same time I did, and their experiences were similar to mine, but more distinguished, or more extensive, or notable for some other reason. They all excelled as infantry combat leaders in the Korean War. Their stories are included here because they are some of the highlights of what we were doing there, top individual achievements of Marines in that year, 1951.

In a chapter called *Musings*, I recount some of my impressions of war and the Marine Corps based on our experiences. Generally, these are the impressions of Marine rifle platoon leaders in Korea in 1951, but they may represent the experience of others who fought on the ground in other wars as well. And, finally, the last chapter includes an update on the lives after Korea of some of the Marines whose actions figure prominently in the pages of this book.

Chapter 1

KOREA, THE PLACE, THE WAR

K orea, the country, is a peninsula extending some 600 miles
southward from the northeast coast of Asia. It is anywhere
from 125 to 200 miles across. Its shores are washed by the Yellow Sea
on the west and the Sea of Japan on the east. Although Korea is at
about the same latitude as San Francisco, its climate is remarkably
harsh. Temperatures range from well over one hundred degrees
Fahrenheit in summer to minus forty degrees Fahrenheit in winter,
when bitter Siberian winds from the Asian mainland sweep across it.
In 1950, Korea had about thirty million people, some ten million in
the north and twenty million in the south. The hills of Central Korea
are rimmed by mountains in the east, running south from the Yalu
River to the port of Pusan on Korea's southeastern coast. Over on
the west coast, the land is muddy and flat.

Because it is a small country wedged in among world powers—
China, Russia, and Japan—Korea has had a challenging history. It
has suffered some nine hundred invasions in the last two thousand
years and has been occupied or in contention for all of the twentieth
century. Shortly after the century started, Russia and Japan clashed
over Korea and ironically, Japan proposed that their differences be

settled by dividing Korea into two "spheres of influence," with the dividing line to be the 38th parallel. When the Japanese proposal did not take, the powers collided militarily in the Russo-Japanese War, 1904-1905. That war was settled by the Treaty of Portsmouth, in New Hampshire, a peacemaking achievement for which then President Theodore Roosevelt received the Nobel Peace Prize. The treaty might have ended the war, but it has not endeared history-sensitive Koreans to the role of the United States. Without any countervailing force, Japan promptly occupied Korea in 1905 and annexed it as a colony in 1910, holding it in an iron grip until 1945 when World War II was coming to an end.

The future of Korea was discussed at least briefly during World War II. At a meeting of the Allied heads of state in Cairo late in 1943, President Roosevelt had endorsed the policy of a free and independent Korea. This goal was later refined at the Yalta Conference in 1945, where Roosevelt proposed a trusteeship of the United States, Soviet Russia, and China to ensure the freedom and independence of Korea. But nothing was done at that time, and Korea continued to the end of the war as a Japanese possession.

In early August 1945, with World War II rapidly drawing to a close, the Soviet Union declared war on Japan and rushed its troops into Manchuria and Korea. That brought the issue of how a Soviet-controlled Korea might threaten Japan straight to the fore, an issue that had to be faced. The result was a proposal for a joint U.S.-Soviet occupation of Korea and a line of demarcation, with the Soviets occupying territory north of the line and the United States occupying territory to the south. Considering how much was riding on it, and especially considering what happened a few years later, in 1950, there was a remarkable lack of attention to establishing the line.

On August 10, 1945, in the course of an all-night meeting in the Executive Office Building next to the White House, two young Army staff officers were assigned the mission to determine where the line of demarcation should be drawn. The officers—Charles Bonesteel, who would later become the military commander in Korea, and Dean Rusk, who would later become secretary of state—went into a room adjoining the meeting in session. Neither had any background for this assignment, nor did they have time for thoughtful consideration. Using little more than a *National Geographic* map, they decided on the 38th parallel as the line that would divide North from South Korea.

Bonesteel and Rusk were not aware that the 38th parallel had been designated nearly fifty years before as the dividing line between Russian and Japanese spheres of influence. Rusk later acknowledged that if they had known this, they would have avoided the 38th parallel because it could suggest that the Allies recognized the earlier proposal as precedent. But the 38th parallel was included in the general order for occupation of Japanese-held territories, and Soviet and U.S. forces took up their positions north and south of that line.

Setting the line at the 38th parallel was an important event, essentially the basis for the border that still divides Korea today. But it was done hastily and not all comments about it have been favorable. As one distinguished scholar of the period has written: "No division of a nation in the present world is so astonishing in its origin as the division of Korea; none is so unrelated to conditions or sentiment within the nation itself at the time the division was effected; . . . in none does blunder and planning over-sight appear to have played so large a role."

It is significant that Korea was divided in 1945, near the beginning of a period when all of Asia was a seething cauldron of change. In China between 1945 and 1949, the Nationalists, with U.S. assistance, battled the Communists until the Nationalist collapse left Mao in control of mainland China. And all across the face of Asia, formerly colonial regimes were undergoing convulsive realignment. Indonesia was freed from Japanese occupation in 1945 and then struggled against the British,the Dutch, and finally, the Communists for years. The British were pushed out of India in 1947. Burma became independent in 1948. Then, for twelve years from 1948 to 1960, the British battled Communist guerrillas in Malaya. And in what was formerly called French Indochina, Ho Chi Min and his Communist forces fought the French first and then the Americans from 1946 to 1975.

Against this background of upheaval, the internal conflict of a divided Korea festered as the United States remained uncertain of what its interest in Korea really was. In 1947, the United States had 45,000 troops in South Korea. It was expensive to maintain them there, and the strategic value of continuing that position was questioned. The joint chiefs of staff concluded that the United States had "little strategic interest in maintaining the present troops and bases in Korea," and it was thought that they might actually be a liability in a shooting war. If we wanted to launch an offensive, we'd probably bypass Korea anyhow. And if a Communist offensive came out of the North, we'd probably neutralize it with air rather than ground troops. Or that was the idea at the time.

So in September 1947, when the Soviets said they would pull their troops out of Korea if we'd do the same, we readily agreed. They did pull out in late 1948, and we left the following June. Then Korea was to be left to the Koreans, but a strong imprint remained from each of the occupations.

In the North, the Soviets had established the Democratic People's Republic of Korea with its capital in Pyongyang. Below the 38th parallel, the South Koreans had elected a national assembly and established the Republic of Korea (ROK) in May of 1948.

Each of the separate Korean republics was headed by a carefully chosen leader. In the North, it was Kim Il Sung, then thirty-six, said to have been personally selected by Stalin with the comment that "Korea is a young country, and it needs a young leader." With a scant eight years of formal education, Kim had fought the Japanese as a Communist guerrilla leader in Manchuria and had served in Soviet training camps there and attended military schools in Moscow. In the South, the United States had supported Syngman Rhee, then seventy-three, a strongly anti-Communist expatriate who had returned to Korea from the United States at the end of World War II. Rhee had been educated at George Washington University, Harvard, and Princeton, and had lived in the United States for forty years. Kim and Rhee were each monomaniacally dedicated to the reunification of Korea, but under totally different systems. In that, they were like two locomotives racing toward each other, wide open on a single track. And there was much to indicate that U.S. military and diplomatic planners wanted to clear out before the crash.

In late 1947, General Marshall viewed our continued presence in Korea as "untenable, even with expenditures of considerable U.S. money and effort." And George Kennan, then chief, State

Department Policy and Planning Staff, wrote that "since the territory is not of decisive strategic importance to us, our main task is to extricate ourselves without too great a loss of prestige." By March 1948, these views had emerged as U.S. policy: We'd turn the problem of Korea over to the United Nations, with only the proviso that we'd support Korea with some economic aid, but we would *not* regard anything that might happen there as a *casus belli* (Statespeak for an act that would justify war).

When General Omar Bradley, then chairman of the joint chiefs of staff, saw the policy, he submitted the specific issue it raised to the JCS staff for study: what would we do if North Korea invaded the South? The resulting paper from the JCS staff started with the then-conventional wisdom that Korea was of "little strategic value to the United States" and went on to suggest that going it alone in Korea would be "ill advised" and "impracticable." The study concluded that we might oppose such an invasion with a "police action" (presumably the first use of that term later made famous by President Truman) by an international force. And we might even contribute "units" to such a force. Of course, studies like this—no matter how confidential or highly classified—become known. And in this instance, it was only a matter of time.

During 1949, there were sporadic clashes between North and South Korean military units along the 38th parallel, with each side building up, probing, seeking to test its strength against the other. And in early 1950, those interested in the military security of South Korea—the South Koreans themselves and the American military advisors working to reinforce their defenses—were jarred by a series of public statements from Washington.

On January 5, 1950, President Truman announced a hands-off policy toward Formosa. To Syngman Rhee, president of the Republic of Korea, this raised the immediate specter that Communist China would first attack Formosa and then come after Korea. If that did happen, would the United States then back away from Korea as it was backing away from Formosa?

Just a week later, on January 12, in a press conference at the National Press Club in Washington, Secretary of State Acheson sought to clarify the hands-off Formosa policy. Without mentioning Korea, he described the U.S. defense perimeter in the Pacific, a line of defense that Korea was not within. His remarks were widely interpreted as a signal that the United States would not defend Korea.

And finally, Senator Tom Connally of Texas, powerful Chairman of the Senate Foreign Relations Committee, suggested in a published interview that U.S. support of Korea might be abandoned "whether we want it or not." And, in response to a follow-up question, he acknowledged that Korea was not an essential part of America's defensive strategy. So South Korea was off to a rocky start in 1950, but that was only the beginning.

When Soviet archives became available to scholars after collapse of the Soviet Union, it was disclosed that in 1949 and early 1950, Kim Il Sung, clearly dependent on the Soviets for any military initiative, had repeatedly sought Soviet authorization to invade South Korea. For the better part of a year, Stalin rejected these appeals. But early in 1950, he reversed his position, and Kim got the green light. He acted decisively.

At about 0330 on June 25, 1950, a rainy, blustery Sunday morning in Korea, the North Korean artillery opened up. Then, seven divisions of North Korean troops, supported by Soviet-built aircraft and T-34 tanks, pushed across the 38th parallel into South Korea. Two NK divisions, each spearheaded by tanks and other armored vehicles poured through the Uijongbu Corridor headed to Seoul. Later that morning, a fifteen-car train carrying an NK regiment pulled into the railroad station at Kaesong.

This was no cross-border raid. This was the invasion! The Cold War had suddenly turned hot on the fault line of the 38th parallel.

At that time, President Truman was spending the weekend at his home in Independence, Missouri, his first visit since the preceding Christmas. At about 2130 that evening—Saturday night in the United States—Secretary of State Dean Acheson called to say, "Mr. President, I have very serious news. The North Koreans have invaded South Korea." Truman's first reaction was to fly to Washington at once, but Acheson persuaded him to stay in Independence overnight and come back the next day.

At his own initiative, Acheson had already contacted the Secretary General of the United Nations to call an emergency session of the UN Security Council for Sunday, the following day.

The council would be urged to condemn the invasion and to call for a cease-fire and the withdrawal of North Korean forces to the 38th parallel.

Truman flew to Washington on Sunday afternoon, gravely concerned that the North Korean attack could signal the start of World War III. He was met at Washington's National Airport by the secretaries of state and defense and the director of the budget. From the airport, the president and his party drove directly to Blair House where they were joined by other officials from the three departments for dinner followed by an emergency meeting on the Korean crisis.

Surprisingly, in view of the developed position that Korea was not essential to our strategic interests, the effort to hand it off to the UN, the public statements suggesting that it was outside our defense perimeter, etc., the Blair House meeting took a different tack from the very outset. To a man, the participants seemed to agree that this was the time and place to draw the line. As Truman later recounted: "[There was] complete almost unspoken acceptance on the part of everyone that whatever had to be done to meet this aggression had to be done. There was no suggestion from anyone that either the United Nations or the United States could back away from it." Apparently, although Korea had been determined not to be essential militarily or strategically, the unanimous view at Blair House was that it *was* essential, at least symbolically. A keener awareness of the global threat raised by the recent Sino-Soviet alignment may have provided the context. And North Korea's brutal invasion may have just been too raw. The lessons of appeasement at the outset of World War II may have been considered. And in the context of the Cold War, failure to confront this naked aggression might be considered appeasement. At any rate, the judgment was that it must be confronted.

Translated into action, this meant that the decision to intervene with naval and air support was taken almost immediately. And within the next few days, it became clear that ground troops would be required as well. Earlier on this Sunday afternoon, the United Nations Security Council at the emergency meeting in New York had voted 9-0 in favor of an American resolution calling for the cessation of hostilities and withdrawal of North Korean forces to the 38th parallel. The Soviets, boycotting the UN because of its refusal to seat Communist China, were absent.

The Korean War had started. And we were headed in.

The bloody and destructive conflict that followed lasted for just over three years and was a turning point in the history of that era. It involved immediately North and South Korea, then the United States, then fifteen other countries contributing to the United Nations' force. Total fatalities are only estimates, but they range as high as eight hundred thousand Chinese and over two million North and South Koreans killed.

The fighting itself was savage and intense. Before the cease-fire, some 54,000 Americans had died in Korea in a three-year period as compared with nearly 58,000 Americans who died in Vietnam in a war that lasted more than four times as long.

Finally, Korea was a turning point because it triggered a sharp reversal in America's attitude toward Soviet expansion in the Far East and signaled our new commitment to that part of the world. Now—more than fifty years later—we still have some 37,000 troops stationed in Korea. And we've had a force of at least that size there throughout the second half of the twentieth century.

Chapter 2

QUANTICO, THE BASIC SCHOOL

W hen the Korean War broke out, I was a newly commissioned Marine second lieutenant, then on leave. My wife, Joan, and I had been married in Annapolis the day after my graduation from the Naval Academy. Following a brief honeymoon, we were vacationing at Rutgers Lodge on Bay Lake in northern Minnesota on June 25, 1950. When we heard about the invasion, we thought that what remained of my leave would be cancelled, but that didn't happen.

My orders were to The Basic School, Quantico, Virginia, an infantry training course for Marine second lieutenants. Because of Korea, the course at The Basic School (TBS) was accelerated from nine months to six, and I reported to Quantico in early August.

The Marine base at Quantico sprawls over several thousand acres of rolling woodland in parts of three Virginia counties about thirty-five miles south of Washington. It includes two small airfields, and the railroad to Richmond runs through the base. Quantico is the headquarters of Marine Corps schools; it is also the place where the Corps develops its strategy, tactics, and weapons. Within a radius of twenty miles, there is terrain available for every type of combat exercise from attack on a fortified position to climbing the vertical walls of a stone quarry. Because of its location on the Potomac River, Quantico includes some training on water and landing in amphibious operations.

We started The Basic School as 356 second lieutenants, designated the Seventh Basic Class. Some fifty had been commissioned directly from NCO ranks in the Marine Corps, others from platoon leader classes and NROTC programs at various colleges and universities. Forty-eight of us had just graduated from the Naval Academy. The former NCOs had been carefully selected. They were all smart and experienced, and they knew the drill. Many had been young master sergeants, and they seemed at that time to be several paces ahead of the rest of us.

Especially on our accelerated schedule, TBS was a full load. We started early and went until late in the day, sometimes into the evening, and occasionally through the night. There was little time to make acquaintances beyond those you had known before or those you might have direct contact with in the classroom or in the field. For me, that was others who had come from the Academy and the fifty or so in my platoon.

Among those I did know well were Bob Oliver and John Sivright. We had been in adjoining companies at the Academy and, newly married then, were living with our wives in an apartment development just off Shirley Highway, south of Washington. We rode back and forth to Quantico each day in the same carpool. We had a lot of laughs.

Jim Marsh, also a good friend, had been captain of the cross-country team at the Academy. We saw less of him because he was not married while at The Basic School and, thus, was required to live in the barracks for bachelor officers on the base. Bill Rockey, another friend, had been the captain of the Navy swimming team. There were two companies at TBS, and Bill was in Company A, the other company. I didn't see him at all. Another of the members of our carpool was Joe Reed, an NROTC graduate from Miami University in Ohio. He somehow happened to fall in with us, and we saw a lot of him, away from TBS as well as there.

There were a few others that everyone knew. Charlie Cooper and Bill Hawkins had played football at Navy from 1946-1949, and Cooper coached, and Hawkins played for Quantico that fall. Eddie LeBaron, who had been a Little All-American quarterback at College of the Pacific, starred at the same position for Quantico in 1950, as he did for the Washington Redskins and the Dallas Cowboys later.

There was a sense of urgency about TBS that summer. It was the Marine Corps, to be sure, but it was more than that. The Korean War was underway, and our course had been speeded up. We were in a hurry. We wanted to learn how to be Marines and get on with it. We were eager, ready, impressionable. And one who made a profound impression on us that summer was our first commanding officer, a colonel of Marines named David M. Shoup.

Even then, Shoup was a figure of towering renown in the Corps. In 1943, as a lieutenant colonel, he'd been the operations officer of the Second Marine Division, at that time staging in New Zealand. There he had planned the assault on Betio Island, Tarawa Atoll, a redoubt so heavily fortified that Japanese Admiral Shibaski boasted a million men could not take it in a hundred years. Then, when the CO of the Second Marine Regiment had a heart attack, hours before the assault was to begin, Shoup was given a spot promotion to colonel and command of the regiment.

The landing is part of Marine Corps legend. Shoup was painfully wounded coming ashore the first day, but he remained in command. Standing by a Japanese blockhouse near the beach with an unlit cigar clenched in his teeth and a canteen of brandy on his hip, he directed the assault until the island was secured. It took three days, sometimes called the bloodiest seventy-six hours in Marine Corps history. The operation had been all Shoup's, from planning 'til the final shot was fired. For this, he was awarded the Medal of Honor.

Shoup was a solidly built man who looked something like the blockhouse he'd stood by. He was a Hoosier, born and raised on a farm in Western Indiana. He was also a man of strong and independent views, highly intelligent, a common-sense philosopher, and— somewhat unaccountably—a poet.

In the early fall of 1950, The Basic School ran six days a week. Each week, the Saturday morning schedule included two hours labeled CO's Time, a period reserved for the commanding officer to talk to the entire class about any subject of his choosing. It was apparent on that very first Saturday that Colonel Shoup would embrace this opportunity with a zeal that may not have been seen at TBS before or since. He had seen war. He had read widely and thought deeply. He knew what he thought about some of the biggest questions in life. And he burned to deliver his message to us, his youthful charges.

Shoup was a natural storyteller. His talks were direct, personal, highly original, and sometimes quirky. Like all of us, he'd been shaped by his experience, and the epochal experience of his life was, quite naturally, Tarawa. He'd thought about it a lot. He'd relived it in his mind, and he'd written poems about it. His lectures included readings of his poetry, some of which was short and inspiring. An example:

'Til Tarawa

That men will die
And know not why
And wear no frown
Or breathe one sigh
I never knew
'Til Tarawa

Other poems were based on specific events of the battle. Over a three-day period, the casualties were horrific. Many of the Marines who died were men Shoup had served with before. Some were known to be among his closest friends. There is no accounting for good intentions. And surely, it must have been with the best of intentions that the bodies of Marines known to have been close to Shoup were dragged or carried to the blockhouse where he was standing and piled there in his direct view. Quite understandably, Shoup had mixed feelings about this sight, but he could not avoid it. He could, however, express his feelings in verse. And he did:

Friend's End

Yesterday we worked and planned and hoped
You were my friend.
Today you look so smeared and wild and doped.
You've met your end,
On Tarawa.
So often I have looked upon your hideous face.
I hate you now.
You fell and bled and soiled my place,
Amid this row,
On Tarawa.
Drag from my sight this blear-eyed thing,
That was my friend.
Return all to mother earth except that ring
To prove his end,
On Tarawa.

Another poem entitled "Ship to Shore at Tarawa" became a Basic School classic, where it would be recognized simply as "Bill." It concerned a Marine, presumably Shoup himself, and a friend named Bill heading in to the beach at Tarawa. The landing boats are raked by murderous fire from Japanese pillboxes ashore. As Shoup is confiding to Bill that after they land he may not be able to kill the enemy, Bill takes a direct hit. His face is shattered by an incoming round, and Shoup is drenched in his blood. Another poem. The last stanza is:

Good-bye and God bless you, Bill,
I go with your blood on my gun,
I'm getting over the side, Bill
And to kill will be mountains of fun.

At the time, as I recall, many in the Seventh Basic Class were uncertain about their reaction to offerings like this. Few were accustomed to poetry readings on Saturday mornings, especially that kind of poetry. But it was memorable; it did stick with you. And it acquired a certain cachet over the years.

Somehow, it sounded better later, when Shoup, as Commandant of the Marine Corps, was the guest of honor at a reunion dinner of our class. Referring to the Commandant, the dinner program noted: "For him we feel a personal bond . . . developed in the early months of the Korean War by the series of Saturday morning lectures through which he sought to prepare us emotionally for the realities of combat."

When we'd started at TBS, the UN forces in Korea consisted of four understrength, out-of-shape Army divisions. Most had come directly from occupation duty in Japan. In Korea, they had been steadily pushed back as they fought in desperation to hold the perimeter around Pusan where they could continue to be supplied and reinforced from the sea.

When the Marines first entered the war, and especially after the Inchon landing on September 15, 1950, the war in Korea was with us every day. It was always the lead story in *The Sentry*, the base newspaper at Quantico, and it was extensively covered in the national press. It underlay much of our instruction, although the fighting had started too late to make the lesson plans.

Most of our instructors had combat experience, but that had been in World War II, rather than Korea. The sole exception was First Lieutenant Gil Hershey, a tall dark-haired officer, one of the first Marines to fight in Korea. He had been wounded seriously and evacuated to the States. After his release from the hospital, he'd been assigned to TBS as an instructor in the tactics section. His father, a retired Army general who had run the draft during World War II, had been called back to active duty to run the draft for Korea.

Lieutenant Hershey lectured on tactics as they were developing in Korea, and mimeographed notes of his comments were distributed to us. His ideas were not strikingly different, but they were up to date and straight from the front. We devoured them. He talked about tactical air support and widespread use of helicopters for reconnaissance and evacuation of wounded, about how communications could be maintained within the platoon and the company, about how important it was to get full use of support weapons that the line units controlled—machine guns and 81mm and 60mm mortars—and, of course, about close coordination with the larger supporting arms, air, artillery, and naval gunfire.

He also emphasized the importance of map reading, a matter of some concern to me because I had no reason to think I'd be good at it. (I wasn't.) He said, "Your reconnaissances have to be supplemented with a map study because you cannot possibly see everything on the ground, even if you have the time. Your map will be your guide when taking your platoon from one place to another, and you are not likely to get many second chances if you miss the first time." These words kind of hung in the air for me. Somehow I thought I might need a few second chances.

Lieutenant Hershey was a positive fellow, and his guidance to us managed to end on a cheery note. He said that the First Marine Division had a lot of platoon leaders who had been Basic School students only a few months before. They were just like us, had our background, and they were doing a good job, so there was no reason we couldn't. If we just kept our heads, we'd come through with flying colors. We hoped so.

The days rolled by, past the end of summer and into the fall. We pushed on through The Basic School against the background of Marine achievement in Korea. Inchon was followed by the capture of Seoul, a surge over the 38th parallel and through North Korea to the Chosin Reservoir. Then the First Marine Division was encircled, surrounded a massive Chinese force. When Chesty Puller, commanding the First Marine Regiment, was told his command was surrounded, he's supposed to have clapped his hands together and exclaimed, "Ha! I've got 'em now. Those sons-a-bitches won't escape me this time!" The Division attacked and broke out.

As the Marines where fighting their way south to Hungnam, we were riveted to dispatches from Korea. By then, we were spending less time in the classroom and more in the field, even on the water. We were on the river almost all of one long, cold, and very wet night, practicing landing in rubber boats on the darkened shores of the Potomac.

In the closing weeks of our course, there was a tragic accident on the 81mm mortar firing range. With a dozen Basic School second lieutenants gathered close around, a mortar shell exploded as it came out of the tube. Two of our classmates were killed instantly, and another ten were wounded, several critically.

Finally, on the first Friday in March, we moved in buses from the parade ground at TBS to Quantico's main auditorium for graduation. Colonel Shoup opened the program with a summary of our class. A total of 356 second lieutenants had started the course some six months earlier, and 348 were graduating that day. Six were not graduating for academic or physical reasons, and "two had died in the performance of their duties," a reference to the mortar accident.

The principal speaker, Lt. Gen. Merwin Silverthorn, then assistant Commandant and chief of staff, assured us, the graduates, that the future reputation of the Marine Corps rested in our hands. Then—somewhat surprisingly, I thought—he proceeded to an accounting of where a class of 356 second lieutenants like us might reasonably end up. He said 320 could expect to be promoted to captain, 222 to major, 147 to lieutenant colonel, and 87 to colonel. (It was not hard to see that this was an all purpose speech; by adjusting the numbers, it could be used for any graduating class.) Finally, he suggested that seven graduates might become general officers.

Then he finished with congratulations and some fatherly counsel for us. We filed on to the stage to receive our diplomas. At the end, the general went down to the auditorium floor to present diplomas to six of our classmates wounded in the mortar accident who were attending in wheelchairs.

That was it. We were through at The Basic School. Through at Quantico. It was a relief, a happy time. We filed out of the auditorium to join wives, families, girlfriends, well-wishers, all fluttering around taking pictures. Next, we were headed out to whatever assignments we had. For some fifty—a group that included me—that was to Camp Pendleton, Oceanside, California, "for d beyond the seas," meaning Korea. The other three hundred or so were headed to various posts, stations, ships, etc., wherever their orders sent them.

At almost the same time, there was another ceremony far away in Korea; Chesty Puller was saying farewell to his regiment, the First Marines. I didn't know this at the time (and I had requested assignment to the First Marines because Puller was the CO), but that was what was happening. Having just been promoted to brigadier general, he was leaving the regiment. No long speeches here. His farewell was brief. He said, "It's with reluctance that I leave you, men, to assume my new job as assistant division commander. I've commanded some of you on Cape Gloucester, New Britain and Peleliu, and now in Korea . . . . You've always served me well, and it's only because of you and your deeds that I'm a general today. I won't say goodbye because I'm not going far from you."

With that, he saluted and strode over to a waiting TBM (a torpedo bomber) and "roared down the dusty strip past the men who lined up to render their final salute." He was off to be the ADC (assistant division commander) of the First Marine Division. I would see him in Korea later, and back in Washington, but only briefly.

It was easy enough for Joan and me to pull our few possessions together, our furniture to be stored in Alexandria, Virginia. Whatever we were taking with us was stuffed into our Ford Coupe, new in June of 1950, and we headed out for the drive across country to California.

One of our first stops was Winnetka, Illinois, on the lakefront north of Chicago. There we visited the parents of my Naval Academy classmate and friend, Will Macfarland. Will was then serving in the Navy, off somewhere at sea. His father, a Chicago banker, had headed OSS in Eastern Europe during World War II and was familiar with world affairs, military as well as civilian. After breakfast, as we talked by a roaring fireplace in their den, coffee in hand, he asked what my next assignment was. When I told him I had orders to Korea, he replied matter-of-factly, "Well, that's what you're trained for. Go out there and do a good job." I had by that time gotten a few reactions to my duty assignment that had expressed shock or denial, reactions I'd found embarrassing. But when I heard Mr. Macfarland's response, I thought it was perfect. That was exactly what I wanted to hear.

At my parents' home in St. Paul, Minnesota, we arrived during a month when the Twin Cities were nearly buried under a record sixty inches of snow. We had a chance to ski a couple of times with equipment borrowed from some of my friends. Then another round of farewells, and we were back in the car. We headed south through

Iowa, across the windy plains of Nebraska, through Denver and into Salt Lake City where we landed on Easter Sunday. Then on to Sacramento, San Francisco, and finally Oceanside, California, a few days before I had to report at Pendleton.

When we arrived at the base, we were to stay the first night with the family of Birch DeWitt, another classmate from the Academy and TBS. Birch's father was a Marine colonel, and Birch's parents lived in quarters on the base. At the gate where we came in, we asked the sentry for directions. He told us that we should drive straight ahead for twenty-one miles, turn left at that intersection, and continue for another eleven miles to officers' country where the DeWitt quarters were located. We got the idea—Pendleton's a big place!

The rest of our class with orders to Korea came out to Camp Pendleton, some by train or plane, but many by car as we did. One such cross-country car pool included Charlie Cooper, Walter Murphy, Bob Whitesell, and Garland Beyerle. They had fallen in together after we finished at Quantico and headed out in Whitesell's car. Riding together and splitting expenses and driving time is about as economical as you can get it. They shared everything with one exception. And, come to think of it, I guess they even shared that.

The possible exception was learning the Chinese language, an activity to which Murph had at that time dedicated himself with the zeal of a monk. Murph is a student, a red-headed Irishman from Charleston, South Carolina. He is serious about intellectual pursuits, but whether he had taken this up as an intellectual exercise before the Chinese swarmed across the Yalu or not, I've never known. I'm told that Chinese is a language that cannot be learned silently. It involves grunts, groans, tonal, and atonal sounds; grunting and groaning and trying to utter the sounds is the best, or maybe the only, way to learn it. Murph may have understood this before the trip started, but the others almost certainly did not. Nor did they understand that learning Chinese in the confined space of a closed car is an experience that all those who are in the car must share, an experience that necessarily blots out much other activity they could be enjoying.

The first day was their awakening, apparently a real trial. But they looked forward to the end of the day when they'd be out of the car and in their motel room, a room that all four were to share. It was not to be. When they arrived at the first motel, Murph broke out his record player and a stack of 78 rpm records essential to the course. There was apparently no escape. This continued for the next several days. And tension continued to build.

Finally, when they had arrived at the Grand Canyon, there was an opportunity to negotiate a settlement. There, over the waters of the Colorado River roaring thousands of feet below, Murph's travel mates suggested a compromise. Holding the record player, records, and all other materials related to the course in a bag extended out over the gorge, they sought an agreement that would relegate Chinese language training to a lower priority, subject to the will of the group. Without that, the hand holding the bag would release its grip, and everything essential to continuing the course would plunge into the river churning far below. Murph relented. The few remaining days of the trip were quieter, if less productive in learning Chinese.

During the short time I was to be at Pendleton, we settled into an $8-a-night motel on the beach in Oceanside, quite literally, a stone's throw from the Pacific Ocean. Joe and Marilyn Reed were right next door. We spent a day or so driving the area, looking for a place for Joan to stay, and after her first sighting of LaJolla, the problem was solved. We found a bungalow overlooking The Cove, where Girard Avenue meets the Pacific Ocean, and there was room there to share the second floor with three other young women. Joan was set.

There were various final arrangements to be made at Pendleton, and we had a week's cold-weather training at Pickel Meadows (named for an early settler) in the nearby mountains. Thus, qualified for the rigors of the next Korean winter, we were through. Finished. And we were needed in Korea. The eighth replacement draft was ready to go.

On a bright, sunny morning, we loaded on buses with all our gear. It was a short trip to the dock in San Diego where we boarded a waiting troopship, USS *Menifee*.

Chapter 3

ACROSS THE PACIFIC, USS *MENIFEE*

April 13, 1951. Aboard the *Menifee*. Because Truman has called up the reserves for Korea, we're all here together. Young and old, reserve and regular, officer and enlisted, some who look too young to be in high school and grizzled WWII vets who were at Iwo or Okinawa six years ago. A few have shaved heads and Mohawk strips down the middle. Others have pistols, revolvers or automatics, or knives. We are going to war.

When we boarded the buses at Camp Pendleton to come out here to the ship, some were still drunk from last night. Others were silent, hung over or lost in their own thoughts.

Those who did talk were funny. Referring to the sentry, "Do you think that son of a bitch at the gate will ask for our liberty cards?" or "Just look out there. Look at those poor fucking civilians—no place to go but home." And the impression of a bo's'n's voice over the loudspeaker aboard ship, "Now hear this: will the duty chicken lay down to the galley and walk through the soup?"

We are on board USS *Menifee*, APA 202, out of mothballs for the Korean War, and clean as a whistle. We sleep in a troop-officer compartment on the main deck with mattresses, pillows, and sheets. There are writing tables, easy chairs, a cigarette machine, and plenty of room. We only half fill the compartment. The wardroom where we eat is the next compartment forward, the barbershop just aft. This may be a pleasant trip.

April 15. We left the Broadway Pier at 0800 for North Island. We are now loading ammo, scheduled to sail early this afternoon.

I've just returned from the barber with a quarter-inch haircut. Others in this compartment are Bob Oliver, Jimmie Marsh, Joe Reed, Sam Carle, Dick Jones, Dave Ridderhoff, Eddie LeBaron, and John Olterman, all from the Seventh Basic Class. Because we were arranged alphabetically, Olterman and I stood next to each other for six months in The Basic School. Now he sleeps in the rack next to mine aboard ship.

We had strawberry shortcake for lunch yesterday, and french toast for breakfast this morning. So much for the food. Our compartment is clean, and we've just received large crates of games, playing cards, and books delivered by the Red Cross. There's nothing I need, but as I look around, there are some things I should have left behind, especially the Coleman stove which now looks heavy and too bulky to be carrying around.

April 16. Menifee plows on through the Pacific. Most of us spend our waking hours reading and writing letters; that is all but a half dozen or so of us. The half dozen usually stay in their racks all day. They may get up for meals, but otherwise, they sleep through everything.

At Pendleton I had a battery of seven shots, and a horrendous reaction, like near death for three days. Today I'm called down to sick bay and asked why I had never gotten my shots. When I understand what this question means, I blanch. Apparently, the corpsman had not recorded the earlier shots in my medical record, and this corpsman says if the shots are not on my shot card, I haven't had the shots. I protest. But no soap. I had to retake five of the seven, just what I'd dreaded. But now I've had the second round, and I don't feel anything. Maybe that first round worked to immunize me—even from another reaction to the shots themselves.

April 18. We are now some 1,200 miles into the Pacific. The weather has been cloudy and cool, hardly any sun since we left San Diego. Today we started working with troops in the morning, an hour of physical drill, and a couple hours of instruction. Afternoons are generally free.

Yesterday and again today, we've fired weapons from the fantail at cardboard boxes and tin cans thrown overboard and riding in the wake. My carbine works perfectly, as I'd expect. But the really good news is that so does my father's World War I service revolver. I don't know that it was ever fired or even cleaned since he brought it back from France. But it works. Even better, it hits whatever I aim at, that is cardboard boxes and tin cans in *Menifee*'s wake.

We have a bewildering variety of handguns here. Joe Reed and a few others have German Lugar pistols, and there are pearl-handled revolvers of various sizes and current vintage pacemakers and masterpieces. Bob Whitsell has a .357 Magnum, the most powerful revolver made, unquestioned king of the handguns. The .357 is prized because one round will knock anything down—man or large animal. But it is also an object of real beauty, the darkest blue steel, finely machined. It's interesting to see these guns, and I like firing them. But I'm well satisfied with my Dad's old service revolver, especially now that I know it works. The .45 caliber ammo will always be available wherever we are.

MacArthur was relieved a few days ago, and last night on the ship's radio, we listened to his triumphal procession to the St. Francis Hotel in San Francisco. Down Market Street to Mason, left to Post, then right on Post and another right at Powell to the front of the hotel, directly opposite Union Square. Just a few short weeks ago, Joan and I were at the St. Francis together. Now MacArthur is there, and here I am in the middle of the Pacific.

This trip is supposed to be fifteen to twenty days to Japan. Then we're scheduled to stop at Yokosuka for a couple of days before going on to Korea. I had forgotten, but life at sea gives one a different perspective, like looking at the ground from an airplane. Out here on the Pacific, nothing seems quite real. We're just out here afloat, removed from the world. For now, that is.

April 24. Today we hear that we'll arrive in Yokosuka on April 30. Probably be there for a day or so, then on to Pusan. All the news we get is filled with MacArthur's return, his "old soldiers never die" speech to the Congress. From here, it all seems like a soap opera, a distraction from the war we're headed to.

———————— —— ————————

Note: MacArthur's speech was an address that apparently led some of his serious fans to think of him as divine. Representative Dewey Short of Missouri exclaimed, "We heard God speak here today, God in the flesh, the voice of God." And former President Herbert Hoover, who had himself tangled with MacArthur, saw him in 1951 as "a reincarnation of St. Paul into a great general of the Army who came out of the East."

President Truman was less impressed. In a remark to Secretary of State Acheson, he said, "It's nothing but a bunch of bullshit."

Acheson responded that MacArthur's firing, and the speech was like "the story of the family with a beautiful daughter living at the edge of an Army camp. The mother worried constantly about her daughter's virtue and relentlessly badgered her husband with her anxiety. One day the daughter showed up weeping and confessed that the worst had happened, that she was pregnant. The father wiped his brow and declared, 'Thank God that's over.'"

———————— —— ————————

A recent issue of *Life* has dejected-looking doughboys of the Army's 40th Division on board a ship leaving for Korea. The photographer couldn't get that picture here on *Menifee*. The big difference is the Marine Corps. Everyone here is a Marine, and now that we're actually underway, everyone seems to be looking forward to whatever lies ahead, even those who might have had reservations about going in the first place.

Still April 24. This is strange because yesterday was Sunday, the 22nd. We passed the international date line at 0700 and lost an entire day. Whatever happened to April 23?

Last night, we had fairly good radio reception for a while, at least long enough to hear an all-night DJ play "Slow Boat to China."

Much laughter. We'd all heard the song before; we just never thought we'd be on one.

Currently, I'm playing about six rubbers of bridge and reading a paperback a day in addition to classes or drills with the men, cleaning weapons, etc. That fills the hours, but it's not a very good use of time. Better to be like Walter Murphy, a recent Notre Dame graduate and apparently a disciplined academic, maybe an intellectual. He has his record player and Chinese language records with him here, but he listens to the records with earphones. We hear nothing, though Murph spends most of every day on his sack, learning Chinese. Wish I had that kind of discipline.

We hear today that the North Koreans have launched their big counteroffensive. They are supposed to have driven twenty miles south across a ninety-five mile front behind the heaviest artillery barrage of the war. This has long been expected. And we'd all rather have them start now than waiting until after we get there.

There's a big criminal investigation going on here. Two Marines each lost $60 or so just before we left Pendleton. They both suspect a third Marine who is also their closest friend. The investigation has now gotten to the point where they are to open the suspect's seabag locked in a storage compartment below decks. Like murder on the Orient Express, interest among the other passengers is running high.

Today we hear that we'll be landing at Kobe, Japan, rather than Yokosuka.

April 25. Perplexing administrative problem: Marines on *Menifee* have been assigned a barber chair, and a barber to cut Marine hair. He was supposed to cut hair without charge from 0800 to 1600 each day. When it was found that he was charging for haircuts, he was given a captain's mast and nonjudicial punishment. Then somebody figured out that even if the barber worked all day every day until we land, he couldn't cut all the Marines' hair. So now the barber has been ordered to cut hair until 2200 each night. His punishment has been revoked, *and* he will now be allowed to charge for haircuts after 1600. The Marine Corps meets the free market!

In addition to us hard chargers from The Basic School, there are about a half-dozen reserve motor transport officers on board. Because they are generally unkempt and spend most of every day in the sack, we think they are slovenly. They are. Their commander, a reserve captain, is the most profane man I've ever heard. And on a Marine transport, this is a singular distinction, believe me. I've just learned that he once spent five years in a Canadian seminary studying for the priesthood.

The commander of all Marine troops on *Menifee* is a lieutenant colonel, a genial Southerner, somewhat overweight. He has been a food administrator running mess halls at Camp Lejeune since the end of WWII. Now the interesting thing is this: all of these guys—motor transport officers, food administrators, etc.—are headed to Korea with infantry specs, 0302 or whatever. That means they're headed for rifle companies, on the line. When the Corps says "Every Marine a rifleman," they mean it.

April 28. At sea. Yesterday was terrifically rough. Beginning at night and continuing through the morning, we ran through heavy squalls that ruined sleep, rocked the ship back and forth, and sent everything not tied down flying around the compartment. The mess hall was hardest hit. Tables flipped over, and at one point, a bench with nineteen Marines on it collapsed sending the lot with all of their trays and food into a pile in one corner. A mass food spill. Through the day, we had to do six knots on the screws to make a couple of knots headway through the water. We may have lost a day in that weather.

April 29. No radio from the States for the last several days. But there is a fill-in, the poor man's Lord Haw Haw, Radio Moscow. It's music and Korean war news delivered in a feminine American voice, somewhat breathless, attempting to be soothing and sexy. So we hear about American capitalistic imperialism and the millionaire tycoons of Wall Street sending our boys off to fight and die in the Far East. It's fairly entertaining the first time around, but they repeat the same broadcast over and over through the day. We are now close enough to Japan to pick up U.S. broadcasts from Tokyo on the Far Eastern Network. This morning we heard a rerun of last night's *Hit Parade*.

Joe Reed has the bunk next to mine. He wears well and is more interesting as I get to know him better. We agree that April 1951 has been the most nothing month we've ever lived through.

The first part was ruined by leave-taking, and our time aboard ship has been like living in a vacuum. The lost month.

Today we heard that UN forces have halted the Red drive down the Korean peninsula and forced them back ten miles. They are claiming seventy thousand Red casualties which, if true, will help. There was a lot of speculation about what the Communist forces might try to do for May Day, their main holiday. But May Day passes uneventfully.

May 2. It is now morning, about 0830. The air is cool, and there is a light haze, a day with the freshness of Japanese spring. We are steaming through quiet blue water just off the port of Kobe, Japan. There are merchant ships of all nations and hundreds of small Japanese fishing boats and junks lining the channel as we come in. In the fishing boats are men and women, old and young, and children of all ages. They look up from their baskets and nets, and some wave as we glide by. From the upper deck of *Menifee,* we can see the Japanese fishing villages, low buildings with dark gray roofs in the valleys coming down to the sea. We're supposed to arrive at the dock about 1100 and to be here today and tomorrow. We've been nineteen days at sea, and this is the first land we've seen. We're ready for liberty.

Yesterday, for something to do, we had contests in fieldstripping our M-2 carbines. I know my family will be proud to hear that I can detail strip my carbine in forty-nine seconds and reassemble it completely in five minutes, fifteen seconds, actually pretty fair time.

May 3. Kobe, one of Japan's largest ports. A city of 750,000 people subsisting mainly on fishing and sea trade. There is a great deal of smoke here, manufacturing, docks, and shipyards, and the city had a singularly tragic WWII experience. It was bombed only twice, but the second time with napalm firebombs dropped from B-29s. During that second raid, some two hundred thousand people, about half the city's population, took refuge in the subways. Napalm and fire burned up all the oxygen, and when those who had fled to the hills returned, they found that their neighbors in the subways had suffocated. At first they tried to recover the bodies, but the task was so grisly that after a couple of days they gave up and instead sealed off the subways' entrances. Kobe is now a thriving city, with half its WWII population buried in vaults under the streets.

Before going ashore, we had to change money for script and yen, a complex ritual. The PXs and all other U.S. installations here use script, issued aboard ship for dollars in the same amount. Japanese businesses use yen, exchanged at the rate of 360 yen to the dollar. For the 1,600 Marines we have aboard the two transports, the money changing took several hours.

Before we finished the money changing, two trains pulled out on the dock alongside our transports. Rumor instantly had it that we were to be whisked by train across Japan to the western side and sent on to Pusan by LST this afternoon. It turned out that the trains were for aviators who came over with us and were being sent on to the First Marine Air Wing Base in Japan. They left late yesterday afternoon. With them went 157 enlisted Marines who were transferred to the First Casual Company here for further transfer to guard duty in Guam, Honolulu, and the Philippines. After coming all this way, I think most of them were keenly disappointed at not getting to Korea. No officers were taken.

I finally went on liberty about 1800 with Joe Reed, Sam Carle, and Eddie LeBaron. We traveled by rickshaw (best way to move from place to place) and after a short stop at the PX ended up at the Oriental Hotel for dinner. Cocktails, hors d'oeuvres, shrimp, plank steak, sherry, cognac, and coffee came to 8,000 yen (something over $22) for four of us. Then on to the Officers' Club in the Shinko Building where we drank and talked until around midnight and where everyone from our ship appeared at sometime during the evening.

Bob Oliver and Jimmie Marsh had come ashore with only script, and when the yen line at the PX was too long, they looked for a faster way to exchange. They thought they had got that idea across to their rickshaw boy, but after going some distance through alleys and side streets, they were dropped before a darkened entrance. Both recently married, they had no interest in finding a whorehouse. But of course that's where they were. They were ushered upstairs and seated in a room where smiling Korean girls paraded before them. When they continued to protest that they only wanted to exchange script for yen, one of the girls stayed with them anyhow. She nodded, and they thought she understood. But when she left, it was to come back with another girl so that they would be paired. Further protests finally produced the madam. They got their script changed, and after promising to be back, they finally got away to tell us about it at the Oriental. Much laughter.

During the evening, we also talked with Army lieutenants just back from the front in Korea and with doctors from the hospital ship *Repose* tied up at the dock next to *Menifee*. In us, they had eager listeners, and they said:

"For wounds that heal in a week to ten days, you stay right at the field hospital in Korea; ten days to two months means evacuation to a hospital in Japan; over two months, casualties are shipped back to the States. All compound fractures and most psycho cases go back to the States. Psycho cases among Marine officers or regulars are practically unheard of. The few Marine cases have been reserves called up and too hastily trained. Helicopter evacuation and the availability of new drugs mean that almost everyone who can be evacuated recovers. Perhaps nine out of ten. Certainly the highest recovery rates of any war in history. Most wounds are caused by shell fragments from grenades or mortars, few by bullets. Also, very few head or groin wounds."

The First Marine Division is considered the best of the UN forces. Outstanding performance from the beginning. It has sometimes been at risk when ROK units on its flanks have bugged out. That happened last week at the start of the Red offensive. The division was on the line when the ROK division on its right flank buckled. The First Marine Regiment was sent up to replace the Koreans. The units passed through each other on the road— Marines going up, ROK soldiers coming back. Apparently, there were catcalls in both languages, especially bitter in English. When the First Marines did get on the line, they took the brunt of the Red assault and suffered heavy casualties.

These Army guys say that Marine rifle platoon leaders are supposed to have an effective life of six minutes in combat. That can't be right!

We are to leave Kobe at about noon today, and the trip to Pusan is twenty-four to thirty hours. When we arrive there, we'll go by bus to an airfield, K-1, and be flown directly to Wonson. That is if we still hold Wonson by Friday night or Saturday morning. We'll get our regimental assignments later this morning, so we'll know soon. From regiment, we'll be assigned to battalions.

Later, May 3. Regimental assignments came out this morning. Earlier I had requested the First Marines because of Chesty Puller. Now he's no longer there, but I got assigned to the First Marines anyhow. Well, that's fine. Over the past couple of months, the First Marines have been on the line for forty-six consecutive days, supposedly longer than any other Marine regiment anyplace. They had just gotten into reserve when the Red offensive started last week, and when the ROK division caved, they were rushed back on the line. So now they may be due for some reserve time.

The Seventh Basic Class is scattered. Joe Reed, Bob Oliver, Jimmie Marsh, Neil Ness, Stan Olson, and about a half dozen other lieutenants are heading to the First Marines with me. About a dozen, including John Oltermann, are going to the Seventh Marines. And a couple of infantry lieutenants have even been assigned to the artillery regiment.

We are scheduled to arrive at Pusan about 1900 tomorrow evening and to fly up to the front the next day. For me, the prospects look good; I haven't gotten sidetracked into tanks or any of the rear echelon positions. Several lieutenants have been assigned to the records section at division headquarters, and a few to tanks. Eddie LeBaron is going to the amtracks at Masan. So far, I'm lucky. The assignments are working out all right for me.

Chapter 4

ARRIVAL IN KOREA

*M*ay 5. We left Kobe yesterday and passed through the Tsushima Straits where Japan defeated the Russian fleet in 1905. Shortly after midnight this morning, *Menifee* eased through the murky waters of Pusan Harbor and tied up at the dock. Here we are alongside the hospital ship *Repose*. Out there in the darkness beyond is the dim outline of wharves and a warehouse lighted by a single incandescent bulb. The air is heavy, and it smells of rotting wood, centuries old, and honey carts with night soil. A light rain is falling.

Reveille was at 0200, and it is now almost 0400. We were to have disembarked earlier and moved by bus to the airfield, K-1, to be flown directly to the front. Now we hear that weather will hold up all flights, at least through the rest of the morning.

At very early first light, we fall in. We are in battle gear with full field packs weighing eighty pounds each. We load fifty Marines to a truck, standing on the flatbed of Army trucks and are hauled over the rutted gravel streets of Pusan in the rain. It's a jarring ride.

As the rain continues, we are all soaked through on arrival at the Army's Pusan Assembly Area Depot around 0630. The depot is a tent city, a vast collecting area for troops from all of the United Nations heading for the front and coming back. The tents they put us in have cots and are dry. But between the tents run avenues of ankle-deep red mud potted with pools of rainwater.

When the rain lets up around noon, I offer to take a young Marine pfc. to have his broken glasses fixed at the Army station hospital in the city. We are gone a couple of hours, and this turns out to be my only look at Pusan. It ain't pretty.

The air is steaming and fetid. The street outside the depot looks like a field of plowed mud. It's jammed with panhandlers and hustlers hawking their wares at street stalls. There are also Americans, mostly soldiers in grimy dungarees. A sleek, busty Army nurse in khakis is having her boots shined on a wooden box at the curb.

And there's action in the street. When a Korean pulls his cart over the telephone line that an Army corporal is stringing, the corporal loses it. He literally blows up. Screaming curses, he lunges after the hapless Korean, raining blows on his head with a coil of telephone line. The Korean bobs and weaves to get away, pulling his cart behind him. The street absorbs all of this shouting and banging. Others move along on their way without even glancing up.

Pusan is a huge Army base with much of the Army's rear echelon here. Could you believe a bath company with three shower platoons? They have them. And they're here.

May 6. Another 0200 reveille. About noon, we board the trucks again for a short ride to K-1 and a flight to Hoensong in Central Korea. For the flight, I'm the commander of flight team 19 consisting of some forty Marines. Our canteens are full. Our weapons are locked and loaded. We are ready.

When we land at Hoensong, to my amazement, the first person I see as we are getting off the plane is one Peaches Hamilton. I can't believe it. This is a flashback to my plebe year at the Academy.

At that time, plebes were required to have posters on the doors to their rooms by noon on Friday before the each Saturday football game. (Maybe they still are.) This was mandatory. No exceptions. Around 1145 one Friday morning, my roommate, Bob White, and I arrived back at our room late from class and realized with shock that we didn't have a poster up. We're playing Georgia Tech the next day. In a burst of inspiration, Bob grabbed a desk blotter and a crayon and scrawled across the blotter: "Sherman marched through Georgia—so can Navy!" We stuck the poster on our door feeling satisfied. We're both from Minnesota, and we thought that would be fine.

Within minutes, we hear the clatter of upperclassmen coming back from class. They are stopping at each plebe room to inspect the posters and comment, usually approving or disapproving. We hear a group stopping outside our door, and we listen, waiting for their approval. There is a moment of silence. Then we hear a scream that might have been a rebel yell, the wail of a banshee, an unearthly screech. The words were something like: "Jesus Christ! Who the fuck is responsible for that?"

Next, a foot slams into the door, and the door flies open with enough force to shatter its panel of translucent glass. By this time, of course, my roommate and I are both on our feet—braced at rigid attention—as Peaches Hamilton of Dalton, Georgia, strides into the room, eyes blazing. He was apoplectic.

We both spent the next month going around to Peaches' room to do push-ups every night before lights out. After that, we just tried to avoid him and didn't see him much until he graduated in June 1948. I hadn't thought of him since.

Peaches had been in the service briefly and then was released to go back to Georgia to run the family cotton mill, or whatever business his family had. But he had stayed in the reserve. Then when Korea started, the reserves were called up, and sure enough, here was old Peaches to greet me on the scene. Out here, he was very cordial as he loaded us back on trucks—this time smaller trucks—for a forty-mile ride to the forward area.

This is a ride through rugged, mountainous country with peaks towering over the road running along a stream on the valley floor. We see our first bomb craters, napalm-scarred slopes, slit trenches, and foxholes. We pass through Massacre Valley where the Army lost an entire battalion a few days earlier in what is said to have been the perfect ambush. Army signs along the road point to CPs, motor transport areas, medical battalions, etc. We are still far in the rear, but it's obvious that American logistical support is massive.

Finally, we arrive at the First Marines regimental CP (command post) where we are to draw our battalion assignments. For just a moment, I stop to wonder. What the hell am I doing here? The moment passes.

After we get off the trucks, I realized—too late—that I'm missing something. I've left my rolled-up sleeping bag on the truck. Losing the bag might be a mistake, but that wasn't the first thing I thought of. We'd been told in Japan that every new second lieutenant reporting to a rifle company was expected to bring whiskey. I had a fifth of Old Fitzgerald stuffed in my bag with the expectation that it would lead to an enthusiastic welcome at some rifle company. No more. Now I was on my own. And of course, I never saw the bag or the bottle again.

At the First Marines CP, we are greeted personally by the regimental commander, Colonel McAlister. He's weathered-looking, compact, an Annapolis graduate who has just replaced Chesty Puller. Off line, we hear that he got hit about a week ago, grenade fragments in the back. I wonder how many regimental commanders get into direct fire and get hit. Somehow I find that impressive, as well as surprising.

We got our battalion assignments. One of my Seventh Basic classmates goes to the Second Battalion. Most others, including Joe Reed, Jimmie Marsh, and Bob Oliver, go to the Third. I've been assigned to the First Battalion along with Neil Ness (considered too gung ho by some in our class, but someone I've always liked) and Hal Needham and Dick Winter who I don't know very well. Company assignments are to be made the next morning.

I like the idea of "First Battalion, First Marines, First Marine Division." To me, it sounds like a good address.

Winter, Ness, and Needham have no further assignments, so their day is over. They get to sack in. I'm assigned sixty-six replacement Marines to set up a perimeter defense around one side of the camp. I haul their asses and mine one thousand feet up the hill and put them in place. Then I climb down to the CP to get my gear and shave. Then back up the one-thousand-foot hill again, this time with a full pack. Not easy.

When I get to the hole I'd picked out earlier, it's almost dark. I don't notice what I had missed before in daylight.

Someone had dumped here earlier, and two large clumps of human excrement remain. I spread my poncho and lightweight sleeping bag over them, carefully, as I discover that a large tube of Desenex has ruptured in my pocket. I don't really care. What I do care about is that it's now cold, and the new light bag I've picked up is too light to help much. Also 90 mm antitank guns used as artillery are firing over our heads at regular intervals, and two enormous searchlights are trained on clouds above to light the area.

After several sleepless hours there, it's dawn. I was too stiff and cold to feel much, but it was a great relief finally to be able to crawl out of that hole.

Down at the battalion CP, I meet Lt. Col. Robley West, CO of the First Battalion, First Marines. He assigns Winter and me to Baker Company. With the others headed to Baker Company, we go about two miles forward of the battalion CP in trucks. A guide takes us the rest of the way to the ridge where the company is on the line. It's probably a mile and a half and two thousand feet up from the road.

We are thirty men and two officers, inactive for three weeks at sea. I know I feel out of shape. Maybe some of the others do also. The climb gets progressively tougher as we go up. We stop often, but still some of the group look like they may pass out or even fall off the trail. When we finally come into the company positions, we pass along a line of real Marines—combat-hardened veterans, those who have been here for months. They stop whatever they're doing and turn to look at us with bemused interest. They comment to each other, but their voices carry, presumably because they are intended to. What we hear is

"Look pretty bushed, don't they?"

"They sure do. Washed out. Don't know how much *they* can help us."

By that time I was trying very hard to look cool, but I guess it wasn't working.

May 10. Of the fifty-three lieutenants who came out here from The Basic School, only twenty-one of us have come straight to rifle companies. The rest have gone to support units, motor transport, amtracks, shore party, etc., many to their great disappointment. Division wants to have the support units at full strength so that officers will be available here if they're needed later in the rifle companies. Everyone is expected to make it to the line eventually.

At full strength, there are just over forty Marines in a rifle platoon. There are three platoons in a company and three companies in a battalion. A rifle company, usually commanded by a captain, has 7 officers and 221 enlisted men and includes a machine gun section and a mortar section in addition to the rifle platoons. At this time in Baker Company, all three of the rifle platoons are commanded by first lieutenants.

Dick Winter had been commissioned shortly before I had. So when we joined Baker Company at the same time, he was senior and was given his choice of the two open billets: the machine gun section or the mortar section. He took machine guns. So I got the mortars. I really want a rifle platoon, but this is okay for now.

The company commander, John Coffey, is a captain, a regular officer in his early thirties. He's an athletic-looking fellow. He seems slow and deliberate but is probably competent.

The company exec. officer is Jim Cowan, a reserve first lieutenant from Santa Monica, California, who has been here since Inchon. Cowan is a large-boned personable man in his late twenties. He looks even tempered and steady.

The first platoon is led by Bob Work, a mustang, somewhat older for a first lieutenant. He is lean and tough with an excellent service reputation. He is expected to become the company exec. when Cowan leaves.

The leader of the second platoon is Tex Lawrence. He was in the class of '49 at Navy where he started at center in football and was the Navy heavyweight boxing champion. Tex is a dedicated Marine. His platoon respects him, but they're supposed to have some concern that his taste for combat might put them at risk.

Ed Dibble has the third platoon. Originally from Staten Island, he was in the class of 1947 at Yale. He's a tall plain-looking fellow with a keen sense of humor and a garrulous, friendly manner. He's been in Baker Company for the past three months.

May 11. When the Red offensive of late April finally ground to a halt, the Eighth Army had fallen back to a line across Central

Korea about twenty-five to thirty miles south of Chunchon. In early May, the First Marine Division broke out of that line and attacked north. The attack is continuing now against light and sporadic opposition. Division recon is ranging out ahead, north of the 38th parallel. Seventh Marines are the division spearhead, followed by the First Battalion, First Marines, my battalion. The rest of the division is behind as a reserve.

Last night, we received the order to fortify our positions here with barbed wire, trip flares, and booby traps. At the same time, it's still not clear whether we'll be staying here or moving on continuing the attack. I spent all morning today on a reconnaissance of the company defense area in order to lay in positions for machine guns, mortars, and artillery concentrations. Interesting work.

Baker Company is on something called No Name Line, generally along a saddle between two peaks. The company CP and the hole where I sleep are on a small knob just above the saddle. The views from up here are great, but that's not why we're here. We're here because this is the high ground, and tactically, this is where we have to be. Always. The road net is far below us, so far away that from up here it seems irrelevant. Baker Company runs patrols out to the front daily to keep the gooks away, or at least to be sure that we know where they are and what they are doing.

We eat C-rations. Some of the Marines here have been eating them for six or seven months and are still hearty and healthy. So C-rations must be okay. Actually, they're supposed to provide a balanced diet, and—strangely enough—I like them. I think they taste better than a lot of the chow I've had over the last four years. C-rations come in cardboard cartons, usually handed out just before noon. If you're moving, you eat one meal then a second that night and the last the next morning. Then there's nothing left to carry when you move out again.

Each carton has seven cans, three of the main food like corned beef, meat and beans, spaghetti and meatballs, hamburgers, etc., and three cans of crackers, coffee, and cocoa. The seventh can has some type of fruit or fruit cocktail. There is also a utility packet with cigarettes, a can opener, matches, more coffee, Scot Tissue, etc. We get PX gear, toothpaste, razor blades, shave cream, candy, etc., about once a week. What we don't get—or don't get enough of—is beer.

It's getting warm here in the daytime now, but it is always cold, very cold, at night. Because the Reds have no air or artillery, life in the rear can be very relaxed. About five miles south of here, they actually have movies every night and soldiers bathing in the streams during the day. The Army is motorized and road bound. We, on the other hand, travel and climb on foot and live on the hills. It's slower and physically much harder, but it's also a lot safer. So far, Marines haven't gotten ambushed.

Despite having taken 293 casualties in one fourteen-hour period last week, the First Battalion still has a good record, i.e., reasonable losses. At this time, most of the Marines who made the Inchon landing last September have been rotated home, although we still have thirty-four Inchon men in Baker Company.

May 15. On Sunday, we were pulled out of the line and brought back here to regimental reserve, a camp just north of Hongchon. Tents, cots, straw on the ground. More important, a shower (my first since arrival in Korea eleven days ago) and change of clothes (same). Most important, steak dinner (first hot meal) and 21,000 cases of beer are supposed to arrive tomorrow.

My mortar section, twenty men, is supplemented by a seven-man section of 3.5" rockets (bazookas), for use against tanks, roadblocks, concrete emplacements, etc. We haven't seen any targets like that, so the rockets are not active.

The 60 mm mortars are another story. Whether used together as a section, or split up with one squad assigned to each of three rifle platoons, the 60s are in the middle of every tactical encounter, every firefight. With the section, I got one Staff Sergeant Stamm who has been here since Inchon and is supposed to be the best NCO in the company. He is good, too good in fact, good to a fault. He not only makes all the decisions for the section but also actually does most everything himself and carries the section on his shoulders. As a result, Marines in the mortar section are less effective than they should be. They know less; they don't take enough responsibility. And if they ever lost Stamm, the section would collapse. I've got to fix that, because Stamm will soon be leaving on rotation. I like mortars, and we're going to start intensive mortar training soon.

Dick Winter, the other second lieutenant who joined Baker Company with me, left today. He was reassigned to the Seventh Marines. They were understrength, and we were overstrength, so either he or I was going to go. He went because the machine gun section is always broken up with one squad assigned to each rifle platoon, and the machine gun officer doesn't have anything to do. The mortar section, on the other hand, stays together as a unit and, thus, needs an officer. I was sorry to see him go but glad that I am staying. I like it here.

May 17. Still in regimental reserve. There is time to tell stories here, and I've heard a lot about the First Battalion, First Marines. They landed at Inchon, fought through to Seoul, and were hauled around Korea in ships to land at Wonson on the Sea of Japan. They advanced to the Chosin Reservoir and, on the way back, Able and Baker companies captured and held the pass at Koto-ri for the rest of the division to come through. Later, in March, the battalion jumped off again in Operation Killer. Finally, the Chinese counterattacked, and they were engaged in heavy fighting again in late April, just before I joined.

General Almond, X Corps commander, and Chesty Puller landed here by helicopter today. Puller, the most famous Marine, is an original who looks exactly like his pictures. In describing that time at the Chosin Reservoir when his regiment was surrounded, he remarked that the Chinese had beaten them to their knees, "but they found Marines fire well from that position." In talking to his men, he's supposed to have said, "If you hurt, or even if you're just feeling low, don't go to see the doctor. Don't go looking for the chaplain. Those fellows are all right, but they can't do anything for you. If you're feeling bad, you come around and see me. I always have a fifth of I. W. Harper in my pack, and I'll be glad to talk with you. You'll feel better after we talk." These quotes may be apocryphal, but you hear them everywhere, and they do a lot for morale. Puller himself is an inspiration.

We awoke about 0400 this morning to artillery that sounded like freight trains going over our heads. Later, we learned that during the night a Chinese regiment had slipped through the Seventh Marines' lines and was coming south along the road when they were spotted. Artillery fire called in by the Seventh managed to destroy that regiment, but we expect more attacks in the next few days. By that time, we'll be back on the line ready to defend.

May 18. Last night we came out of reserve and relieved C Company, Thirty-eighth Infantry, Second Army Division, back on No Name Line. From the standpoint of comfort, the position is great: deep, solid, well-constructed bunkers, neat paths and steps, close to the road with supplies readily accessible. But tactically it's no good. We are strung out too far and exposed in too many areas. We know we are going to be hit tonight, and we think we know just about where.

May 19. We were hit all right, but what we didn't count on was the weather. There was a flash shower late in the afternoon and then after dark, lightning, thunder, and a wild electrical storm. At its height, I'm in the bunker that serves as a CP with Captain Coffey, the company commander. It's cold and wet. We're laying out the defense plan for the night and with the light of a single candle. I show him where the mortar concentrations have been registered, and he marks them on his map. There's about three feet of headroom in the bunker, and we're lying on our stomachs wrapped in ponchos. A Marine wireman is crouched at the entrance to the bunker, listening on a sound power telephone connected to the rifle platoons on the line.

Suddenly, the wireman jerks up, lurches forward, and falls full-length into the bunker, literally on his face. Our first thought is a sniper. We douse the candle and lie there for what must have been minutes, cold, wet, and shaking in the darkness. The wireman is conscious and apparently not wounded. After a corpsman restores him with a couple shots of gook whiskey, we are able to determine that his feet were in a pool of water at the entrance, and he had been struck by lightening. It's raining too hard to get him back to his hole. We bundle him into a sleeping bag and lay him in a corner of the CP where he stays until morning.

The lightning and rain continue. We have rigged trip flares and booby traps across our front, and they go off like firecrackers through the night, each one triggering a flurry of grenades, and small arms fire from the line. Tex Lawrence's second platoon is on the high ground—Hill 736 on our extreme right flank—and they get most of the action. Tex has rockets, four sections of both heavy and light machine guns, and one squad of my mortars. The mortar squad alone fires sixty-two rounds through the night. By morning, I've spent the entire night in the company CP, most of it on sound-power phones to the line.

At dawn, everything is still in place, but shortly after dawn, five rounds of Army artillery, not cleared by their artillery FO, come slamming into our position—Tex's platoon—on Hill 736. The results are bloody. Six seriously wounded Marines are evacuated. Later that morning, we move out to take up new positions. We're all glad to be moving.

May 20. Last night about 2200, I finished registering concentrations for mortar fire in front of our new positions. The mortars were set up in a small draw just back of the line, and that's where the men and I were for the night. I dug a shallow hole and rigged my shelter half over it. The night was quiet, the moon nearly full. I set a 50 percent watch, and I was off the first half of the night. I turned in and fell asleep right away.

Just before midnight, I was jolted awake by a tremendous explosion on the rise slightly above me and about ten feet away. Something that felt like a rock hit my left leg just above the knee. At about the same time, I heard one of the men yell out, "Lieutenant, I'm hit!" I pulled on my boots and rolled out of the shelter half to look for the damage.

Before Doc Williams, the corpsman, arrived, our check showed that three Marines were hit, none seriously. Williams gave them morphine and penicillin, and while we're waiting for a Jeep ambulance to take them down to battalion, I felt something wet and found that my left leg was bleeding, just above the knee. Before I could ask the corpsman to take a look at it, a second incoming round landed close. This one—plainly from a large mortar—landed a few yards farther away. But it was still close enough to knock us all to the ground and also close enough to wing me with a second shell fragment, this time in the right elbow.

After we had carried the wounded down to the Jeep trail where the ambulance picked them up, the corpsman gave me a shot of penicillin, and I returned to the shelter half. Through the rest of the night, several other mortar rounds fell in our position, but nobody else was hit. At around 0600, we had another salvo of incoming mortar rounds and burp gun and rifle fire from directly in front of the line, apparently the gooks were trying out a little H&I firing and a light probe.

This morning, I had a chance to check for damage more closely. My shelter half and sleeping bag were basically shredded. The down filler in the bag was spilling out through long tears, and the bag was beyond repair. My dungaree jacket had several large horizontal tears across the chest where shrapnel had torn through folded cloth. If I had been in a shallower hole—or had a deeper chest—I might have gotten hurt.

I had promised the corpsman that I'd go down to get checked out at the battalion aid station this morning. And, when it was understood that I was going down to battalion, I picked up an unwelcome assignment.

The mortar section in Charlie Company had gotten a 60 mm mortar round stuck in a tube. They asked if I could take the tube—with the round stuck in it—back down to the battalion armorer. Frankly, I could think of things I'd rather do. If the round became unstuck and slid the rest of the way down the tube, it would detonate, not a particularly good thing to have happen. And in bouncing a mile or so down the rutted Jeep trail, I thought it could become unstuck. Actually, I had no idea how likely this might be, but I'm a mortar officer. I'm supposed to know about things like that. So I agreed to take it. Holding the tip of the projectile gingerly in one hand and cradling the tube like a baby on my knees, I did get the tube and its stuck round down the trail and to the armorer. Then the battalion surgeon picked a couple of shell fragments out of my leg and elbow, and I was back with the company by midafternoon.

That was just in time to watch our air and artillery pound a ridge about five thousand yards to our front. The Chinese were massed there. Our air was Marine F4Us, Corsairs, dropping napalm, and firing rockets. The artillery was 155s and 105s located far behind us and firing high over our heads. It was a beautiful sight, and effective. The Chinese must have taken a beating.

A new first lieutenant joined our company today, Ike Cronin, a reserve officer from Philadelphia who graduated from Notre Dame in 1948. That might mean one more officer between a rifle platoon, and me, but I can't worry about that now.

May 21. A couple of days ago, there was a change of command here at regiment. Colonel McAlister, who had replaced Chesty Puller as CO of the First Marines, was relieved by Colonel Wilburt S. Brown. I haven't seen the new CO yet, but he is universally known as "Bigfoot" Brown. And he's famous.

It seems presumptuous for me to call him Bigfoot. I've never even met him. But that is what everyone calls him. He is supposed to wear a size 16 or 18 shoe, and there are a lot of stories and jokes about him. Most are obviously apocryphal.

Like, he's supposed to wear his headgear always askew, so that anyone meeting him will look at his head rather than his feet. And like, it would be five days' piss and punk (Marinespeak for bread and water) for any enlisted man caught staring at his feet. Of course, there are the references you might expect to skis, snowshoes, etc.

The story I like best is why Bigfoot Brown hates aviators. It is said that when Bigfoot was a young officer in the Marine expeditionary force to Nicaragua in the late '20s, he led a patrol out into the jungle on the heels of a band of Sandinistas. The jungle was a rain forest, intense sun, temperature over one hundred degrees, and total humidity. The patrol was to be out for several weeks. Supplies were dropped to them from an ancient Curtis Jenny that Marines in the jungle communicated with in Morse code flashed with a mirror.

The patrol was out so long, and the Nicaraguan heat and humidity so bad, that Bigfoot's boots rotted away, just fell apart. A signal was flashed to the supply plane: "Bring a pair of new boots, big ones." And next day, the Jenny was back again to carry out the mission. Banking low over the Marine patrol waiting in the jungle, the pilot dropped his delivery, a large packet. And in the packet was a single boot with a message inside. The message read:

"Sorry, but this one was a full load. I'll bring the other one tomorrow." Despite stories like this—or more likely because of them—Bigfoot is known and widely revered throughout the Marine Corps, one of the most distinguished figures of the Old Breed. I look forward to meeting him.

May 22. Last night, we got the order to send out a company-size reconnaissance patrol to leave at 0800 this morning. Reconnaissance means go out and get information. You don't seek direct contact with the enemy, and you don't fire unless fired upon. This patrol is to be led by Jim Cowan, the company exec., and is to include the first and second platoons reinforced by squads of both heavy and light machine guns and a squad from my 60mm mortar section. This is well over one hundred Marines moving several miles forward of the lines. I've never seen anything this big, and I want to go along. Cowan says fine.

Our patrol objective is Hill 736, the same peak where Tex Lawrence had such a hairy time and caught the short artillery rounds a few nights ago. Able Company started out for there yesterday, but they drew fire at about the halfway point and were ordered to come back. Today's patrol is uneventful. At one point, we do sight a Chinese patrol over one thousand yards away, but we don't fire on it, and moving steadily along, we're on the objective at about 1300. We scan all of the area to the north, seeing nothing, and after blowing up some ammo and grenades that Tex's platoon had left there earlier, we return. By map distance, the patrol only covered about seven miles on the ground, but there was a lot of climbing, and by the time we get back, we know that it has been a full day.

About 2200 this evening, I'm sitting in the darkness with Jim Cowan and Ike Cronin, smoking and drinking Coffee Royale (unlike me, Cronin has brought whiskey as he was supposed to) when the captain returns from a conference at battalion. Our patrol and other patrols along the front indicate that the Chinese have pulled back. In addition, information from prisoners suggests that our artillery has been effective in destroying Chinese replacement battalions. Their casualties are reported to be high and their morale low. So this is considered the right time for a counteroffensive. The Eighth Army is to jump off in an attack across the entire front at 0800 tomorrow.

May 23. Reveille at 0600. The battalion moves out with Able and Charlie companies up and Baker in reserve. Our objective is Hill 736, the same hill we patrolled to yesterday, but with full sixty-pound packs, the going is slower. We capture three prisoners along the way but encounter no real resistance. We are on the objective by 1700, tired and hungry, only to be told that our work for the day is about half over.

Before tying in for the night, we are to push across the valley floor below and climb to the top of the next ridge about five thousand yards to the north. The climb down is not easy, and the sun is below the horizon before we start up the hill leading to the ridgeline. It is well after 2300 before we have the mortar section in position and all defensive concentrations registered. Another long day.

May 24. It's damp and foggy, and all our gear is wet as we tie on our packs and move out about 0730. We climb for a half hour on to a saddle from which we have a clear view of Hill 660, the battalion objective, one thousand yards to the north. It is honeycombed with heavy log bunkers, and in the early morning light, it looks menacing. The gooks have been there in strength for some time, and they're dug in to stay. We've had reports of heavy activity around Hill 660 over the past few days. But we see no movement there now.

Baker Company is up, and Ed Dibble's third platoon is to lead out. From the saddle, we set up the mortars and register artillery and mortar concentrations. Heavy machine guns on both flanks of the saddle fire tracers into the objective to adjust their sights and check the range. The only approach is a low ridge running from the left side of the saddle up to Hill 660, and as the three rifle platoons of Baker Company move into concealed positions along that ridge, the artillery and mortar preparatory fires begin.

About 0930, when we've finished working over the objective, Dibble starts to move his platoon forward. They go cautiously, slowly at first, using cover, advancing with one fire team at a time, moving through the trees. There's no firing now, and no other sound. It is very still.

Then it starts. First we hear the gook mortars, rounds going into the tubes on the reverse slope of Hill 660. We hear the high-pitched whine as they come up and over, exploding where they had been registered along the only approach. Dibble's lead squad seems to get through the mortars all right but is soon pinned down by fire from the bunkers farther up the hill. His second and third squads swing to the right and left and continue the advance. Our artillery is hitting the objective, and our heavy machine guns open up, firing just ahead of Dibble's lead squads.

Then I get the order to move the mortars up for close-in support of the attack. We chuck our packs into the cover alongside the trail and run down through the underbrush to our new position, moving as fast as anyone can lugging base plates, tubes, and extra rounds of 60 mm ammo.

On the way, I'm able to catch a glimpse of Bart Bartholomew, a corporal squad leader in Dibble's platoon, much talked about in the company for his earlier combat exploits. Bartholomew is out well in front of his squad. He's running forward, grenading bunkers, and firing at anything that moves. It's a superb performance, like watching a 100-yard touchdown run.

Just as we are setting up the mortars, I get the word that Hill 660 has been secured. There were eleven Chinese bodies there, no prisoners. Some Chinese, pursued by fire, were running off the ridges to the north. The shooting part of the assault has taken about a half hour.

Tex Lawrence's platoon, right on Dibble's heels in the approach, passes through on to the objective. Tex catches a grenade fragment in the side of his face. We have nine other casualties, six serious enough to be evacuated by helicopter.

After we arrive on top, I notice Bartholomew, Dibble's celebrated squad leader, sitting alone off to one side, with his head down. He's reading a comic book.

We are immediately joined on Hill 660 by a forward air controller and forward observers for artillery and 4.2" mortars. They spend the afternoon working the ridges to our front. We watch, absorbed. For us grunts who only climb hills to shoot at gooks at close range, this is a spectator sport. And it's fascinating. At one point, the forward air controller spots a Chinese convoy about five miles north of us headed our way. Within minutes, his call produces a flight of F-51 Mustangs flown by South African pilots firing into the convoy with .50 caliber machine guns and raining bombs and napalm down on them. No more convoy. Later patrols confirm that the Chinese are gone. Those that are left have pulled back to somewhere farther north.

May 26. We come off Hill 660 in a downpour and march along the road eight miles to the south. This is a regimental assembly area where I meet Stan Olson from the Second Battalion and Bob Oliver, Jimmie Marsh, and Joe Reed from the Third. Except for Oliver who is with an 81mm mortar platoon, they're all in rifle companies, waiting for rifle platoons. We have a lot of recent experiences, a lot to talk about. And no time to do it. We move on.

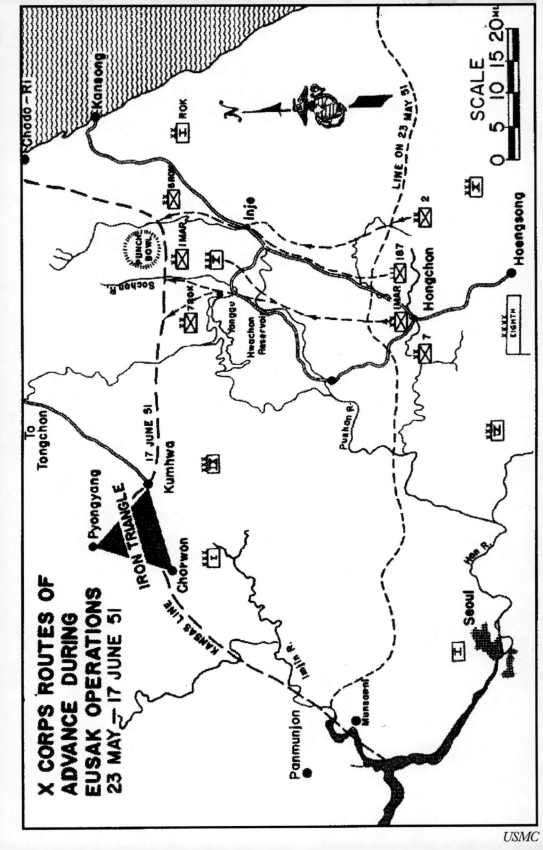

X CORPS ROUTES OF ADVANCE DURING EUSAK OPERATIONS 23 MAY — 17 JUNE 51

SCALE

0 5 10 15 20 MI

USMC

Chapter 5

EDDIE LEBARON
HITS THE LINE

Late May and early June, 1951 saw a remarkable shift in the balance of forces on the east central front. The powerful Chinese offensive had been stopped in its tracks. Then the Chinese, overextended and undersupplied, finally started to crack. It wasn't smooth.

To Walter Murphy, seeing it up close, it was a spectacle: "The People's Volunteers blackened the ridgeline as they trotted toward us, at least ten zillion of them. Then, as dozens of their soldiers were incinerated, riddled with 20 mm shells and blown to shreds, the lead elements whipped around and galloped north, whereupon they collided head-on with troops from the next unit jogging south. While the Corsairs were doing their gruesome thing, the Chinese were pushing through each other in utter terror and chaos, shoving comrades out of the way and, thus, often off the ridge, even knocking casualties off stretchers, sending wounded and well plummeting down the steep incline. When the planes finished, we called in artillery, using air bursts. It was a massacre, truly."

And in more open terrain, it could have been a sweep. But here in the rugged mountains of eastern Korea where the steep, heavily treed pitches run up to soaring granite walls and summits look out on the Sea of Japan, where sometimes the only roads give way to two-lane gravel trails running along the streambeds, defenders have a great advantage. And they use it.

The Chinese were still in charge, but when Marines closed with the enemy, they found that the enemy was no longer Chinese. They'd been replaced by conscripts of the North Korean Peoples' Army (NKPA). The NKs were perhaps less well trained, but they were tougher in this kind of fighting. Their mission was to hold until the Chinese could pull out to take up positions farther north, or in some cases to hold to the death. And their mission was enforced by political commissars with each unit ready to shoot the NKs to keep them in line.

Some still did manage to get away—for a time, at least. Walter Murphy recounted an example: "During one of those shellings, as we lay in a rice paddy, three NKs dashed for the north . . . . Willie Hammond, a black squad leader from Winona, Mississippi, where the White Citizens Councils were to be founded a few years later, stood up, pointed at the NKs, and shouted to his men, 'Git those muthuh fuckin' muthuh fuckuhs!' His troops obliged with a few shots, and the NKs chose prison camp."

This was the environment along the front as those of us who had started with the machine guns or mortars were working our way up to the rifle platoons. Sometimes the assignment to a rifle platoon came without a lot of advance notice. Eddie LeBaron was a good example.

Back at The Basic School, the only widely known member of our class was Edward Wayne LeBaron Jr., known universally as Eddie. His renown came from playing quarterback at College of the Pacific in the last coaching seasons of the venerable Amos Alonzo Stagg. At five foot seven inches and 175 pounds, Eddie was never the biggest, but he was usually the most outstanding player on the field wherever he played.

Eddie's other distinction at TBS was that he was the youngest member of the Seventh Basic Class, as he had been the youngest in earlier classes. He tells the story of being sixteen, and looking even younger, as a freshman on the College of the Pacific football team. The team was on a train, headed to Chicago to play Northwestern, then one of the top teams in the country. It was shortly after World War II, and many of his teammates were older veterans who had just returned from the war. On the way to the dining car one evening, he overheard an elderly lady ask a friend who those boys were and be told that they were a football team on the way to play a game. Then the lady, looking at Eddie, said, "Isn't that nice. Look, they brought their little son along."

Eddie had joined a Marine reserve unit, an amtrack company, while in college. Later, when he was in training for the college all-star game, his reserve unit was called up for Korea, and the manager of the college all-stars got a thirty-day extension for him to play in the game. During the extension, he also played two preseason games for the Washington Redskins. And at the suggestion of a former Marine playing with the Redskins, he applied for a program under which Marine reserves could get a regular commission and be assigned to The Basic School. Eddie arrived at Quantico only a week after being commissioned, and after our class had finished rifle firing on the range. He was in time for classes and, of course, for football practice.

Generally, Eddie did well in class, and he thinks he even learned something of close order drill. But he may have been the only regular Marine officer ever to go into combat without even having fired a rifle on the rifle range. Not unexpectedly, on the football field, he was superb, leading the Quantico Marines to the all-service championship after its best season in years and winning the Washington Touchdown Club Award as the outstanding player in the armed forces.

Eddie is also personable and intelligent. But the most impressive thing about him was that he was serious about service in the Marine Corps. Unlike some who avoided duty in front line units but later sought recognition as combat Marines, he played everything straight. When we finished at TBS, Eddie had orders to the First Marine Division in Korea. But after Quantico's spectacular season in 1950, every base in the Marine Corps wanted him. The athletic administration at Quantico wanted to hold him there, and Pendleton and Pearl Harbor also sought to have his orders changed and to hold him, at least through the fall of 1951. Then when we landed in Korea, he was assigned initially to an amtrack company in Masan. Somehow he managed to avoid all of those takeouts, and he actually arrived at the Seventh Marines about the same time the rest of us got to other rifle regiments.

At the Seventh Marines, Colonel Herman Nickerson, the CO, told Eddie that the commanding general of the First Marine Division didn't think he would want to go through the war commanding an amtrack platoon, and Eddie agreed. So, he was assigned to Baker Company, 1-7, and ended up as the officer in charge of the mortar section. From there, his active military career went on fast forward. He moved on from being a replacement, the extra officer, to being the *senior* platoon leader in the company in the next week. And he was among the very first of our class to distinguish himself in combat.

The place was near the Hwachon Reservoir of east-central Korea, the date May 29, 1951. Here's the story in Eddie's own understated words:

"In the last week of May, we were hard on the heels of the enemy, then mostly Chinese. We ran up against fortified positions at the Hwachon Reservoir, and we were attacking up ridgelines so narrow that you couldn't do much maneuvering. So it got down to digging them out bunker by bunker.

"As our platoons were attacking, I set up the mortars, and we were trying to put pressure on the bunkers. But the only place you could observe was out with the guys attacking and, with a radio, that made a good target for the Chinese. I didn't know enough to be afraid, with bullets snapping around, 'til someone right next to me was shot. Then I guess I understood that being out there was dangerous.

"I brought up a rocket launcher, and we tried to work over the bunkers with that, firing directly, and the launcher did enough damage, so we could move ahead.

"Then I was called back by the company commander to take over a platoon. Two of our platoon commanders had just been hit. Because we were never on level ground in Korea, platoon leaders always had to be up front in the attack and were prime targets for fire from bunkers as well as mines and booby traps. We learned early not to wear bars or other indications of rank that would make you an instant target."

There are many challenges, of course, in the world of substitutions. The distinguished conductor or soloist is stricken just before his performance; the star collapses in the dressing room; the quarterback or place-kicker is felled at the critical moment. In situations like these, an untried substitute may be thrust forward to take over. But to take over a Marine rifle platoon, under fire, in the attack—forty or so Marines, many combat-hardened veterans— and to command them successfully through what comes next, is another kind of a challenge. And it has to rank right up there on the challenge scale, especially when the substitute has never done it before. Fortunately for the Marines in his platoon and for the success of the attack, Eddie was up to it.

His laconic description continues: "After I got the second platoon of Baker Company, we advanced up the ridge and, with the other platoons, kicked the Chinese off the hill. We had a lot of help from Marine pilots flying Corsairs loaded with napalm. We put orange panels in front of the troops, and the Corsairs came in low and slow with .50 caliber machine guns blazing right over our heads and napalm pods dropping right in front. You just hoped the pilots could see the orange panels.

"Immediately before we jumped off, the young Marine next to me was shot. Then a piece of shrapnel from enemy artillery hit me in the shoulder and knocked me down the side of the hill. It wasn't that bad, so I got it patched up; and I took off with the platoon. I was so sore from getting knocked down off the ridge that I didn't pay much attention to the wound, and the action was over by nightfall. This gave me a good opportunity to get acquainted with the guys in the platoon who turned out to be good guys, and great Marines."

So Baker Company, 1-7, moved forward. The battalion took its objective, and the momentum of the Marines' attack was maintained. It sounds easy now. But attacks like this "ain't beanball." And when platoon leaders are hit, success may depend on having someone like Eddie there who can take over on short notice.

Chapter 6

JOE REED TAKES HIS FIRST HILL

Eddie LeBaron wasn't alone in being thrust suddenly into leading a rifle platoon under fire. Joe Reed's start was equally fast. For Joe, it happened on June 3, 1951, a few days later and a few thousand yards away. Joe makes it sound almost like going to a ball game. In his words:

"The approach march that day was uneventful, in lovely weather after the rainy night. I remember a wild sense of pride when we fell out on the road. As I looked ahead to the other units of the battalion, there was a display of flags flying from the whip antennas on the radio and command jeeps representing many of the states of the Union. There was also a startling number of Stars and Bars, not acceptable today. We had been out there for several weeks by then. We really did look like the Raggedy-Ass Marines they sing about.

"We pretty much knew we were going into a real fight because the chaplain said Mass on the hood of a jeep. Actually, it was a jeep stolen from the Army (serial no. 1234567). I remember, being then still a Methodist, how the guys seemed to be really focused. It impressed me greatly, and later, as I was taking instruction in the faith, I counted that experience as a factor in my conversion.

"I began that morning as the machine gun platoon leader [How Company, 3rdBn, 1st Marines]. So I didn't take over the second platoon until after a series of disastrous casualties. First, Dan Evans, the company commander, was hit and evacuated. Then Morris (Sam) McGee caught a round that ricocheted off a tree; he was hit in the spine, and he remains a paraplegic to this day.

"At that point, the company exec. ordered me to take over Sam's platoon to assault the next objective, about one hundred yards away. We had to cross a ridge running between the two laterals of an H-shaped hill mass. The NKs had mounted Maxim heavies on both ends of their lateral, and they were able to rake the ridge we had to cross in a murderous crossfire. By the time I got with the platoon, our artillery FO had been hit and evacuated. We had to find some way to drive the gooks back into their bunkers long enough for us to get out on the ridge. That's where Hal Artunian and his 60 mm mortars came in.

"The problem was he had to fire almost straight up through the overhanging branches of trees, and any branch could detonate a mortar shell. If they got through, he should be able to drop them right on the target. I remember, just as we started across the open ridge, hearing the rounds come out of the tubes and watching the branches sway, although there was no wind anywhere. But Artunian's accuracy was superb. Everything landed on target and detonated there, not in the trees above us.

"We had fixed bayonets, because this was going to be a very personal matter if the NKs stayed in their holes to the end, as they had in recent days. We were running uphill and about twenty-five yards from their position when they finally got their heads up and realized we were almost on top of them.

"I saw a couple of small branches rise up with a helmet underneath, and I fired a whole thirty-round magazine at it. It disappeared at that moment. We found out later that it was an NK major who died with a lot of valuable papers in his pack.

"By then we were in defilade against the hill, but a shower of grenades was falling on us. Mike Robatin, squad leader of the first squad, was right next to me when a grenade landed between us. I was stunned, but I heard him say, 'Oh, shit!' and when I looked down, I saw that the blast had taken off his left leg, right at the boot top. Boot, foot, and that part of the leg were lying there next to him. The wound had been completely cauterized; there was not a drop of blood anywhere but at the end of his leg. Mike showed no sign of shock as he called on one of the fire team leaders to take over the squad."

In the final minutes of the attack, Joe and his last few Marines were locked in a grenade duel in the center of the approach. Joe had apparently not heard the old saw that three-second fuses only last two seconds, and when they found their own grenades coming back, they started holding. That is, they'd let the spoon fly and count to two—against a three-second delay—before throwing. That's dangerous, and it requires exquisite timing. But when you do it right, it works, and they did it right. The grenades didn't come back

At the very end, Joe had to make up his own fire support. He and four other Marines took two grenades each and hurled them up in two volleys. Then they charged up and over the top, firing from the hip, bayonets flashing in the sun, everything on full automatic. That was enough. They had the hill.

While mopping up gook bunkers farther along the ridge, Joe got his wounded evacuated and the rest of his men dug in. Fearing incoming mortars that the NKs typically registered on positions they had to evacuate, remnants of the platoon worked as fast as they could. And expecting a counterattack, Jim Barnett, who had taken over as the company commander, managed to get artillery registered on the gook ridges to their immediate front. Then the artillery fired H&I (harassing and interdiction) fires through the night to protect what remained of Joe's platoon on their precarious perch.

At the end of the day, Joe's platoon had tive Marines dead and eighteen wounded, nearly 60 percent casualties for the day's work. They counted twenty-five enemy dead there and took fifteen enemy prisoners, all wounded. They estimated another thirty or so NKs had been able to pull away at the last minute to head north.

What impressed Joe—and what is impressive—is that he was able to take command of a platoon of Marines he had not trained with and did not know, Marines who could scarcely have known who he was, and together they could accomplish what they did. As he put it, they "never questioned my taking over thirty minutes before we assaulted . . . not a one hesitated to follow me." Part of that is the Marine Corps tradition, of course, for both the officer and the men. And part of it is Joe. But, however, credit is shared, the attack that day was outstanding.

This attack showed, once again, that driving hard pays off. The assault didn't have to turn out like it did. At the outset, when there was no air and no artillery, the Marines could have been stopped in their tracks. Just charging ahead could have cost that entire platoon and other platoons to follow. It was only resourceful use of the 60 mm mortars that got the attack launched. And later on the approach, it was speed in getting in close and effective use of grenades that made it work.

At any rate, it was a successful attack for the Third Battalion. And a great start for Joe.

Chapter 7

BAKER COMPANY IN THE ATTACK, MAY 30-JUNE 9

May 30. We came off the line yesterday and are here in division reserve at a place called Oran-ni, about ten miles east and six miles north of Hill 660. We have been here for two days. I spent the entire first day cleaning everything I have and the second on patrol. The Fifth and Seventh Regiments are out to the northwest, heading toward the eastern end of the Hwachon Reservoir. We expect to join them, or relieve one of them anytime now. Meanwhile, we sit here alongside the MSR (main supply route) as trucks, tanks, and supplies headed north rumble by at all hours of the day and night.

I learned later that Walter Murphy—with the keen eye of a born naturalist looking for fauna—had thought of Oran-ni as Frog Town. Murphy recalled that "there, we were assaulted by millions of lustfully fornicating frogs. They leaped into our food, our packs, our sleeping bags, even our clothes, and wherever they hopped, it was in pairs, with one mounted on the other, madly humping away. During the day, we brushed the frogs away and took out patrols that vacuumed up Chinese by the gross. The Third Battalion, Jim Marsh's, took more prisoners in those few days than the battalion had suffered casualties since Inchon."

May 31. With the Chinese retreat, we've captured a slew of Chinese horses and donkeys, both with packsaddles. When these were passed out to the line companies according to need, Baker Company's mortar section got two horses, a gray and a bay. They are small and have saddle sores, but they are sturdy. With heavy loads of mortar ammo on their backs, they just keep plodding along. They stumble, but they don't fall.

For some time now, we've had Korean laborers, called *yobo*s, to haul food, water, and other supplies up the ridges we climb. We got sixty-three additional Korean laborers last week, and the battalion hopes eventually to have one for every Marine. They can carry tremendous loads on big A-frames, and they are fun to have around. But because of the language differences, there isn't much we can say that they can understand. You get them by yelling, "Yobo! Yobo!" when you need them, and they come running, usually laughing in a noisy pack. A Marine battalion fully reinforced by a full complement of Korean laborers with Chinese horses and donkeys added will be quite a sight.

June 3. For the last couple of days, we've been moving. We're going north with the First Marines in the attack, and our battalion in reserve. At about 1800 today, we get to where we think we're going to dig in for the night, just as big dark storm clouds are rolling in. I head out on the line to get the mortar section in position and get my men in place. When I get back to where I'm going to start digging a hole to sleep in, the rain is coming down in sheets. It fills in after each shovel full of earth I take out. So I'm soaked and actually relieved when word comes to pull all our gear together and move on to the next ridge.

We do the entire move in darkness. In the driving rain, our packs are sodden as lead. We have to go down a thousand feet or so and then climb about that far up again to the top of the next ridge. We get there shortly after midnight.

I have no thought of digging in this time. I just want to get through to morning. I wrap up in a poncho and drop to the ground, leaning back against a tree. Finally, I doze off. When I wake up at daybreak, I'm amused to remember that Joan and I were married just a year ago today. In that year, I've come from the relative luxury of the Wardman Park Hotel in Washington, DC, to a mountainside in Korea where I don't even have a hole to crawl into. I'm sleeping sitting up against a tree, in the rain. Somehow, that doesn't seem like progress. It doesn't even seem like going in the right direction.

June 5. Hwachon Reservoir, Central Korea. The reservoir is a large irregular body of water running generally east-west about ten miles north of the 38th parallel and just southeast of the so-called Iron Triangle. Our main supply route from the south runs around the eastern tip of the reservoir, and the Reds have registered artillery and heavy mortar concentrations on this vulnerable point. They fire for effect on everything coming up, and they have ambushed a couple of truck convoys here. So it's necessary for us to take the hills north of the reservoir, for planning purposes called X-ray, Yoke, and Zebra. First Battalion gets this assignment, and Baker Company is to secure the ground on both sides of the MSR from which the attack will be launched. The company manages to get this done with light firing and no casualties. We settle in for the night.

June 6. Attack. We're up at 0600, and we move out at 0800. The weather is clear and cool today, and visibility is good. Baker Company is to take objectives X-ray and Yoke, and Charlie Company is assigned Zebra, the next high ridge to the north.

We get both of our objectives by late morning, and Charlie Company has Zebra before evening. The enemy, two NK companies, is well dug in and puts up a stiff fight. But by the end of the day, battalion intelligence has counted seventy-four enemy dead on the three positions. The battalion has captured a lot of military hardware and fourteen cases of 57 mm recoilless rifle ammo and has taken four NK prisoners. We have some wounded but no KIA.

I might say a word about attacking well-built defensive positions in this phase of the Korean War. Marines attack generally along a ridgeline, or directly uphill if there's no other way. The assault troops have BARs, rifles, grenades, and sometimes bayonets. But effective use of all supporting arms is an essential element of a successful attack as well. We have the air, the naval gunfire support, and an overwhelming advantage in artillery and heavy mortars. Marine commanders use all of this—everything they have—so that the objective is pounded before the first rifleman starts up. That's Marine doctrine, not only the best way to do it, but also important to holding casualties to a minimum and to maintain the troops' morale (also their confidence in their commander).

The same coordination of supporting arms is important after an objective is taken. If an attack has resulted in the enemy pulling back off the position, effective use of artillery and air is necessary to finish the job. It's also essential to ensure that we won't have to fight the same enemy again, the next day or the day after, a few ridges to the north.

Before an assault is launched, the commander and any forward observers usually gather on the OP (observation point), a vantage point with the best view of the objective. Included there will be the forward air controller, the artillery FO (forward observer), and FOs from the 4.2" and 81 mm mortars. They will have registered concentrations on the target earlier and will fire for effect. The impact of this firing is watched intently, and any part of it may be fired again, maybe over and over. When the air and other heavy stuff have done all they can do, the assaulting troops are ready to move. The battalion's heavy machine guns, and sometimes the heavier .50 caliber machine guns, are set up, usually around the OP. They may start overhead fire, every fifth round a tracer, and hold it on the objective as the lead fire teams move out.

That's about all that can be planned. The rest depends on what the assaulting troops run into and how hard they can hit. There are a lot of possibilities.

In Korea, the OP is usually on a ridge with the objective the next tactically significant high ground, almost always the next ridge to the north. We're below the tree line here, and the hills we're on are covered with trees when we arrive. But that doesn't last long. This war is hard on tree-covered hills. Bombardment from both sides first strips the trees of foliage and then blasts out the stumps. Soon it all looks like moonscape.

When any cover is available, we'll use it to get closer to the enemy without being seen. It's greatly to the attacker's advantage to be able to stay out of sight while moving forward, especially if the gooks have their heads down to avoid incoming fire.

But at some point, the approach comes to an end. You're there, right in front of the objective, whether it's a bunker, a gun emplacement, a trench line, or gooks in fighting holes. Then there's no more cover, and it's just a question of how much fire you can lay down and how fast you can move forward. Firing on full automatic helps. Speed helps. Grenades are essential. But sometimes all of that may not be enough. That's what you have bayonets for, and you use whatever you have. You do whatever you have to do. And you don't have any time to think about it.

Generally, the platoon leader is behind the lead squad or even the lead fire team. He has to be close enough to see what's happening and see it early. So he's as far forward as he has to be.

If you get stopped by fire, you have to figure out what to do next. Usually, there are only a few choices, but you may have to make that call pretty fast. Of course, that's why you're there.

Today I had set up the 60 mm mortar section and registered on the objective, X-ray. When the first platoon, lead platoon in the attack, moved out, I moved along behind it with the company commander and his radioman. We were held up by fire on a knoll short of the objective with the fire coming from an enemy bunker ahead and off to the right. Luckily, we had registered the mortars on that bunker the night before, and I could call fire on it from where we were pinned down.

With the 60 mm mortars and our light machine guns firing on the bunker, we see two North Koreans get up and walk slowly along the ridge very close to where our lines of fire converge.

Because we need prisoners and someone thinks this pair may be trying to surrender, we hold up everything, and a Korean interpreter calls to them on a bullhorn. We hold for several minutes. Finally, still ambling along, they disappear over the ridgeline unto the reverse slope, the back of the objective. They're gone!

Everything opens up again, full blast. Bob Work and the first platoon roll up and over the objective. X-ray is ours. The third platoon, working its way along a ridge a hundred yards to our right, and also headed to X-ray, has a firefight all the way. When they finally arrive on top, we consolidate. There are twenty-six NK bodies there and on the approaches. There are no prisoners and only negligible casualties in Baker Company.

In this kind of action, where the North Koreans are defending and withdrawing, there are always some who stay and die in their bunkers. The others stream off the back of the hill to take up positions on the next ridge to the north. That's why pursuit by fire with air and all other supporting arms is so important.

Today we had the full support of all heavy weapons from the moment we took the hill. Heavy machine guns were in place in a matter of minutes, and artillery and air worked over the ridges to the north for the rest of the morning. Our second platoon took Yoke in the late morning, and before nightfall, we watched Charlie Company capture Zebra. With everything working on schedule, the First Battalion had a good day.

In addition to the usual number of burp guns and other gook weapons, the battalion recaptured a truckload of our own mortar ammo, a couple of our own 81 mm mortars, several Russian books, plus diaries, maps, papers, etc. From the captured papers, we learn that we've been fighting remnants of the Sixth North Korean Division. As of yesterday morning, they were supposed to be nine hundred men strong, but that total must be much lower after today.

We are on the very crest of objective X-ray with a beautiful view out over the lines to our front and the Hwachon Reservoir about a mile to our rear and below us. We expect to be here for a few days.

June 7. Today is Baker Company's change-of-command day. Captain Coffey, promoted to major, is leaving to take over Weapons Company at battalion; Jim Cowan becomes company commander. Bob Work moves up to company exec., and I replace Work as platoon leader of the first platoon. I'm surprised at this happening now. I'm not the senior lieutenant in the company. As a matter of fact, I'm the only *second* lieutenant in the company. But those are the orders, and that's enough for me. The first platoon is first rate, considered experienced and steady, a solid outfit. I couldn't be better satisfied.

I really like Bob Work. When I talk with him after the changes are announced, he's pretty matter-of-fact. "I think they're okay, John. I think it's a good platoon. But you won't really know what you have until you come under fire with them." He was tactful enough not to add, "and neither will they." But that's what I was thinking, and that's the only thing I was concerned about.

My concern was a nagging uncertainty lying just below the surface, simple but very real: What could I add to this first-rate platoon? Some of these guys had been here for almost a year. Everybody, of course, had been here longer than I had, and the platoon itself had done everything in the war. What could I possibly have gotten out of a few months at The Basic School that would stack up against the Inchon landing, the Chosin Reservoir, and that spectacular attack southward to Hungnam? They've already proved that they're world class at what they do, and now I'm going to be doing it with them. What gives me the edge to command them? Well, whatever the answer is, we'll soon find out. This is what I've wanted, and now I've got it.

June 8. Our new company commander, Jim Cowan, is a seasoned veteran who has been with Baker Company since the Inchon landing last September 15. He is twenty-eight, born and raised in Hawaii—actually one-eighth Hawaiian. A landscape architect, a lover of plants and flowers, Jim took degrees at USC and Berkeley and was working in Los Angeles when he was called up with the Marine Corps Reserve for Korea. He's inclined to make the best of everything, says he'd have felt left out if he hadn't gotten out here.

Cowan is cool. He is calmly self-confident and deals easily with people. He's able to make the difficult and dangerous sound like the most natural thing in the world to do.

He is like that always, even in the face of uncertainty. More than a few times I've heard him say, "I'm not sure what this order means, but it looks like we're in for a good thing." That's a great quality to have, especially in a rifle company under fire. Just like fear, confidence is contagious. It carries directly through to the officers and men in the company. Cowan is going to do all right.

June 9. As it turns out, this was a big day. But it started like any other.

About 2200 last night, Jim Cowan called the platoon leaders, a group that now includes me. He had just gotten off the phone from battalion. As usual, his voice is casual and easy. If we were back in the States, he might be calling with tomorrow's weather report.

"We're going to be on the move again tomorrow," he said. "We'll be attacking north, straight to the front, those next two ridgelines. We'll have plenty of artillery, and we'll have them really work those ridges over. We jump off at 0800, third platoon, first platoon, second platoon—that order. Any questions so far?"

Everyone grunted. Cowan went on, "This doesn't look too bad actually. They're there, but we'll start early and soften them up. We don't have to move out until we think it looks good up there, and we'll have air on standby if we need it. Anything now?"

Again nothing. Tex and Ed Dibble had heard orders like this before, and I was thinking of other things.

And then to me, "John, that's a really good platoon you've got. That used to be my platoon you know; those are my boys. So I know you'll take good care of them. Are you all set?"

Actually, right at that moment, I didn't know how set I was. But if I wasn't set by this time, I never would be. "Sure, Skipper, we're fine."

"All right, men, get some rest. We move out in the morning."

I head back to my hole to sleep. Generally, platoon leaders are not supposed to have their platoon sergeants in the same hole with them. The idea is to avoid getting hit at the same time. That makes sense. I don't disagree with it, but somehow, I never followed it. When I was assigned to the first platoon, I got Bill Landon, the platoon sergeant, with it. We started out sharing the same hole, and I never changed after that. When I do get to the hole, Landon is there asleep, snoring. I feel edgy as I settle into my sleeping bag.

Physically, I feel great. But a couple of things are bothering me. First, this is the real test coming up, and I'm still not sure how much difference I can make. How can I improve on what they would do right, just by reflex? The other thing is simply that I don't know them. I've seen them around for a month or so, but I don't even know most of their names.

It's too late to worry much about that in the few hours left before dawn, and I drift off to sleep.

We're up at first light. No steak and eggs, what I've heard of as the traditional Marine Corps attack breakfast. Just spaghetti and meatballs warmed over a Coleman stove. It's easy to pull our gear together, and we're saddled up. The air is fresh and cool. There is some haze in the valleys below, but it's otherwise clear. When the sun gets high enough to burn off the haze, it is perfect weather for anything. I have Landon form up the platoon to be ready to move out. In a few minutes, he's back. He looks serious.

"Lieutenant, one of the squad leaders has just turned in. We need someone to replace him. It should be Howard Allmain to take over that squad. Allmain is right over here, but if you want me to tell him, I will."

I was surprised, "What happened to the squad leader?"

"He's had it," Landon says. "He's a good man, but he just turned in. He was with us at Kojo last winter when the Chinese came through a snowstorm in the middle of the night. We had sixteen men bayoneted in their sleeping bags, and he hasn't gotten in a bag since that night. Like some of the others, he never got over it. He was due out on rotation last week, but that was cancelled, and this morning he just ran out of gas."

"Okay, Bill. Tell Allmain he's got the squad. And, Bill, . . ."

"Yes, Lieutenant."

"Which one is Allmain?"

When Landon pointed him out, I felt better. I did recognize Allmain as someone I'd noticed earlier, though I didn't know him by name. Much later, someone told me that he was wild—reckless, with little concern for his personal safety—especially since he'd gotten a Dear John letter from home a short time before. But of course that wouldn't have bothered me, even if I'd known it. Allmain was fine. We're ready to go.

The company moves out quietly in a long column, heading to the OP where we set up a base of fire. The attack starts from there.

On the OP, we huddle again with Jim Cowan. Tex, as always, looks ready for anything as he is squinting ahead at the ridgeline to our front. Cowan explains, "Okay, Tex, I want the second platoon here on the OP. Set up to support Dibble in going after that first ridge. Get your machine guns and 60s in place and register. Be ready to move out and then to move through them after they've secured that first objective."

Then, turning to me, "John, you've got the second ridge ahead. Let's see how it works out with Dibble, but you'll attack from there—the first ridge—with Dibble's platoon as a base of fire. Then Tex will move up and through you after you get the second ridge secured."

Cowan holds up for a minute as the first rounds of the 105 mm artillery and 4.2" mortars start coming in over our heads to land on the ridge directly to our front. It sounds great. We love it. We could never get enough of it. We like to hear Cowan requesting it, and we like to hear the FO calling it in. Now we do feel ready as we sprawl on the OP to wait for the first act, the third platoon's assault on the ridge ahead.

The artillery barrage winds up, and Ed Dibble and his platoon move out. They have to descend for a few hundred yards, and then they have a steep climb. There is some light firing from the ridge ahead, but they seem to be moving steadily forward. Finally, they come up on the objective. In less than an hour, Dibble radios back that the hill is secure. We move out in a long file to take up our positions there, on the ridge Dibble has just taken. The artillery and 4.2s adjust to firing on the next ridge, the one we are going for. As the artillery prep winds up, Jim Cowan and I are kneeling at the crest of the new OP, looking through binoculars for any movement on the objective. Smoke rises slowly where the artillery rounds have landed. But except for that, there is nothing. No movement. No sound. Finally, Cowan turns to me with that slow, confident smile.

"Okay, John. You can move out whenever you're ready."

I feel like I've been ready for a year. I've talked to the squad leaders, and I nod to Landon to get the platoon started. The first squad heads out, and I join them, just behind the lead fire team. The trail heads off to our left and down along a spine several yards wider than the trail on both sides. We move on down, staying off the trail at this point to take advantage of all available cover, anything that will keep us out of the enemy's sight. Whenever the objective comes into view, we strain to see any sign of movement that will tell us what's there. But we see nothing. If there are gooks there, they must be lying low.

After half an hour, we've covered several hundred yards, maybe halfway to the objective. It's warm and humid now, and we're sweating freely. I'm trying hard to see the ridge ahead, even when it's obstructed by trees. I'm trying to think ahead. I may have been trying too hard.

We reach a point where the spine we're on is joined by a spur running off and down to the right. The lead fire team moves past the junction with the spur, and I look right at it as I'm moving along, but somehow it doesn't register. Just as I'm starting to pass it, still moving ahead, I'm startled to hear a Marine close behind me.

"Lieutenant, do you want someone to go down there and check out that spur?"

Do I? *Of course, I do.* How the hell could I be going past it?

I hold up the lead and direct the next fire team in line out to the spur to see what's there. I wait with the rest of the platoon, spread out on both sides of the trail.

We don't have to wait long. The stillness is broken by the sharp racket of firing, automatic weapons and exploding grenades, ours and theirs, from down on the spur.

With that, I pull up the next fire team and head out to the spur on a dead run. We arrive just as the firing is ending. The first fire team has flushed a heavy machine gun nest manned by four North Koreans. Their gun was facing to the front, directly at our objective. If we had advanced in the open without taking out that machine gun, we could have had more trouble than I like to think about. But with the advantage of surprise, our first fire team had killed the NKs at the gun and in the bunker close by.

Now we control the gun, and we bring down two of the light machine guns attached to our platoon and set them up there, with the captured machine gun, to support our attack from that position.

Back on the trail, we continue our advance, now supported by the three machine guns on our flank. Howard Allmain, at the head of the lead squad, ties a brilliant yellow air panel on his pack, so our machine gunners can fire just ahead of the air panel, the lead element of the platoon. I plan to go up on the objective from the front slope to take advantage of that covering fire.

We pick up speed and soon arrive at the corner where the spine we're on swings to the right and runs directly up to the objective. As we advance around the corner, we are okay at first because we're in defilade behind a hummock of ground to the front. But as soon as we came into view over the top of that hummock, we draw heavy machine gun and burp gun fire.

A couple of Marines are hit in that opening exchange, and the rest of us dive to the ground, flattening ourselves into any slight depression that will keep us out of the line of fire. The slightest movement brings another hail of fire, bullets snapping viciously just over our heads. We're on a hot corner, not a comfortable place to be.

I figure that if we try to rush the top from there, we won't get very far. We are directly in the gooks' sights. Our machine guns are firing in from the flank now. That sounds good, but it's obviously not enough.

We could try to pull back and call in an air strike, but we'd have a hard time pulling back, and the strike could be a long time coming. Meanwhile, we're pressed flat against the ground—really trying to burrow into it—with bullets snapping right over our heads. There must be another way up, I think. But I have no idea where it might be. I don't even know what's on the reverse slope, the back of the objective, but it couldn't be much tougher than this.

I call over to Allmain to hold his squad in place where they are. And still pressing against the ground, I wriggle backward to get behind the hummock and pick up the rear squad that has not yet come into the line of fire.

When I get there, I talk to the squad leader, Sims Morse, a quiet Louisianan with eleven months in Baker Company. It was easy to explain to him that I want to get around to the back of the objective and try to get up that way. Sims nods that he understands, and we move around pretty fast. When we're on the reverse slope, Sims lays out his squad in a line of skirmishers across the hill. He and I are together on the right end of the line. We start up.

For the first few strides, everything is quiet. I can't believe this will really work. As we're moving, I look over at our line moving up through the trees to my left. They look good. They are spaced well, about five yards apart, climbing slowly, straining to see ahead. Maybe this will work.

Then for just an instant, Sims and I see something move or flash, ahead and slightly to our right. We pause. I think it's too close to where the squads we left on the main approach may be. We don't fire in that direction.

We continue on up. Then, without warning, with no other sound, the morning silence is shattered by a volley of automatic weapons and burp gun fire that rakes our line from end to end, across its entire length.

Sims is hit. He crumples to the ground, just to my left, almost at my feet. Other Marines fall all across the line. Those still on their feet are firing, but the line is stalled. We're taking heavy fire from automatic weapons, and the air is thick with NK grenades, although most of the grenades bounce on down the steep incline to explode below.

I leave Sims for a moment to head toward the center of the line where I get Corpsman Gary Spalding and send him back to Sims.

I can see at a glance that nearly half the squad has been hit. Because we don't have enough men left to go forward there, I leave the wounded to Spalding and another corpsman. I head back around the corner of the hill to where the rest of the platoon is still pinned down.

They are there, in place; most of the first and second squads are still firing. But they're down. They're not able to move without drawing fire. We're still stalled.

This was the critical moment, the tipping point. There are only two approaches to our objective, and we've tried them both. Now we're in too close for an air strike or even supporting artillery. And we've lost enough men to seriously limit whatever choices we might have left.

It seems to me we have a couple of options. We could either pull back, or we could hold there and call for Tex to come through with the second platoon, still fresh and at full strength. I don't like either of those, but there doesn't seem to be any other way up.

Or maybe there is. Maybe we can take it straight ahead from where we are. Trying to get a feel for that, I listen hard. Then, wondering if I may be imagining it, I seem to sense that the enemy firing is less intense, not as heavy as it has been. Maybe this is a better shot from here now than when we'd first tried it.

I huddle briefly with Allmain and the other squad leader. If we're going to do it from here, it's not complicated. We just have to get up with everyone firing to the front and run hard, straight to the front and up. We have to provide our own covering fire. And once we commit, we have to drive ahead, fast!

The hard part is just to get started. But these are Marines. They get the word right away, and they understand. They look to me for the signal, but no one questions the order. No one balks or even hesitates. When I'm sure that everyone's in place and ready, I take a deep breath and yell.

"*Let's go!*"

Rising to start forward, I glance to both sides to be satisfied that we're all together, up and moving. We are—almost.

After one step, I'm right on top of two Marines who'd been just ahead of me, struggling to their feet. I hear one, looking to the other, ask, "Who's going to go?"

At that moment, I'm right over the questioner. In a reflex action, I duck down and yell "you are!" in his ear just as I swing my foot into his rear. In that split second, he reacts. Like a shot. Like he's coming off a catapult. He bounds all the way up and goes by me in a stride, the other Marine with him.

When I see how this kick start worked for him, I wish someone had been there to kick me. And from that point on, the Marine I'd booted keeps on going, out in front of the rest of the platoon. As we come up over the crest of the hill, he is well in front, running in a crouch, firing and grenading bunkers and shouting the rest of the platoon on. His buddy is right there, a few paces behind.

By that time, we are all firing. Everyone with an automatic weapon is blasting a path to the front. The carbine I'm carrying feels like a fire hose, blowing out everything before it. Firing on full automatic—750 rounds a minute—it is an enabler.

The example of the Marine in front is exhilarating, and the momentum of our charge carries us forward. We go on over the top, killing some twenty or so gooks in their positions and grabbing a couple of prisoners on the way. It's over fast, the final minutes a rout.

We set up a hasty defense and radio back to the company that the hill is secured. Then Tex's second platoon passes through us and on out to a continuation of the ridge we'd just taken. The artillery and heavy mortar FOs set up in our position to fire on the enemy streaming off the back of the hill.

While this is going on, the rescue helicopters fly up into the ravine behind us to evacuate Sims Morse and our other wounded. We expect that everyone taken out fast like that will recover, because most do. In this case, that was true of everyone but Sims. With a string of bullet holes across his chest, he lived long enough to get to the field hospital, but they couldn't save him. He died there a week later, an especially tragic fatality. He was overdue for rotation back to the States, and this would have been his last action under any circumstances.

For Baker Company's first platoon, those few hours must have been a great relief. They had taken on a fresh new second lieutenant and still gotten by fairly well. Their record of outstanding performance had been extended, and they had gotten through the day without unreasonable losses.

For me, the action that day was a break, and the timing was good. My first scrape with the platoon had gone okay; the business of building confidence, which otherwise could have taken weeks, was shortened to a couple of hours. This was, after all, the fastest way to get to know the Marines you were with.

Most of what I didn't learn about the platoon on the hill, I did pick up over the next few days in recapping the action. This was a great exercise in getting more detail about what happened and also learning more about the individual Marines. Surprisingly, the impressions I gained in those first few days remained mostly unchanged for all the rest of my time in Korea.

Vic Heins, for example, was a stalwart on June 9, as he had been in a score of earlier actions. He was later promoted to sergeant and served as our platoon guide until he was rotated back to the States at the end of the summer.

Howard Allmain, who became a squad leader at the very last minute before we jumped off, was in the thick of everything that day. He came off that hill without a scratch, although bullets had ripped through the bright yellow air panel he'd tied to his pack and shattered the wooden handle of his entrenching tool. When I talked to Allmain nearly fifty years later, he still called me lieutenant. And referring to the action on June 9, 1951, he said, "To be truthful, Lieutenant, there hasn't been a day since then that I haven't thought about that particular battle."

Marv Burnett, one of the leaders in the final charge, caught a jagged piece of shrapnel in the shoulder. At the field hospital, they thought some of it might have come to rest in his lung cavity, so they held him for ten days. At the end of that time, he was back with us and ready to go again.

And, finally, the Marine I'd booted at the start of our final push was a discovery. He was Bernie Hletko, then a pfc. His performance that day was so spectacular that it inspired the entire platoon. He was painfully wounded in the final charge but refused evacuation until the others were taken out, and then he was the first to return to the platoon. He was later awarded the Silver Star for his actions that day. His buddy, close behind him in the last charge, was Vic Heins.

Actually, I had noticed Hletko, even before June 9. Somehow, you noticed him—a non-reg looking guy, rangy, bony, hair sticking out from under his cap. By that time, I may even have heard that he was an outstanding baseball and football player from a high school on Chicago's south side. His coach had taken him to the recruiting office to enlist in the Marine Corps Reserve, so he wouldn't be drafted when he turned eighteen. Later, Hletko would explain it by saying simply that "the reserve unit needed a second baseman." That did keep him out of the draft. But after the North Koreans invaded, President Truman called up the Marine Corps Reserve, and Hletko was called to active duty. When he got to Camp Pendleton, on his way to Korea, he'd never had a rifle on his shoulder. He had a couple of weeks at Pendleton on the rifle range and the drill field. Then he was on a transport headed for Korea in an early replacement draft.

Hletko was a natural leader, regardless of rank. When Allmain left on rotation, Hletko, still a pfc., took over the squad. Later, he was promoted to corporal and then sergeant, and he stayed as the squad leader as long as he was there. He would have stayed as long as I was there; any replacement NCO with higher rank would be assigned to one of the other squads.

The firefight on June 9 was also an awakening for me. I'd never again wonder why the platoon leader is there or what he is supposed to do. And I better understood Bob Work's comment about not knowing what I had until after the first firefight.

I just hoped the platoon thought as much of the day as I did.

Chapter 8

BILL ROCKEY ATTACKS

I n early June, 1951, when Bigfoot Brown inspected his regiment's
position on the Kansas Line, he was shocked. The First Marines
did not have the high ground, and their positions were dominated by
the enemy on the next ridge to the north, some three thousand
yards away. Bigfoot didn't hesitate to bring this up, and when he
did, he was given authority to move out. The First Marines
attacked to the north, pulling the rest of the line up with them.

As it turned out, this was no minor line adjustment. The gooks
were on that high ground because it was the controlling terrain for
a vast area. They were well dug in and heavily bunkered. And the
Chinese had ordered them to hold there at all costs, to fight to the
death. The result—especially for Second Battalion, First Marines—
was Armageddon, some of the most savage fighting and heaviest
Marine casualties of the entire war. And in these actions, Bill Rockey
and Walter Murphy, two rifle platoon leaders in the Second
Battalion's Easy Company, stood out.

At 1000 on June 8, Easy Company jumped off in the attack.
When the lead platoon was stopped by fire, Bill Rockey's third
platoon was moved up to the point. Bill, a trim, square-shouldered

Marine with an all-year-round tan, is the son of Lt. Gen. Keller Rockey, USMC, the distinguished Marine who had accepted surrender of some fifty thousand Japanese troops near Tientsin, China, at the end of World War II. Bill had served as an enlisted man in the Corps before going to the Naval Academy. Consistently modest and understated, he acknowledges the pressure in this his "first challenge under fire," or as he says "the first time I had to stand up and advance against an enemy firing real bullets trying to kill me."

When several of his men were hit almost immediately, Rockey developed his plan. He gave the hand signal to commence firing and bounded forward himself, calling "Follow Me!" to his troops.

That is exactly how the Marine Corps teaches it at Quantico, just how it's supposed to be done. But this time, as Bill tells it, he jackknifed "right into a foxhole left by the enemy! My helmet flew off, and in spite of my struggles, I couldn't get out of the hole. My runner came over, handed me out of the hole, and gave me my helmet back. It was not a spectacular start of my active combat experience . . . except for the laughs."

With that, one would expect that the runner, Charlie Kimmel, was off to a good start with Bill. But first impressions can change. A few minutes later and a little farther along the ridge, Charlie hurled a grenade up to clear the crest they were heading to And to his and Bill's profound shock, the throw was short!

Bill again, "In horror, we watched as the grenade began to roll back down toward us, gathering speed as it came. We could do nothing except attempt to melt into the ground on each side. By a miracle, neither of us was hit when it blew."

Next a burp gun opened up on Bill at close range, splattering small stones in his face and sparks on the rocks in front of him. Then two concussion grenades exploded alongside his helmet. He was stunned.

When he recovered and the platoon was again moving ahead, the gooks had pulled back. The platoon had engaged an outpost, and they moved through it and on up the hill. Later, when Bill had a chance to look at his gear, he found two bullet creases in his helmet, the chin strap had been shot off, and there were two more bullet holes in the blanket roll on his pack, just above his right shoulder.

While this fighting was going on, General Whaling, the assistant division commander, had arrived at the battalion OP to view the action up close. And long after he left, Easy Company was still at it, slugging its way through a series of seesaw battles along the ridgeline. In early afternoon, the company finally broke through, aided by a stunning display of close air support. Here, for a change, the planes were available. Rockey's Marines got the support when they needed it, with the planes directed by a savvy forward air controller (FAC). For Easy Company, this was the best air show in the world as the Corsairs swept in, mixing strafing, rockets, napalm, and dummy runs to keep the gooks hugging the ground deep in their holes and bunkers until Bill and his Marines were on top of them.

The company was able to take its first objective with only one KIA, a rifleman who stuck his head into a gook bunker *before* dropping in a grenade. Of course, that's not the right sequence, not how it's supposed to be done. And, sadly, in this case, the rifleman paid with his life.

Chapter 9

WALTER MURPHY MOVES UP HILL 676

F inally, at 1755 hours, Easy was on top of the final objective for the day, a horseshoe-shaped hill called 421. The top was taken by Easy's second platoon led by Walter Murphy, the Notre Dame graduate from Charleston, South Carolina, who had so thrilled those traveling with him across country by his devotion to Chinese language records. In no way was Murph your typical Marine second lieutenant. Under a shock of copper-colored hair, he looked out on the world with a puckish sense of humor and a power of concentration that could be startling. That concentration had now shifted to the rugged terrain of the east central front— and to the enemy forces awaiting the arrival of Murphy's platoon of Marines.

In describing their ascent to the crest, Murph said, "The only hairy part of taking it was that scaling its rim required us to climb up single file, hand over hand, with the leadman giving his weapon to the man behind him and retrieving it when he was on top. I didn't think much about it at the time, but one of my sergeants would later have nightmares about being unarmed and meeting NKs with burp guns."

The company took up positions along the ridge with their wounded on the ground below, inside the horseshoe. The night was long and scary, punctuated with intermittent enemy mortar fire. It ended when the gooks came in for an early morning attack in the rain. The attack was repulsed, but between the enemy mortars and our own 4.2s falling short, there was a lot of big stuff exploding in the Second Battalion area; the battalion suffered forty casualties before the day even started. Among the wounded was Robert McClelland, the battalion commander, evacuated with a piece of shrapnel in his back. Someone later reported that McClelland was a good Marine: he took a place at the end of the line at the aid station and waited until all his men had been treated before letting a corpsman examine him.

Meanwhile, as Murph described it, "the inside of the horseshoe that was Hill 421 was a wild scene. Not only were there lots of wounded Marines lying there, but every one of the four Chinese horses we had rounded up near Oran-ni for pack animals had also been hit. The poor devils were running around madly, bucking, rearing, and screaming. We decided the kindest thing would be to shoot them. We did, with difficulty as well as regret. Shooting them was certainly the safest course: horses are big beasts whose hooves can do a lot of damage, especially to men lying helplessly on the ground."

With McClelland out, the battalion exec. officer, Maj. Clarence Mabry, took over the battalion. They jumped off again. Easy Company headed to the left, the west approach to Hill 676—a steep and irregular monster, a hill mass topped by three jagged peaks that looked as if they'd been cleaved from one other by a gigantic axe. The battalion diary described it as "a steep-sided hill surmounted by a rocky crag and with extremely difficult approaches to the hill from all sides." Hill 676 was defended by a full-strength NK battalion, and quite naturally, the battalion CP was located on the highest crest, atop a steep pitch of almost sheer granite.

The NK battalion's defensive positions had been exhaustively constructed: trenches, fighting holes, and deep bunkers were layered with heavy timbers and covered with sod—not just near the summit, but down on the approaches, the forward slope, as well. From the lower slopes, the gooks had cleared interlocking fields of fire, so as to engage the attacking Marines well forward of the main positions. This also allowed them to hold their own men in place on the forward slope, in case any of them might be tempted to bug out.

So the terrain was tough, and the gooks were ready to execute a carefully prepared defensive plan. Late on the morning of June 10, they held their fire until the Marines were at close range and then opened up with everything: machine guns, automatic weapons, satchel charges, and grenades—all of this fired into Marines on ground so steep they had to drop to their hands and knees just to keep moving. Progress was agonizingly slow and the fighting sometimes hand-to-hand.

This was the big day, and a lot that the Marines had counted on went wrong.

Close air support had been ordered, more than twenty-four hours before, to be on station throughout the day, but as daylight faded, it had not yet arrived. The weather was certainly a factor: heavy rains and the cloud cover blanketing the mountains limited all air operations that day.

Tanks supporting the attack from the road below were masked by the side of a mountain and so were unable to fire into the largest bunkers on the right side of Hill 676. The seventy-five recoilless rifles, effective for a time, had run out of ammo at a critical point in the afternoon.

On the plus side, the Korean porters' performance was outstanding. From early morning well into the night, they hauled great loads of ammo up the hill on their A-frames and carried Marine casualties back down. But they paid a heavy price: they suffered some two hundred casualties, killed and wounded, on this day alone.

Around noon, with Easy Company committed to the Second Battalion's attack, Walter Murphy's second platoon moved out on the point. The company commander, Johnny Little Carter, was a Mustang from Georgia and, at thirty-two, the oldest officer in the battalion, renowned for the fine detail of his orders. To Murph, he said, "You see that peak on the left? Go up the second ridge over there and take the peak. Call me when you're on top. You can have this extra SCR 300 radio."

That may have been shorthand, but Murph got it. How could he miss? All he had to do was take the hill and call back.

Murph picks up the story, "At shortly before 1600, we were about a hundred yards below the west crest, with the first platoon pretty much abreast on the ridge to our left. To our right, Dog's firefight was still going full blast. I again asked for artillery and this time got a battery, five rounds, of 105s. Alas, we were too close, and some of the rounds landed behind and to the side of us. Fortunately, most of the short rounds landed in the open space between Easy's two assault platoons, and we took no casualties.

"The face of the crest was now completely bare as we came up slowly toward the last fifty yards, moving out of the ridge's line of scrub pine trees that had given us concealment. We were surprised to see that we were in front of a sharp rise that climbed at nearly thirty degrees—and looked twice as steep.

"My platoon sergeant, Bull McKinnon—Leather Lungs, the troops called him—set up our two machine guns down the slope a bit, where they could cover us, while I moved with one squad up and to the right, east of the line of rocks. There was a tree at the north end of those rocks: now shattered, it must have been decent sized for Korea. I stood by that tree, planning.

"If we met resistance, we would maneuver our second squad to the left (west), between our unit and the first platoon. I distinctly recall giving the command, 'Drop your packs and fix bayonets!' and motioning the lead squad leader to take his troops up the hill. He was immediately behind his point fire team, with me and my radioman, a young man named Sullivan who usually acted as my bodyguard, following immediately behind. After that moment, my memory is jagged.

"Unconnected, badly blurred images: bullets and fragments sloshing into the mud and cracking human bones; grenades rolling down, exploding, and flipping Marines down the slope. These scenes are more like a disorganized potpourri of snapshots that pop in and out of focus than a coherent, moving picture. My first image, distorted, is of stopping at the tree near the end of the rocks, then moving up, behind a fire team, going slightly to the right of the rocks. Sullivan, packing his SCR 300 radio, was a half step behind me and just to my right. The machine guns straight ahead and to our right opened up, but I couldn't see either one, only Marines falling.

"Suddenly someone shouted 'grenade!' and the first volley of grenades came down on us. One exploded up ahead. Another rolled between Sullivan and me. He dived to the right, and I to the left. I could feel the explosion, but not as painfully as Sullivan. It tore the radio off his back, broke his arm, and sent him tumbling down the slope.

"The next thing I knew I was sitting up on the ground to the left of the rocks. NKs were still screaming; bullets were still splashing in the mud all around, and grenades were still rolling down the hill. A light concussion grenade that had exploded against my helmet had set fire to its camouflage cover, and the twigs and leaves I had stuck there.

"I must have gotten up and moved a squad into the gap between us and the first platoon. I do remember committing the squad but have no recollection of getting up, only of standing there motioning to the squad leader. I wanted this squad to get the machine gun to our left, and I fired a few shots myself toward the gun whose position I had seen. Others joined in my fire, and the machine gun shut down briefly, though it later opened up again.

"Another grenade landed a few feet in front of me and slowly, very slowly, rolled between my legs. I prayed it farther down the slope, where it blew up. I remember thinking, 'You don't have to know Sigmund Freud to be terrified by that.'

"The leader of the squad I was trying to maneuver was about ten yards down the hill in the line of rocks. He'd cracked. He was lying in the mud screaming, 'Don't send my boys up that hill! Don't send my boys up that hill!' I motioned for his people to move out, and they stepped over him and, without hesitation, attacked.

"One of the men in our attached machine gun section deserted; he didn't crack; he deserted. And he was the gunner we were depending on to counter the NKs' machine gun fire from the right. Instead, he stood up muttering, 'I can't take this anymore,' and slowly walked down the hill, leaving his gun unmanned. I both hated and envied him, but I had no time to bother with him.

"Aside from those two—although the squad leader had been strong under fire until he reached his limit—I cannot find the words to describe the determined heroism of those seventy-five young Marines. Commanding them was like leading a pack of ferocious wildcats. They were not going to let gooks stop them, no matter what the cost to themselves.

"Slipping, sliding, and rolling through mud, seven of our nine BARs jammed—but that hardly slowed the BAR men. They simply swung their weapons as clubs, holding on to the hot barrels, as they closed with the NKs. One squad leader was blown down the hill by a grenade blast. He came rushing back up, covered with slime and blood, only to be blown down a second time. He came back up yet a third time, firing his weapon and screaming in rage. When the fight was over, the battalion surgeon picked twenty-three pieces of shrapnel out of him.

"Back in the rocks we had been pinned down so tightly, we couldn't lift our heads. Bullets zinging around and splattering us with chips of rocks were enough reason to keep our heads down. A black sergeant, blinded by a grenade blast, claimed that his ears told him where the center machine gun was. When he insisted, we gave him a few grenades that he threw toward the sound. He didn't destroy the gun, but he did hold it up briefly—long enough for Charles Abrell to get a free run at the bunker.

"Abrell, a pale white-blond kid from Indianapolis clearly deserved his reputation of being the toughest and bravest man in the company, maybe in the entire Corps. He had won the Navy Cross the previous winter near Hung'nam, coming out from the Chosin Reservoir. Now, he pulled the pin from a grenade and dashed up to the bunker and partially into its opening. The explosion killed the machine gun crew, but Abrell's lifeless body came tumbling down at my feet. His skin was alabaster white, his eyes still open.

"I don't think he meant to sacrifice himself, though I can't be sure. I had actually yelled at Abrell to take cover the week before, asking if he was trying to get killed. His reply at that time was 'Lieutenant, I'm so tired I don't care.' But I was—and I am—absolutely certain that he was willing to lay down his life to silence that gun and save our lives. I wrote him up for the Medal of Honor, and *mirabile dictu*, his family got it. What he would have considered more important was that he got the gun. And in that, he did save lives."

Finally, around 1700 hours, with fire support from Easy's platoon on a ridge to their left, Murphy's platoon managed to kill all the remaining NKs on the westernmost of Hill 676's three peaks. Murph and his men had achieved their part of the objective, but there were only fourteen of them left. They were now separated from the rest of their company, with no radio, and they were almost completely out of ammo. The gooks remained solidly in control of the remaining two peaks and were pouring a steady stream of fire into the Murphy group. Just at that point, Murph had some welcome visitors:

"I heard a noise behind us; I turned and saw Han, an NK deserter who had joined Easy Company earlier, crawling up through the slime, grinning and muttering something about 'the hucking gooks.' (Like most Koreans, Han had difficulty with Fs.) More important, Han was leading a group of Korean workers with cans of ammunition and sacks of grenades lashed to their backs, who would carry our wounded down the hill on their return trip. Largely through the medical skill and quiet courage of Doc Roberts, our platoon corpsman, and the brave assistance of those Korean workers, all of those wounded would live. We lost only the three men killed earlier that day.

"A few minutes after Han and friends came up, I heard the rattle of equipment and the heavy breathing of overloaded Marines struggling up the mountain: Bill Rockey and his third platoon had arrived. His face was a worried gray.

"But Bill Rockey's face also showed a grim determination that no man in his right mind should want to confront, as he prepared his troops to continue the assault, now to the east."

Chapter 10

ROCKEY, WHEN THE CLOUDS OPENED UP

Bill Rockey's platoon had been ordered to follow the advance through the afternoon and be prepared to pass through for the final assault. In the closing hours of daylight, that point had been reached. Rockey led his platoon up the steep side of the ridge to pass through Murph and the few men he had left.

Bill's first sight in the area was of a young Marine in full combat gear, yellow leggings and all, lying on his back by the side of the trail, spread-eagled in death. His next was of one of Murph's NCOs, stumbling downhill, holding his crotch. When Bill asked if the Marine was hurt, he answered that he'd been shot through the penis.

Then Rockey was up on the ridge. Ahead lay a deep saddle along the ridgeline and then the steep rise to the highest peak on Hill 676 and, with it, the gook CP. Rockey and his men headed down into the saddle.

As Bill describes it, "About 35 yards to our front across the open ridge, the ground rose sharply into a jumble of rock boulders among which the enemy was hidden. They had a perfect view and field of fire down the ridge to any of us. When we tried to advance, we were met with deadly fire, and a number of my men were hit. Advancing across the open space along the ridge against a hidden enemy would have been extremely costly, and because we were on the ridge, there was no possibility of an envelopment. We couldn't get at them from the side."

So Bill renewed the call for an air strike. Although the entire area was still socked in, a heavy rain falling and the summits smothered in clouds, calls for air support had now become a sore point. This was the umpteenth call from the Second Battalion that day, but this was especially *urgent*!

The other calls had been urgent too. But not like this. This was the last shot. They were right at the gate, the crest of the gooks' CP. And daylight was rapidly going. Without much faith that it would be different this time, Rockey ordered his men to pull the air panels out of their helmets and lay the brilliant red and yellow squares out on the ridge to mark their positions. Tension was thick as the weather. The platoon waited.

Finally, they could not wait longer. They were going. But at the last minute, just as they were taking off, the message crackled through from battalion: "Hold up!" Battalion said the airplanes were on the way. Of course, Rockey and his Marines didn't believe it—it had been a very long day—with nothing. But they were ordered to wait, and they did.

First, they heard the planes, but they'd heard them before. That didn't necessarily do it. The rain had stopped by then, but the clouds and fog still blanketed the objective, and the ceiling was zero.

Then, as Bill describes it "by some miracle, a hole opened in the sky almost directly overhead." With daylight fading fast, the clouds parted to allow the sun's last slanting rays to flood through and light up the objective. And diving through that hole came the Corsairs, two F4Us, loaded with everything they could carry: 500-pound bombs, .50 caliber machine guns, and big tanks of napalm.

To Bill, it was a vivid experience, "After a dummy run, they came in hot. In the mountains—especially in that kind of weather—it takes real guts to drop through a hole in the clouds like that.

Their landing gear was down, wing flaps full down, speed just above stall, their .50 caliber machine guns blazing. They were so close to us; they seemed to be firing into our positions. God! What a thrilling sight to see those planes come in, "MARINES" painted large on their sides. We could see the whirling yellow tips of their four-bladed propellers. We actually cheered!" With their bombing and strafing runs completed, the Corsairs finished off with napalm, the jumbo tanks tumbling out on the crest, splashing flame into gook emplacements.

Of course, that didn't do it all. But it was all Bill and his men had been waiting for. He gave the command to fix bayonets and led his platoon across the saddle and up against the final objective. Not surprisingly, there were gooks still there. And these didn't leave as others had before them. They stayed. They fought viciously, and they exacted a bloody toll of Marines, but eventually, they died.

Along the way, Sergeant Bruce Henry, a machine gunner with Bill's platoon, already wounded, jumped into a hole with four NKs. He shot three and strangled the fourth with his bare hands. With that kind of spirit, it didn't take long. Bill and his men closed out the final objective after an hour of savage fighting, the last of it in darkness.

It had, indeed, been a long day.

Chapter II

HILL 676, RECAP AND AFTERWARD

In sum, as Murph saw it, "The slaughter the NKs had earlier wreaked was now turned on them. We didn't do a systematic body count, but at least two hundred NK corpses were strewn along the three suddenly and eerily quiet crests."

And as Murph much later acknowledged, before the battalion went into regimental reserve the next day, some of his men had a chance to play another round of their favorite after-the-battle game: roll the gook. It may not have been a candidate for Olympic competition, but the rules were simple. Murph's description follows, "They would line up enemy dead, bend their heads between their feet, and, on a count of three, push them down the hill. The Marine whose gook rolled the farthest won. There were enough bodies for several rounds. It was a game that offended me, but early on, I had sensed that the sight of friends killed, blinded, and crippled, the fear, excitement, and hatred generated by close combat, cut gaping holes in what we deemed to be morality. It was less wrong that, after battle, these people desecrate enemy dead than kill or torture prisoners. Whether there was a connection, here I am by no means certain, but it always struck me as curious that Marines could fight ferociously and ten minutes later treat prisoners well. I often had to stop my men from feeding Chinese and NK prisoners and giving them cigarettes. Intelligence officers say interrogation is much more productive if the prisoner is tired, hungry, and nervous about how he will fare in captivity."

On June 10, the Second Battalion lost 14 Marines killed, and another 114 wounded, not counting those with slight wounds who were not evacuated. There were, additionally, some two hundred yobo casualties. The NKs lost an estimated one hundred to two hundred KIA, including their battalion commander killed in the final assault. And eight wounded NKs were taken prisoner on Hill 676.

For Bill Rockey and Walter Murphy, as for the Marines they commanded, the fighting on June 10 was something they'll never forget. Hill 676 was widely acclaimed. The battalion commander later said the assault on Hill 676 was "the most difficult made by this battalion since the landing at Inchon," some nine months before. But, perhaps not surprisingly, the best tribute may have come from Bigfoot Brown himself.

Bigfoot, a legendary artilleryman, had spent hours on the phone that day with Colonel Winecoff, CO of the artillery regiment. He wanted to be sure his men had all the heavy fire support they needed, so he stayed in his regular CP until he was sure he'd done all he could do there. Then he "went forward to see the finale."

His judgment: "It was a glorious spectacle, that last bayonet assault. In the last analysis, 2/1 had to take its objective with the bayonet and hand grenades, crawling up the side of a mountain to get at the enemy. It was bloody work, the hardest fighting I have ever seen."

The Marine Corp's history of the Korean War points out that, a comment like that coming from Bigfoot, was hardly faint praise. As a distinguished veteran of combat in Nicaragua, China, and three major wars, he'd seen a few other scraps. But in Korea, in the month of June 1951, he knew that the First Marines had suffered more casualties than they had coming out from the Chosin

Reservoir. And he thought that Hill 676 was the toughest fighting he'd ever seen.

The individual performances of Murphy and Rockey were recognized as well. In July, Murphy was summoned to the First Marine Division CP where in a field surrounded by H&S personnel and a band playing the Marine Corps hymn, General James Van Fleet, commanding general of the Eighth Army, presented him with the Distinguished Service Cross for extraordinary heroism. This was the highest decoration to be received by any living member of the Seventh Basic Class. Murph modestly wonders why he got the medal, says he can't think of anything he did to deserve it. That is not—I might add—a question raised by any of the men who served with him or anyone who'd witnessed his performance. The view of Murphy's men, in fact, was summed up by a young pfc. from the platoon who declared, "We'd storm the gates of hell if Mr. Murph would lead us." Murphy says that this tribute has been worth more to him than any medal, and in that, he undoubtedly has the right perspective.

Bill Rockey was also highly decorated for conspicuous gallantry and intrepidity in action on Hill 676. He later became the only member of our class to command a rifle company in Korea for any significant period of time. And as the Easy Company commander in late September, Rockey led the company through Operation Blackbird, one of the very first company-size helicopter operations of the war.

As a final note on June 10, it's now apparent that was the day that broke the NKs back. On that day, the First Battalion moved ahead to seize Hill 802, suffering 9 KIA and 97 WIA in an effort that lasted from early morning until well after dark. And there were other advances all along the line in the next several days.

But after June 10, enemy resistance was not as determined or fanatic as it had been. The First Marines' juggernaut was rolling forward, and the NKs were no longer staying to fight to death.

When the First Marines' advance ended on June 14, the regiment was holding the high ground across a front referred to, unofficially, as the Brown Line. Bigfoot had made his point. The advance had carried the line forward some three thousand yards to the north, to heights that dominated the area. Thereafter, it was officially designated the modified Kansas Line.

Chapter 12

ATTACK AND ON LINE,
JUNE 10-JULY 6

*J*une 10. Because we're thought to have delivered the First Battalion's mail yesterday, Baker Company is out of it today. We're in reserve.

June 11. In the beginning, this looked like a tough day for us, but it turned out to be the battle that wasn't. In brief, I got a better understanding of artillery today—how it can be conclusive—and Tex Lawrence and I climbed a mountain.

We get up about 0600, and the rain from last night has stopped, replaced by mist and fog denser than any I've seen in Korea. Straining to see through the fog, we see nothing. Then it clears for a few minutes, and we look out to Baker Company's objective to our immediate front: It's a mountain, literally, bigger in every way and particularly higher than anything I've seen here.

Jim Cowan gathers his platoon leaders on the OP. Dibble's platoon is going to provide fire support, so the assault on the objective is up to Tex and me—sort of. It's either up to Tex, or to Tex and me. Jim leaves the decision to us.

I guess he thinks we're both trade school boys, so we're eager, and we can be relied on. And after the first platoon's performance on Saturday, he may think that I know nearly as much as Tex. If so, Jim's mistaken. Tex learned a lot in the year he spent training with schools' troops at Quantico, enough to be a year ahead of me in every way. In fact, Tex is superb, the best lieutenant I've seen at work.

But at any rate, the company commander has turned it over to us, so what do we want to do? Tex wants to take the hill, and the sooner he can take off, the better. He is squinting up the hill, trying to see through the fog, and he looks like he can't wait. He really doesn't care what anyone else does.

I think the hill above us is a monster, the biggest thing I've seen in Korea. I don't particularly want to climb it, much less climb it under fire while trying to shoot gooks. But I can't imagine any one platoon taking it on alone.

We talk it over and agree that we'll do it together, Tex's second platoon on the right and my first platoon on the left. He and I will stay near the middle as we go up, to maintain contact for whatever may happen on the way.

All of the artillery prep has been fired, and we are about ready to take off when the whole plan changes. The top of the objective has been shrouded in fog, and the fog blows away briefly; we see gooks in the bunkers on top, and they see us. They open up, firing on our OP with heavy machine guns. Because of the distance, their firing is not effective, but it triggers a dynamic response from our side.

Our heavies immediately open fire to engage the gooks in a machine gun duel. More important, battalion holds up the attack, and our artillery starts firing all over again. This time, they are registered exactly on the crest of the objective, and when the first rounds land, it looks like an erupting volcano. The crest explodes. Bunker after bunker goes up from direct hits. Logs and timbers fly through the air. We know that we're watching the artillery in a peak performance. And no one can appreciate it more than someone like us, Marines waiting to go right up there where the rounds are landing.

The second barrage finally ends, and we move out. By the time we start up, the fog has moved back in. I can only see twenty feet or so ahead, but through the trees, I can see most of my platoon. And to my right, I can see Tex. The climb is so steep that for much of it, we are on all fours, using our hands. It may have seemed longer than it actually was. But finally in looking up, I see several Marines on the skyline above me. They're on top. A minute later, we're all up there, and we've gained it without firing a shot.

What we find there wows us. There are a lot of NK dead and a few wounded. One of the wounded tells us that there were six hundred NK soldiers there this morning, and the bunker and trench system we find confirms this. The rest of the company joins us, and we hold up here for the rest of the day, preparing the position for defense and patrolling to the front and the flanks. Tex certainly would have liked it better if we'd had to strangle gooks to get there, but for me, this was just fine.

June 13. The third battalion is attacking on our right flank, and Baker Company is ordered to go out a couple of miles to the front and set up on the high ground there to support their attack. Our company, as now reinforced, is a powerhouse. We have the artillery and 4.2" mortar FOs and the TACP (tactical air control party) to call in close air support, bombs, and napalm. They are to clobber anything that comes off the back of the hill while third battalion is assaulting. Obviously, for us this is a pretty cushy assignment, a front-row seat at the war. We spend the day watching the attack through glasses. I find that the TACP officer is from St. Paul and attended the same high school I did, four years ahead of me. I hadn't known him before, and now we meet out here, thousands of miles from home.

We are now about ten miles north of the eastern tip of the Hwachon Reservoir. We hear that the reservoir is to be an anchor in the final defensive line and that we've come this far north to destroy enemy artillery and mortar positions and to mine a wide belt in front of the line.

We also hear that the Marine rifle regiments are supposed to have taken 25 percent casualties in the past two weeks, and there is talk of the division going into Army or Corps reserve for a month very soon. There we would have a chance to get replacements and reorganize. Marines who came here for Inchon, or in the first-replacement draft, have now seen some of the toughest fighting in the Korean War, and those still here are wearing out fast.

June 15. What's the title of the song, "Little Things Mean a Lot"? We've now been in place for several days, and this morning, along with a batch of mail, we get PX rations, hamburger meat, fresh eggs, fresh bread, and clean new fatigues. This afternoon, we're supposed to get beer. These are things I've never noticed, always taken for granted. It's funny how much they can mean when you go a few months without them.

In today's mail delivery, I got a letter from a friend, now in college at Yale. Apparently, I'd written him earlier about life in the platoon. He wrote back to say, "I'm glad to hear that you like running up and down hills in Korea shooting at people. But, incidentally, do you know what you are fighting for?" The question stopped me for a minute, and when I thought about it, I thought it was something coming from another planet, the farthest out thing I've heard in a while. Actually, I never had thought about that, and I don't know anyone else who has. Not out here. If I had to answer that question, I suppose I'd think first of the Marines in my platoon, maybe the Marines in Baker Company. Certainly nothing beyond that. I can't imagine anyone out here having a much different answer. Now I realize how totally war concentrates your attention, once you're in it.

In truth, I find that I can get along pretty well here without much. At the moment, there are only a few things I'd like to have that I don't. I'd like to know more about what's going on, especially in the war, but also in the Marine Corps and the world outside. Also, I need a regular supply of airmail envelopes. And it would be good to get a bottle of whiskey once in a while. Whiskey is great for morale and great as a social lubricant. It helps in getting to know other Marines in the outfit. It seems funny to me, but I think that's all I really do need.

Today I heard about Fritz Muer, the oldest and most experienced officer in our Basic School class. He had thirty months' commissioned service before reporting to Quantico. At our level, that's an impressive background, and he really did know a lot. But maybe he didn't know as much as we thought, or maybe he was looking the other way. Fritz came over with our replacement draft, and today, I heard that he was killed in early May, shortly after arrival. It wasn't from enemy action. He was disarming a booby trap that he had set himself, and apparently, he pulled the wrong wire.

I've been used to thinking of 41 as the number of Marines in a rifle platoon. But today I realize that I've got more than 62, now in the first platoon.

The difference is a light machine gun section attached more or less permanently to us and what might be considered the platoon staff. That is Bill Landon, the platoon sergeant, and Sergeant Hunt, the platoon guide. Landon is just my age, a clean-cut outdoor type from Oregon. He's a reserve now, but he likes the Marine Corps and wants to ship over as a regular. He's a good man, steady and cool, and I like having him.

Sergeant Hunt is young but looks old. He's loyal and conscientious, always in the background, always working. He handles supplies, draws them, and passes them out to us. And he carries everything with him, at all times. The man is a walking hardware and confectionery store.

There are at least a couple of others who make this platoon work as well as it does. Our messenger, Milas Butcher, is, of course, called Butch. He's about twenty, short, chunky, with quick, bright eyes and a probing curiosity. As a messenger, he's outstanding. He gets everything exactly right the first time, and he'd go through hell to deliver a message. He seems indifferent to danger and to his own safety. His curiosity leads him to search enemy bodies after an attack. He goes after them all, no matter how gory, and he comes up with the damnedest things, not necessarily because they have intelligence value, although some do.

Parks, a Korean boy who is my personal helper and friend, is sixteen but looks younger. He makes fires to heat C-rations, washes clothes, and keeps my M-2 carbine gleaming and well oiled, inside and out. We now have Parks completely outfitted with Marine gear, and he always looks ready for inspection, clearly more squared away than any of us who are supposedly his role models. There is another young Korean with us, Butch, the company interpreter. He and I are working on Parks's English, now on almost a daily basis. Parks should qualify as an interpreter soon. He's very bright.

June 16. Today, we got an extraordinary message from our regimental commander, Bigfoot Brown. It reads like he actually wrote it himself. Running on to a second mimeographed page, the message expresses Bigfoot's "boundless admiration and heartfelt congratulations for [our] conduct of the operations of the past two weeks." The essence is in a few lines where he says:

> You have used sheer guts and determination to close with the enemy and destroy or rout him with grenades, bayonets, clubbed rifles and even with bare hands on at least one occasion.
>
> I have never in my life been so proud as I am to be permitted to command this regiment.... I have served in infantry with the 5th Marines as an enlisted man in the First World War, and as a junior officer in the Nicaraguan Campaign. I have supported a lot of infantry regiments while I was an artilleryman before and during the Second World War. It is my carefully considered opinion that this is the best regiment of infantry that I have ever seen. I am glad to be allowed to join your club.
>
> This memorandum is written to tell you how one old Marine, who isn't about to fade away as long as he can serve with men like you, feels about you young Marines.
>
> I think you are grand. Thank you for all your most gallant and effective work.
>
> W. S. Brown
> Colonel, U.S. Marine Corps
> Commanding

There must have been other messages like this from other commanders. Maybe it's just that I haven't seen one before (as a matter of fact, I still haven't even seen Bigfoot). But, for me, this was unique. What a great tribute to the First Marines who gave their lives in this last offensive, to those who were seriously wounded, and to those who so distinguished themselves, including Walter Murphy, Joe Reed, and Bill Rockey.

And—as for Bigfoot—what a great guy!

June 18. We've been on the line but inactive for the last week or so, and I feel relaxed and rested. The current hot topic in the battalion is rotation, meaning, essentially, when do we go home? I'm not directly involved because I just got here, but I listen. What I hear is that rotation is not working, that it is slowed down because there are not enough Marines to rotate in. Supposedly this is so because we had heavy casualties recently and because Marine reserves called up for Korea are now being released.

It's certainly true that the Marine Corps reserves have carried more than their load here to date. In Baker Company at full strength, we'd have 221 Marines, and there are only 63 regulars in the company. All the rest are reserves. If they are all released on a speeded up schedule, there won't be much rotation for a while.

In the Marine Corps, there must be a lot of junior officers available, both regular and reserve. We have heard this week that a new policy will have officers rotate out of rifle companies after four months. That seems too short a time to me. I feel like I just got here.

Ed Dibble, platoon leader of Baker Company's third platoon, has been here a little short of four months. He's had an active time and is beginning to feel the strain. He's moving back to battalion as the S-2 (intelligence officer) on July 1. We have had two replacement lieutenants join the company since I arrived. Ike Cronin, from Notre Dame, and Barry Diamond came in a few days ago. They're both in Baker Company but have not gotten assignments here in the company yet.

June 20. On the line. We work every day to strengthen our position, building and reinforcing bunkers, laying barbed wire, putting in trip flares, and storing ammunition. Rumors have it that the Chinese are coming back this way sometime soon, and we want to be sure we're ready for them. I think we are. I don't know about the rest of the line, but I can't imagine them ever getting through here. We run patrols forward of the line every day. That means that the first platoon goes out every third day, but none of the patrols has been eventful so far. This is a quiet time, and there are always more rumors in a time like this. Currently swirling around are stories that General Ridgway has a surprise for the First Marine Division and that the war will wind up in the late summer or early fall.

June 22. We had a long and interesting patrol on Saturday that took us farther north than any Marine unit has been since the Chosen Reservoir last winter. We crossed the Suip-ch'on, a small river about twenty yards wide and fordable in many places. Our mission seemed more than a little strange. It was to support a platoon-size patrol from Charlie Company that was going out to high ground to the east and above us. When I looked at it on the map, I was puzzled because I couldn't see what good we could do for the Charlie Company patrol. From where we were supposed to be, we couldn't even see the top of the high ground they were heading for, but anyone up there could look right down on us. At any rate, that was our mission.

When we got to an observation point on the south side of the river, we could see the patrol area laid out below us. I left a rifle squad and our machine gun section on that point to support us, and with the other two rifle squads, I headed down into the valley. We crossed the river at a point where it was about hip high and started down the valley, working our way along the hedgerows and irrigation ditches that would afford some cover if we were being observed. We passed through a small village with one of our squads cautiously working each side of the single street. Butch, our interpreter and radio operator, and I walked down the middle of the street staying in touch with both squads. There was no evidence of the enemy there.

When we came out of the village, we were back on the riverbank again with another crossing to reach our patrol objective. The second crossing was deeper; only my helmet and carbine were dry by the time we got over.

But there we were, on our assigned objective. We had the river and a road at our backs. We were on flat ground, actually a field, and the high ground we were to observe was directly before us, and we couldn't see the top of it. There was no sign of the Charlie Company patrol.

We were in the tall grass, and we settled down into it to wait. Within minutes, we had first one and then a second sighting of someone moving on top of the high ground. There was no firing and no other sound, and we couldn't tell who was up there. I thought to myself, "This is crazy; we're like sitting ducks here in the grass." So we quietly pulled out of the tall grass and worked our way back up the valley to the point where we'd crossed the river first.

On the way back, we sighted a column of troops crossing directly in front of us about a half mile away. Because we couldn't tell who they were at that distance, we held up until they got out of the way. While we were watching them, we saw about fifteen to twenty mortar rounds land in their midst. They took off on the double, hightailing it back toward our lines. Later, we learn this was the Charlie Company patrol we were to have observed. They were coming back without having gotten on to their objective. They had four Marines hit, all but one walking wounded. Actually, this was not too bad, considering their exposed position and the number of rounds they took.

For us, we'd had plenty of exercise. We'd crossed the river several times, gotten farther north than anyone else, and had run through the village as well. After that, battalion shortened the patrols and started using squads to observe to the front from selected observation points on high ground. The whole idea of the patrol was dumb, and our role in it made no sense. From the first platoon's standpoint, we were just lucky that the Charlie patrol was out there to attract the gooks' attention. Otherwise, those mortar rounds probably would have been fired at us.

June 25. My boots had worn out, just in the time I've been here. Yesterday, I decided the requisition was taking too long; I'd go back to X Corps headquarters and get a pair of boots for myself. I arranged for a jeep and driver, climbed down off the line, and hiked back a mile and a half to meet the jeep on the road. It turns out the driver is from Minneapolis. His name is Mangin. We drove fifty-five dusty road miles south to the X Corps, General Almond's headquarters. It was a long, hot drive, and after coming that far, I would have gotten the boots if I had to pull them off someone. For a while, it looked like that might be necessary.

First, I encountered a sergeant who told me there was no supply there. Then I met a captain who asked if I was acquainted with my regular supply and repair channels. Finally, I got to a lieutenant colonel who looked at the boots I was wearing and believed my story. He picked up the telephone, and that's when we started to roll.

As a result of the call, the sergeant I had talked with first joined us. Now he was smiling and agreeable, even when the lieutenant colonel had him carry off my old boots and bring back a pair of brand new Army combat boots, size 9D.

The entire trip took from 0930 in the morning to 1900 in the evening. But it only took about ten minutes from the time I met the lieutenant colonel until I had pulled on the new boots. So even though it was a long day, it worked.

My major impression from the trip was how luxurious the living is at a Corps headquarters. They have stuff there that I haven't seen since I arrived in Korea: things like chairs, tables, electric bulbs, and tablecloths. And everyone has them at X Corps. They have stout people there also, some of them actually fat. And in the office tent where I got the boots, there was an open half case of Seagram's VO. I didn't know things like that existed out here. But they do.

June 26. Still on the line, improving our positions and patrolling to the front. This is now called our permanent defense line. The definition of "permanent" is any place we stay for a week or more. That means bunkers rather than fighting holes with light canvas overhead. Bunkers are usually dug in the side of a hill. Sides above ground are banked with sandbags. Roofs are layered with timbers and sandbags and covered over the top with dirt. For us this is good enough, the last word in safety. It will stop bullets and shrapnel and should withstand anything but the direct hit of an artillery shell.

We're comfortable here. We're still working on bunkers, clearing fire lanes to the front and laying double-apron, three-strand barbed wire just beyond grenade range. Farther out, we lay trip flares and booby traps. All of that adds up to security, and that's why we are comfortable. On the reverse slope (backside) of the hill, we're building a road for supplies and evacuation, so we can move anything in or out without being observed.

The longer we're here, the more domestic it looks. We now have signs, and I suppose tables and chairs will soon sprout up. The rainy season has ended, and the days are sunny and beautiful.

A few days ago, the battalion commander declined the opportunity to go into regimental reserve, a decision that everyone applauded. Our only excitement is the patrols.

June 28. Parks, my boy, is the greatest. He speaks fluent Japanese and is learning English rapidly. If I ever got evacuated to Japan, I'd want to have him along. And for a far out fantasy, I could see him in a white jacket serving drinks in an apartment on Russian Hill in San Francisco.

Another thought, this about wounds. Of course, there are all kinds. And sometimes wounds that are not serious have advantages. That is, the one who is wounded gets a break, rest, excellent care, and if it happened at the right time, a trip to Japan. We had seven Marines evacuated after our firefight on June 9, and five of them are back with the platoon now. Thankfully, they're all well.

And a song: Here's a song the machine gunners attached to my platoon sing to the tune of "That Old Gang of Mine":

> Oh, I get that lonesome feeling
> when the big shells whistle by.
> Mortar shells are breaking up
> that old gang of mine.
> There goes Taylor, there goes Fenn,
> right down White Cross Lane.
> Though we'll see them all again,
> they won't seem the same.
> (sotto voce . . . *no arms or legs*)
> Mortar shells are breaking up
> that old gang of mine.

There is understandable concern here about Marines getting killed or hurt shortly before they are due to be rotated home. Sims Morse getting it last week—after eleven months in a rifle company—is only one example. Since then two men in Charlie Company were killed on a combat patrol. One of them had come in at Inchon, nearly ten months ago. He had served all of that time in the company, had been recommended for the Silver Star, and was scheduled to go home at the end of this month. To prevent casualties like that in the future, there is now a division policy that all Inchon men and everyone due for rotation will not go out on patrols. I still have several Inchon men in the platoon, and before our last patrol, they came to see me as a group.

"Lieutenant, we want to talk to you about the patrol."

"Yeah. I know about the policy. You don't have to go."

"No, Lieutenant. That's not the point. We checked with the first sergeant, and he said we're right. How the policy is carried out is up to each individual Marine."

"So?"

"So we want to go out on all the patrols the platoon goes on while we're still here."

"You sure?"

"Yeah. Yes, Lieutenant. We're sure."

I hadn't expected that. I could only reply, "Okay then. Check with the platoon sergeant. We'll be going out at first light tomorrow. Oh, and by the way—thanks."

Thinking about it, I guess I liked this as much as anything that's happened since I've been in Korea. It's the Marine Corps of course. But it makes me feel proud to be here, proud just to be serving with men like that.

June 29. Today our battalion is relieved on the line by Third Battalion, First Marines. We head for an assembly area in the rear. Baker Company is relieved by George Company, 3/1, the company Jimmie Marsh is in. He was hit and evacuated in June, but he is now back with the company and okay, except for a small scar on the side of his head. As I'd expect, he's getting along great. He had a rifle platoon for only three days before he was wounded.

Tom Parsons, another friend and former football teammate of Tex's, was relieved by Joe Reed on the line. Joe is in great shape too. We are to be in reserve for a week or so, and Jack Benny is supposed to come in with a troupe of entertainers on July 4.

July 1. In reserve. Because the battalion was on the line for the entire month of June, maybe we have to be in reserve now. But from Baker Company's perspective, we'd much rather have remained in our positions on the hill. We are down here now on flat ground where sun bakes the entire area from 0900 to after 2000 in the evening. The heat is terrific. I'm with the rest of the company officers on cots in a single BOQ tent. It's good that we all get along, in play here as well as on the line.

Morale in the company has improved sharply under Jim Cowan's leadership. We can feel the difference. It feels like a company now rather than three platoons and a headquarters, each going its own way. It really makes a difference to Tex who used to hang out with his platoon and stay away from the company.

July 5. Still in reserve. This area is just north of the town of Yanggu, and only a couple of miles behind the front line. We are scheduled to move out of here tomorrow to relieve the Second Battalion back on the line. We are to be on the line there until July 23 when we're supposed to move back to a training area in the rear to train for night attacks. There is also some talk of the cease-fire this month, but I find that hard to believe.

Yesterday morning, I went up with the company commander and the other platoon leaders to look at the position we're going to be on. This is an area that the Second and Third Battalions took in early June with rather heavy casualties. They've had trouble there ever since, a lot of incoming rounds, both mortars and artillery, and the patrols that they've sent out have all been fired on. From our reconnaissance, it looked like there will be more work there than if we were moving in to an unoccupied position. The bunkers are weak and poorly constructed, and the barbed wire is too close to their holes to be of much use. The gooks could stand by the barbed wire and lob grenades into the position.

Yesterday was the big Fourth of July show with Jack Benny, Marjorie Reynolds, Benay Venuta, June Prunner, a tap dancer, a mental wizard, and a guitar soloist. General Thomas and General Whaling were here, and we had a huge assembly of Marines, all of the motor transport people and other rear echelon pogues. Benny and his troupe performed in 108-degree temperatures under a scorching sun, but they stood up quite well.

More scuttlebutt about Eddie LeBaron: he was hit twice in early June, in actions about a week apart. He is now back with his platoon, so the wounds can't have been serious. Stan Olson was also hit and evacuated about the same time.

We've had a lot of fun here in the last couple of days. The night before last we had a real party with steaks from the galley grilled over a charcoal fire on ammo rods and short barbed-wire stakes. Much drinking and singing. John Coffey was here. He's a major now and headed for home. We sang "For He's a Jolly Good Fellow" and wished him the best. But we're thankful that Jim Cowan now has the company.

Tex and I—with great reluctance, but bowing to popular demand—sang several times. It's a song we do a duet on. We are probably the least musical pair on the planet; we couldn't carry a tune in a basket, independently or together. But we were stimulated by having seen the entertainers, and I feel that with enough beer, anyone can sing. The party lasted until after 0200. Tex is the only one who didn't have a drink all night. After it was over, he said it was the best party he'd ever been to, and he obviously meant it. Somehow, I thought that was sad.

Last night, I sat up again until morning with the first sergeant, Jim Cowan, and a friend of Jim's named Doug Miller, a former quarterback at USC. Then I woke to a steady rain and a hangover, so I was slow to get up. This was our last day in reserve, and I noticed I wasn't the only one dragging.

July 6. Big day for the First Battalion. We got a new battalion commander today, and we come out of reserve to relieve Second Battalion on the Kansas Line. The new battalion commander is a trim-looking officer who has come out here from officers training duty at Princeton. He is said to have been the CO of various seagoing detachments during World War II. The relief of lines is easy. We pull out of reserve in midmorning and are solidly in position on the line by afternoon. Once again, my platoon occupies the high ground, a bald knob some 800 meters above sea level. We are on the extreme left (western) flank of the company where we tie in with Able Company. Baker Company's second and third platoons extend down the ridge to the right, to a road about 1,800 meters east of here. The regimental antitank platoon is set up around that road, and they tie in with Charlie Company on their right flank.

The enemy is directly to our front about a mile away. They are on a ridgeline parallel to the one we're on and a hill mass called Hill 983. On cloudy days when our air couldn't get at them, the second battalion watches gooks scurrying around, digging holes, chopping down trees, etc. There is supposed to be an enemy battalion with heavy mortars, artillery, and antiaircraft weapons there, and they have been very active. Another ridge runs north from our position toward Hill 983, and there are two objectives designated number 1 and number 4 along this ridge with number 4 being about midway between our line and Hill 983. Second Battalion patrolling was focused on those objectives, and we expect that ours will be also. And we expect to patrol actively.

Because our platoon has the high ground, all attached units are attached to us. We have an extra section of heavy machine guns, two sections of light machine guns, the tactical air control party, forward observer parties for the artillery, 4.2" and 81 mm mortars, and an Army artillery flash-and-bang ranging unit. For supply and for keeping track of them, that means that I have 111 men to take care of. Now, this is really a big platoon.

Chapter 13

CHARLIE COOPER, HILL 907 AND AFTER

C harlie Cooper came out of Clarksdale, Mississippi, self-styled "Golden Buckle on the Cotton Belt," and Ole' Miss where he'd been a starting tackle on the Rebels football team in 1945. He also started in the line for Navy and was the line coach of the Quantico Marines 1950 championship squad.

Charlie is personable, enthusiastic, and he doesn't give up, ever. It was apparent at The Basic School that Charlie and the Marine Corps were a good fit and that he was going to do well leading Marines. After we'd landed in Korea, Charlie was assigned to Baker Company, First Battalion, Fifth Marines, a high-spirited outfit that called itself the Baker Bandits, and he was off to a fast start. By June 17 with more than a month in Baker Company, Charlie had made enough of an impression that the battalion commander designated Charlie and his platoon as the point, to spearhead the assault, in the Fifth Marines' important attack on Hill 907. He wanted Charlie in the lead.

Hill 907, a towering peak, dominated all of the surrounding area. It was heavily fortified, and no one thought it would be easy to take. But the actual assault turned out to be much tougher than expected. As Charlie and his platoon worked their way up the hill, they encountered murderous fire from fortified bunkers and machine gun emplacements, and their casualties mounted as they continued. Midway in the assault, Charlie's first radio operator was killed, and a short time later, his second was shot through the neck and evacuated.

The platoon's advance was dependent on almost continuous air and artillery support as they punched their way on and up, a few yards at a time.

Finally, reaching the crest of Hill 907 with the platoon seriously understrength, Charlie was at the point of no return. He couldn't hold his position because he and his men were still in the gooks' sights, subject to killing crossfire. He had to go forward, but he needed at least another air strike to do that. Fortunately, two Air Force F-80s fully loaded with napalm were available overhead. With his last WP (white phosphorous) grenade, Charlie was able to mark the target for a strike (by hurling the grenade thirty yards through the trees), and the F-80s came screaming in to drop their tanks of napalm right into the middle of a North Korean counterattack.

That incinerated the North Koreans at the last minute, but not before Charlie was seriously wounded by a burst of machine gun fire that caught him on the left side. Still conscious, he continued firing his carbine until the weapon was literally shot out of his hands. What was left of his platoon clung tenaciously to the part of the crest they still held. The enemy forces withdrew after dark.

The rest of the objective was taken next morning by other units of the Fifth Marines without firing a shot. Charlie was evacuated to a field hospital for emergency treatment and surgery and then transported to the Navy hospital ship USS *Repose* at Pusan. There, he remained in critical condition for several days with a fractured spine, paralysis, and massive blood loss. His heroic effort on Hill 907 had cracked the North Korean defenses. And he had managed to hold on there against staggering odds.

But that's not the end of the story. After further surgery on the *Repose*, Charlie was loaded on a special hospital plane for transport to the Navy hospital in Yokosuka, Japan. He was one of six patients—all combat casualties on IVs, all listed as critical—on litters strapped aboard the airplane. When one of the plane's two engines conked out over Southern Japan, the pilot managed to crash land on a highway. The landing sheared off telephone and power lines, and the impact was severe enough to pitch four of the six patients (not including Charlie) off their moorings and on to the deck. Finally, a break. They had crashed a scant half mile from the huge Army general hospital in Kyushu, Japan. Ambulances with sirens screaming arrived at the crash site almost immediately. Charlie was able to start on the long road to recovery that few thought even possible when he was carried off Hill 907.

Difficult and violent as this experience was, it is only one brief episode in a long and colorful Marine Corps career. What came before and after is set out in Charlie's book, *Cheers and Tears*, published in 2002, a compelling account of a Marine who always stayed close to the troops and the fighting and who shouldered some of the Corps's most important responsibilities in a series of top assignments.

Chapter 14

AGGRESSIVE PATROLLING, JULY 7-17

July 7. This is the beginning of a different war, or at least a new phase of the war we have. Recently, there have been proposals for truce talks both by the Soviet UN delegate and by the Chinese. We assume that this is done primarily for tactical reasons. Over the last month, the North Koreans and the Chinese have had staggering losses and have been pushed well back to the north. They badly need a respite, time to regroup and resupply. Representatives of the UN are to meet with the enemy today at Kaesong, west of here, in an effort to set up truce talks.

This development has a direct impact on what we're doing. We are now back on the Kansas Line, and we expect that we will maintain this position and run patrols, generally platoon size or smaller, to the north. In other words, we will no longer be attacking.

Today was the first patrol. Ike Cronin's third platoon headed out to the hill directly to our front. It is called objective 1, and they gained it without incident. From there they sent a squad on out to their final objective for the day, called objective 4 That's where they stumbled into real trouble. About midway to objective 4, the squad was ambushed by NKs firing automatic weapons from concealed positions on both sides of the trail. In the resulting firefight, the squad suffered six casualties, including one Marine killed.

The trail for this patrol runs out from our position, so our platoon was closest to the third platoon and its ambushed squad. Before we got the call from the company, we had pulled together all the stretchers at hand and were standing by. Then I called company to clear it, and we headed out to help the third platoon with their wounded. Carrying the wounded along a narrow trail is hard work, and it took the rest of the afternoon. But by the end of the day, we finally got everybody back.

July 8. From the way this is starting, we may be running platoon-size patrols out along this trail from our line. This is the only way out, and it looks like the patrolling duty will just be rotated among the three platoons. Today was our second day here, and Tex's platoon gets the assignment. We watch from the OP as they move out slowly and carefully. As they draw close to objective 1, they come under mortar fire. Watching through binoculars, we can see frenzied enemy activity on Hill 983. The battalion commander, with us on the OP, orders Tex back and calls for an air strike and artillery to blanket the gooks. It seems to quiet them down.

July 9. Today our platoon has the patrol, and now, everyone is very serious about where we're going and what we're doing. The air strike and artillery barrage yesterday must have been effective. But the battalion commander is taking no chances. Before we take off, he has arranged for a rocket barrage that seems to saturate the objective. Then as the patrol moves out, we have a moving artillery barrage, a wall of fire rolling ahead of us, all the way out. With that kind of continuing, advance support, we move through to objective 4 with no delay, and we set up there to stay for a while.

The fun part of sitting out on objective 4 for several hours is that we have the battalion's artillery forward observer party with us. The FO is transported by the opportunity to sit there in the gooks' front yard and call artillery fire down on them from that close. The gooks understandably enjoy it less, and we soon draw heavy mortar fire. When it's coming in like hail, we finally get ordered to return to base. We continue to take incoming on the way back, but we get there without holdup and without casualties. Then the gooks fire 76 mm artillery at the OP for a while, but that doesn't do anything either.

At the end of the day, I feel great. It's been an active and interesting patrol. Maybe we really did accomplish something; part of it was exciting, and best of all, nobody got hurt. These happy thoughts come to an end when I think of what happens next. Apparently, we are going to run these patrols over the same path every day. That means that our platoon is going to be out there every third day. We're certain to attract a lot of unfavorable attention, and it's not easy to see what we might be able to do about it. Oh well, I'm tired, and I fall into a deep sleep.

July 10 and 11. On July 10, Ike Cronin goes out again with the third platoon but is called back by the battalion before they reach their final objective. The patrol route was wrapped in a blanket of fog. It was raining and visibility was so poor that they couldn't have seen anything from the objective if they had gotten out there anyhow.

The next day, Tex goes out, gets all the way to the top of objective 4, and back in safely. The day after that is our turn again, and this time, we do have a lot of trouble.

July 12. On the approaches to objective 4, we start receiving mortar rounds, and we have three Marines hit when the first two concentrations land. Over the radio, we get the order to return, but we need stretchers to carry the wounded before we can move. That means a wait of a half hour along the trail, and during that time, we take a lot more incoming. We're pretty spread out, so it isn't as bad as it might have been, but over the last week, the gooks have registered concentrations all over that trail. Some of their rounds miss the ridgeline on one side or the other, but everything they fire lands between the front and back of our column. They know exactly what they're doing. It takes a long time, but eventually, we get everybody back.

We've now been here almost a week, and by this time, battalion realizes what we're up against. We do have to patrol. We can't just sit on the line, or the gooks will move right in and nuzzle up next to us. But our patrolling is severely limited by the terrain. There's only one way out from our position, and the gooks have everything they have registered on that route. We can change the size and timing of the patrols. We could use different kinds of supporting fires or send the patrols out with air cover all the way, but we don't have a lot of flexibility.

July 13 and 14. For a couple of days, battalion does mix it up: squad patrols, night patrols, and night ambushes. There's not much direct contact, but the patrols reach their objectives. The situation remains tense but relatively quiet. We have only one more day running patrols from this position, but that is the fatal day.

July 15. This is our last day here. The last patrol, and Ike Cronin's third platoon has it. They are to leave at 0900 and go out over the usual route to objective 4, the path we've all been on so many times. This is a reconnaissance patrol; just go to a designated objective to look around, come back, and report. If fired on, they are to return the fire. Otherwise, no firing.

It's a warm, sunny day with perfect visibility. After the patrol has cleared the line and moved out along the trail, I settle down where I can watch them through binoculars. The rest of my platoon is cleaning weapons and getting their gear ready to move off the line tomorrow. As I watch, the patrol moves along the route going out for an hour or so. Their progress is steady, quiet, and uninterrupted. Watching them, I wonder if our time on this part of the line—ragged and nerve-racking as it has been—is to end quietly after all.

Objective 4 is perhaps 1,000 yards away. I see the patrol's lead fire team moving up the incline that leads to the crest. Then they reach the crest and move out to the flat, the top of objective 4. They are followed by the rest of the platoon, and when most of them are on the objective and moving across it, I'm startled to see what happens.

There is no sound. I hear nothing—maybe because of the distance and wind carrying the sound away—but I realize that something is going terribly wrong. From where I am, it looks like there are explosions. First, one Marine and then another is picked up, tossed into the air, and dropped back on the ground. I wonder if they're getting hit with mortars.

I still can't tell what's happening, but I know it's bad. For the first minute or so, the Marines around me are busy and not watching. They're oblivious to what I'm seeing.

I grab a sound power telephone and call the company CP. They are on the radio to the patrol. They tell me what's happening out on objective 4. It's mines!

The patrol had gotten well into the field before kicking the first mine. Then one after another, every step they took was a detonation. *Bang!* A second Marine starts to help the first. *Bang!* Another Marine steps on a mine. *Bang!* He falls on a second mine. *Bang!* Ike Cronin, the platoon leader, goes toward the closest wounded Marine. *Bang!* He never gets there. *Bang!* Someone starts for Ike. *Bang!*

These are shoe mines, so called. They take off a foot at the ankle as cleanly as if it had been surgically amputated. The initial explosion is clean, but then there's the foot, in a boot, six feet away. And the next moment, there's blood all over. It has happened so fast. The Marines in the minefield in that instant are shocked, stunned, and bewildered.

Ike's platoon thinks they have a dozen casualties. Only one KIA so far but several others serious. Mostly single or double amputees. The rest of the platoon is trying to pull their wounded out of the minefield.

Meanwhile, from where we are, we're in the best position to help fast. We're on the high ground, next to the trail that leads out. We know the way. We've come in under mortar fire earlier, and we've gone out to pull back another patrol only a few days before.

I don't have to say much. The Marines in the first platoon know exactly what we're going to do. They're pulling on their helmets and cartridge belts and grabbing their weapons at the same time as I am. We're all ready, well before we're able to leave.

Unlike the last rescue, this is a much bigger deal. In every way. We'll need more of everything, stretchers and stretcher bearers, corpsmen, and especially blood plasma. All this stuff is available somewhere in our battalion area. But it is down the line in Able or Charlie companies or all the way back at battalion. It takes minutes (seems like hours) to get them up to us. Meanwhile, we wait, chafing at the delay.

Finally, we have most of what we need. And we arrange for the rest to catch up with us. We start out at a fast clip on the trail. I'm trying to think about what could be involved when we get out there, and I'm worried.

First, I think, how do we get into the minefield to get these guys out? How do we avoid kicking over the mines that they may not have hit so far? And while we're doing that, how do we guard against an attack? What if the gooks come over the hill in force and take us on when we're there in the minefield?

Beyond that what if the gooks have a bigger plan? What if Ike's platoon is only the bait, and we—or whoever the rescue force is—are the real game? Maybe the idea is to ambush us on the way. Or maybe they'll wait until we're all the way out there. While I'm thinking of this, we're still moving rapidly ahead. Pretty soon, we're there, on the approaches to objective 4.

As we come up to the objective, it looks like a train wreck, but strangely, everything is orderly and quiet. The wounded have all been pulled out of the minefield and are laid out on solid ground. We move through rapidly to set up a defense on the far side of the objective, so we can't be surprised.

With us, we have all the corpsmen in the battalion. Each corpsman moves to one of the wounded Marines; stretcher bearers fall in there as well. Still, only one Marine is dead, but several others look bad, plainly in shock, their faces drained and lined with pain. Those in the worst shape are moved to the head of the column as it forms, each with a corpsman holding up the plastic bag of blood plasma. Carrying a stretcher over the narrow twisting trail pocked with roots and boulders is a backbreaking effort, so there are relief bearers by each stretcher.

Finally, we are ready, and the column starts to move. We set up a rear guard at the tail end of the column to cover us as we head back toward our own lines. The gooks can't surprise us from that direction. The bearers are going slow—agonizingly slow—but they're moving. For a few minutes, it stays quiet. We only hear boots scuffling along the trail, twigs snapping. But the quiet doesn't last.

We haven't gone far when we hear the familiar sound of mortar shells dropping into the tubes and firing. They must be very close, just on the other side of the objective. We can hear it all. First, the firing. Then the long, slow whistle as the rounds—one after another in sets of three—sail up into their high trajectory above us. Then the low whine getting louder as they come over the top of their arc and start down. Finally, the explosions, *one, two, three*.

The gooks have had a lot of practice on this ridge. Their concentrations have been registered and reregistered. They know exactly where they are. They know what they're doing.

But we have some advantages too. The trail we are on runs over a narrow spine, and anything that doesn't land directly on top of the spine falls off to one side or the other and usually explodes harmlessly hundreds of feet below. On the other hand, there are small trees along the top of the spine. Any round that goes into a tree may detonate there, and we do have some air bursts. They are bad, worse than anything but a direct hit. But back on our line, battalion has an eye out for us. As soon as we're off the objective, and they can fire safely, they start to cover our return with artillery and 4.2" mortars firing on to the reverse slope of the objective. I'm sure that helped, but the gook mortars don't stop. We're too easy a target. We're moving slowly, and it's a long way back.

After the first few salvos, I understand that we can time the incoming rounds exactly. We hear them all the way from the tube, and we can tell within a fraction of a second when they will land. This is not much fun for anybody, but it must be agonizing for the men on the stretchers. At the start of each salvo, the stretcher bearers put down their stretchers, and they themselves hit the ground. After the rounds land, they get up again, pick up their stretchers, and move ahead. Stopping like this slows down our progress, but it's the best we can do.

During this trek, I'm working my way up and back along the column. I don't want to be standing when the mortar shells hit, but at the same time, I figure it's unseemly for the platoon leader to be the first one to dive for cover. Because we can time this so closely, I listen with everyone else, but when they dive, I stay up a little longer. By the time everyone else is down (and for the most part they're not looking around), I drop down too. After I do this a couple of times, I think of a way to do it more safely. While the incoming rounds are in the air, I look around for a tree. Then when I drop, I curl around the base of the tree, figuring that whatever part of me is pressed against the tree is as safe as anything can be at that time. It sounds funny to me to describe this now. But that's what I did, and why.

I don't know how long it took to get everyone back, maybe two or three hours. Whatever it was, it seemed much longer, interminable, really. But finally, we got there. By that time, everything was set up for getting the casualties out fast. They went by helicopter to the field hospital at battalion, then by airlift to Japan and back to the States. For the first platoon, it had been a long, trying day, a sobering experience. Obviously, it was a lot worse for the wounded and dead of the third platoon, including Ike Cronin, their platoon leader.

As the sun went down, the men in the platoon and others who had helped in the rescue were totally drained. They could scarcely mumble as they were cleaning up, washing blood out of their dungarees and pulling their gear together to move out the next day. A pall of stillness hung over the platoon as the battalion commander, cheery and chipper as always, came into our area on a visit, working his way from one end of our line to the other. He meant well, and it was a thoughtful action on his part, but the men were just not up to it. They responded—mostly in one-syllable answers—to his questions but, otherwise, remained silent. I regretted that, but there wasn't much I could do about it. That was just the way it was.

July 16. Moving day. No one here is sorry to leave. We moved out, headed for the reserve assembly area.

Yesterday, a corporal named Davison, a BAR man in the third platoon, was killed going to the aid of two wounded Marines. Because the peace talks have started, someone thought that Davison might have been the last Marine to be killed in the Korean War. For that reason, the reserve area we are headed to is to be called "Camp Davison." *Stars and Stripes* wrote a couple of feature stories about this, but of course, the hope for an end to the war was wishful thinking. Corporal Davison's death was but another marker in the course of the war. The peace talks went nowhere for months, and the war roared on with mounting Marine casualties for the next two years.

I would have to say that for me this was a particularly difficult period. Unlike being in the attack, where the pressure would last until the firefight was over, here the pressure seemed to build slowly but persistently over the entire eleven days of our stay.

The patrols took their toll, not just in casualties but also in the strain on individual Marines. Right after the patrol, every third day, the pressure seemed to be released, and it was possible to get a good night's sleep. But after that, the tension built steadily until we were heading into the next patrol and coming back.

I slept only fitfully on each of the second nights back and very little on each of the nights before the next patrol. Lying awake in the sleeping bag, I was still trying to think of all the variations. What could possibly happen? That might have produced one or two good ideas, but usually it was just wasted time and lost sleep. I knew it would be better to get some rest. I just couldn't manage to do it.

Today, we were relieved on the line by elements of the Thirty-eighth Infantry, Second Army Division. Fortunately, the relief of lines proceeded on schedule. Everyone was glad to get out.

This was our first close contact with an Army unit in some time, and First Marines headquarters was concerned enough to warn its battalions about the hazards of such interservice contact in the following message:

"DURING FORTHCOMING RELIEF BY ELEMENTS 38th INF, RIDICULING OF ARMY PERSONNEL, NAME CALLING AND MAKING OF DOG LIKE SOUNDS STRICTLY PROHIBITED X"

We tried very hard to follow that injunction, with only mixed success. At any rate, they relieved us, and we did get off the line.

John Nolan, platoon leader, Baker Company's 1st platoon, shortly after the firefight on June 9, 1951.

Jim Cowan, Baker Company Commander. He'd landed at Inchon and come out from the Chosin Reservoir in 1950.

"When any cover is available, we'll use it to get closer to the enemy without being seen."

Vic Heins

Bernie Hletko. A natural leader, regardless of rank. Got into the Marines "because the reserve unit needed a second baseman."

This was about as secure and comfortable as it could get. And sometimes there was even a view.

Hletko's hard chargers. A Marine rifle squad at its best.
Breen, Elder, Osman, Mueller, Winger (front row, l to r); and
Churchich, Knight, Hletko, Heins, Burnett, Wiffenbach (back row).

Joe Reed...."when they found their own grenades coming back, they started holding....they'd let the spoon fly and count to two. That's dangerous and it requires exquisite timing. But when you do it right, it works."

Eddie LeBaron, a football All-American who excelled in infantry combat as well. Eddie was in the thick of it at the Hwachon Reservoir in late May 1951, and was still going strong at the Punch Bowl in September.

Baker Company's Bugle Call Rag.
Kitchen, Brady and Hays, the
Division Bugler (l to r).

Bill Rockey, Easy Company, 1st
Marines, commander for Operation
Blackbird. It was Rockey and
Murphy's earlier assault on
Hill 676 that Bigfoot Brown called
"a glorious spectacle...the hardest
fighting I have ever seen."

Walter Murphy, rifle platoon leader
on Hill 676 and a one-time Chinese
language student. One of his men
said: "We'd storm the gates of hell
if Mr. Murph would lead us!"

Charlie Cooper, ready to land in Korea and kick-start an outstanding thirty-five year career in the Marine Corps.

J.J. Morrow, one-of-a-kind platoon sergeant, "whose handlebar mustache and natural dignity made him seem older than his twenty-five years."

Marines clear a hootch as the enemy withdraws on the East Central front, Summer 1951.

Breck (John Cabell Breckinridge, III) a few days before he was killed in an ambush.

Tex Lawrence, rifle platoon leader, Baker Company's 2nd platoon.

The Old Breed and The New. Generals Thomas and Whaling flanking Tex Lawrence and Tom Parsons, July 4, 1951.

Questioning an NK prisoner after
the September 25 raid.
John Nolan, Jim Egan (standing).
Dick Kitchen (seated, second from left).

Jim Marsh. When other 2nd Lts left rifle
companies after four months, they usually
went back to battalion staffs. When Jim
left, after nearly seven months, he took
command of the regimental tank platoon.
Hardly the rear.

Marsh with two paddles,
ready to beat the dust
out of his sleeping bag.

Vic Heins

Pak Yon Kun, called Parks.
He'd seen more combat at
16 than some professional
military see in a lifetime.

Butch, Baker Company,
Korean interpreter.

USMC

Helicopter control tower of type built for 1st
Battalion's Guerilla Sweep, October 22, 1951.

Some of the 1st platoon's 1st squad, resting. Hudson, Carfagno, Churchich, Georges (l to r).

A Marine heads up. Some hills were steeper.

Camp named for Corporal Robert Davison, killed going to the aid of two wounded Marines near Yanggu, July 15, 1951. Truce talks had just started, and it was thought that he might be the last Marine to die in Korea. He wasn't.

Chapter 15

DIVISION IN RESERVE, JULY 18-SEPTEMBER 10

July 18. Just eleven days ago, truce talks started at Kaesong over on the west, and today, the First Marine Division pulled off the line after 150 consecutive days. We are now in Corps reserve, something we had heard rumors about for so long that no one believed them anymore. We thought it was myth, but now we're actually here. We expect it to be here for a month, maybe longer.

We are located near Hongchon, a few miles south of the 38th parallel and about forty miles from the front. Comfortably settled in tents, we have fires and lights after dark and movies every night. Last night, I slept on a cot for the first time since I got to Korea. I'm in a large pyramidal tent with Tex Lawrence and Barry Diamond, now the leader of the third platoon in place of Ike Cronin. Ike, who lost part of his leg on that last day on objective 4, has been flown out to the Army hospital at the Presidio in San Francisco. He's there with others in his platoon who went into the minefield together. The artillery FO has gone back to his battery while we're in reserve. So Tex, Diamond, and I are all that's left. We are to start a training schedule on the 23rd.

Joan has been kind enough to send scotch regularly. She fills the bottle to the top with water, so it won't gurgle if shaken (something the postal inspectors are supposed to do); replaces the cap tightly; and packs the bottle with popcorn in a sturdy cardboard box. The popcorn packages come right through, and everyone here is grateful. Any number of Marines—even two—can take care of a bottle in a sitting, and it never lasts for a second—a second sitting that is.

Last night, I hiked over to the Third Battalion area to see Joe Reed, and while there, they called to say that I had visitor back at the company. My visitor turned out to be a young Army pfc. named Bobby Scott, a son of my mother's best friend from her days of teaching school in Montana. Bobby lives in Choteau, Montana, and I had never met him before. A few years younger than I am, he seems like an okay guy. He's been here since Inchon, first in one MP company in the Seventh Army and now in another MP company attached to X Corps. He works for an older Army NCO, first sergeant of something or other in X Corps, and apparently a figure of power and authority in the vast Army supply establishment here. The first sergeant is Bobby's mentor, and I guess also his pal. They were here together tonight, and I visited with them for a while. It sounds like they are gatekeepers for a horde of everything usually in short supply in a war zone. If it's scarce out here, they have it, and they've invited me to visit them at X Corps. They receive and store everything that comes to X Corps, and additionally, they run the MP function and confiscate alcoholic beverages and other contraband.

From the perspective of someone in a rifle company, these guys are the ultimate rear echelon pogues, in the rear with the gear, as the saying goes. But these two are also roguish characters who look and act like they just stepped out of a Bill Mauldin cartoon. Bobby said that three weeks ago they threw a couple cases of beer and some whiskey in a jeep and drove fifty miles north looking for me. At that time, we were on the line, and they weren't able to get up there; so I didn't see them. But today, they did get through, and Joe and I are going to visit them tomorrow night to see if they are really living as high as they claim.

Joe Reed, my friend, is great as ever, though I hardly recognize him. He has a full black mustache and is rail thin. I may have gained a few pounds here, and Joe must have lost thirty-five. He looks lean and hard and says he feels great. He's been in much fighting over the past two months, and between casualties and rotation, his platoon has turned over a couple of times. At one time, he was down to fourteen Marines.

We talked about Stan Olson, the Old Swede, who was hit in the stomach on June 10 and spent three weeks in a hospital in Japan. Joe said he's back in the Second Battalion now, and I hope to see him soon. Bill Rockey also has been in some very heavy fighting and has come out well, as we know.

July 20. Here we are, lying on our bunks in a tent in the reserve area with the rain pouring down outside. We have pulled in rocks as a tent floor, just to keep us from floating out on a sea of mud. We skip from rock to rock in the tent, so moving around in here is like playing hopscotch. We have been joined by another Marine, Ted "Goose" Kennedy, a tall gangling second lieutenant who seems like a nice guy. He smiles constantly. He came out here in the fifth replacement draft months ago (we were in the eighth draft), and for some unknown reason, he's been at Otsu, Japan, since. Maybe that's why he always smiles.

Back here in reserve, of course, rumors swirl. One rumor is that the war here will end before our tour of duty does. That might actually be helpful, because rotation has slowed down so much. Great grumbling and dissatisfaction about that. Also speculation that if the war ended the First Marine Division might be the first unit to leave, and further speculation that the division might go to Camp Elliot, California, or that the division might be split up with one regiment going to Japan, a second to Okinawa, and the third to Hawaii. Obviously, all these rumors are official and extremely well informed. The straight scoop.

Here in reserve, the First Marines are located a couple miles east of the main north-south highway through Hongchon. Our battalion, together with the Second and Third Battalions, is sited on a flat, grassy area with the river below us, between us and the road. Regimental headquarters is on the high ground to our front, just on the other side of the river. We are actually comfortable here.

Our regiment is one-third of the First Marine Division, and the division is now a city of 25,000 living in tents that popped up here in an instant last week.

July 29. Last night the deferred visit to Bobby Scott and his friend the first sergeant at Golconda, their cache of all material goods available in the war zone, finally took place. Joe Reed and I got a jeep and driver to take us to the X Corps CP, along the main road about five miles south of our reserve area. It is necessary to understand that for months now Joe and I have been living in fighting holes or bunkers, miles from everything, even small villages, even hootches. The things we use are simple. If we can't pick them up and carry them with us, we don't use them. And we don't go anyplace except to come down off one hill and up another to shoot at more gooks. Our visit last night clearly showed us that our lifestyle is not the only one that exists over here.

When the jeep drops us off at X Corps, we are taken to the first sergeant's tent. Bobby is there. He and the first sergeant are cordial and hospitable. They have drinks waiting for us. The tent has everything in the way of food and drink that we haven't seen since leaving the States. The bar is fully stocked, but they're drinking Canadian Club and grapefruit juice, so that's what we have.

In due course (after many drinks), dinner is served: grilled steaks appear as if on a magic carpet. They taste great. They are a treat for us because we haven't had any for so long we've almost forgotten the taste. For Bobby and the first sergeant, this seems to be their usual fare, like they eat like this every night.

When we are all full, we tell war stories for a while. Our stories are interesting to Joe and me but seemingly much less so to Bobby and the first sergeant. To them, war seems simply an inconvenience. It requires them to be in this faraway place, roughing it, as it were. This is especially true of the first sergeant who is pleasant, maybe even a little more than that, but plainly not engaged. After a time, he excuses himself like he was just going to step outside for a minute. Much later, when we realize that he has not come back, we ask Bobby about him. Bobby explains that Top has had a tough day, and that he's probably turned in. He has gone to his tent that he shares with a young Korean girl who takes care of all of his needs there.

We continue with Bobby. He is really working hard at playing host, and there is more drinking to be done. By about 0130, the conversation is beginning to run down, and Joe and I make motions to leave. Bobby rises to his feet, somewhat unsteadily, and announces that he will drive us. We wonder about that, but we agree to go back with him. I think to myself that it's probably okay. There's not much on the road at that hour.

But it is raining very hard by then. The river alongside the road is a raging torrent, and the water is rising fast. When we get to the place where we are to cross the river—here, that means driving *through* the river, not around or over it—we find that we do have a problem. Joe says we slipped off the built-up section where the river is usually forded, but at any rate, the jeep is swamped, and we stall in the middle of the river.

Then, Bobby passes out!

By that time, it is after 0230. The rains are torrential, and the river is white froth and far up over its banks on both sides. Joe and I manage to get Bobby to shore—not the shore we were headed for, but the one we had just come from—and we get a wrecker from regimental motor transport to haul the jeep out of the river. Finally, we revive Bobby. We help him get his jeep started, and we get him on the road, pointed south, back toward X Corps.

While all this was going on, a group of returning Marines has piled up on the riverbank, looking to find some way across. The wrecker agrees to take us with the group. Once again, the big wrecker heads down into the stream, but the water is higher now, and the river is still churning by. We do get farther this time, maybe within one hundred feet of the other side, but then the wrecker stalls out, just as the jeep had earlier.

The water is about chest high and moving with such force that it's impossible to stand in it. I look hard at the water. It's very tempting, and it is inconceivable to me that if I just dived in I'd have any real trouble getting to the other side, even if I had to land a few yards downstream. But I stay with the group. There are nine of us there, and we form a human chain, linked by arms, and we move slowly across the rest of the river, leaning against the current. We do make it this time, and we get back to our camp sometime after 0430. I climb into the rack and sleep to 1000 this morning.

July 30. This morning, Baker Company goes up into the mountains a few miles away to test fire weapons. Jim Cowan has been in charge of a crew of Inchon men who are going back to the States on rotation. They've worked for the last week building a range, and today we fired everything, rifles, BARs, carbines, handguns, machine guns, and 60mm mortars up there. Jim, no longer the company commander and due to leave here for the States next Saturday, knows how to relax. He runs his crew, but his spare time now is spent on his rack with a cigar and a pocket book. His conversation has turned to the watering holes of Malibu and Tahoe where he plans to spend time after arriving back in the States.

Bob Work is now the company commander, and we have a new company exec. who arrived today. He is First Lieutenant John Cabell Breckinridge III, called Breck, a square-shouldered first lieutenant from a distinguished Marine Corps family. His father, for whom Breckinridge Hall at Quantico is named, founded Marine Corps schools there, and his brother Jim is a rifle platoon leader here in the Fifth Marines now.

July 31. Today, I have the guard again, a very simple affair. I post sentries and check them from time to time. Tomorrow, we have a general's inspection in the morning, and the next day there is some kind of ceremony down at the division headquarters. Generally, these days, we train or have lectures in the morning and play volleyball or softball in the afternoon. Not bad for the time being.

August 3. Personnel changes. Bill Landon, my platoon sergeant and friend, is leaving to go home on rotation. Expecting that, I had arranged for Howard Allmain, who was great in our first firefight in June, to take over as platoon sergeant. Now Allmain is going home on rotation too. Ordinarily, this would be a problem, but today, it has opened up an exciting new possibility.

When Tex heard that I would be looking for a platoon sergeant, he came to see me. He has an outstanding squad leader, J. J. Morrow, in his platoon. J. J., a tall slim sergeant, whose handlebar mustache and natural dignity make him seem much older than his twenty-five years, is impressive, clearly one of the best Marines around. He is from a small town in South Carolina and is well qualified to be a platoon sergeant anywhere. But Tex already has a platoon sergeant who will probably be with the platoon longer than Tex will, so he offered to make J. J. available to me if I wanted him for the job.

Did I want him? Hell, yes! I said he could start immediately. It's great for the platoon, and it should be for J. J. too. I appreciated it as a thoughtful and considerate gesture on Tex's part. There are other changes today also, Marines going home or being shifted to other units. We'll have a very different team when we pull out of here, whenever that might be.

August 4. Reserve drones on, except that today we actually did have a little excitement. At noon, with Marines standing around in chow lines, someone up in the hills behind us started firing rounds over our heads. Way over. No one was hurt, but still you wonder where it's coming from. Tex was the OD, and he took off with a search party, heading into the hills to investigate. Then scores of Marines, bored with inactivity here, fell into ad hoc search parties and headed to the hills as well. I assembled the first platoon, but by the time we got a radio operator, and our machine gun section joined us, and we got all the way out to where the search was going on, everyone was ordered back. So our job was just to round up the rest of the Marines out there and herd them back. There was speculation that some trigger-happy KMCs just decided to crank off a few rounds, but we never did find out. It was interesting for an hour or so, and it relieved the boredom.

August 5. Here in reserve, with the help of yobos, we've built a large recreation building constructed of timbers and screened in. Tonight we had a battalion party in it, nominally, for Jim Cowan on his last night in Korea. There wasn't much in the way of food, but the building was christened with song and plenty of strong drinks. The regimental commander, Tom Wornham, and a few officers from division came, but the rest was all our battalion.

One feature of the singing was the Raggedy-Ass Marines. A couple of stanzas:

> A thousand gobs laid down their swabs
> To lick one sick Marine.
> A thousand more stood by and swore
> 'twas the bloodiest fight they'd seen.

The Army and the Navy
And the lousy Engineers
Could never lick the Leathernecks
In a hundred thousand years.

Chorus:
As we go marching
And the band begins to P-L-A-Y
You can hear them shouting
The Raggedy-Ass Marines are on parade.

One of the visiting officers was a Tom Bohannon, formerly Able Company commander and now a staff officer someplace. He's about six feet three, a colorful type, well known for bright red scarves and other nonreg clothing and for hard drinking with his men. As Jim Cowan puts it, "Bohannon has always approached the fleshpots of the world with a big dipper." The officers in Baker Company didn't think much of him, but I'm told that his men and the platoon leaders who served under him thought he was first rate, tops for brains as well as guts. That's certainly an important judgment, maybe one of the most important.

Then there was Buck Schmuck, Lt. Col. Donald L. Schmuck, thirty-five. He was the CO of the First Battalion from Koto Ri to last February, and he remains a legend to the officers and men who served under him. Schmuck is a Westerner, raised on a cattle ranch in Wyoming. He played hockey at the University of Colorado and at the end of WWII was a lieutenant colonel at twenty-seven. Stocky, with a blond crew cut, he looks something like a tougher version of Jimmy Cagney, and he's obviously has a lot of confidence in himself, i.e., he doesn't look like he'd disagree with the high esteem in which Marines here hold of him.

Our present battalion commander is a very different cup of tea. Apparently, he was seagoing through all of WW II and has had various administrative assignments since. He looks good and seems conscientious. He's friendly, even personable, but it's hard to tell much from a few weeks in reserve. When Marines out here talk about a new officer, they wonder what he did in World War II, and seagoing doesn't quite do it. We'll see.

Where combat achievement is concerned, our present regimental commander, Tom Wornham, is a near legend. On Iwo Jima, he was as the CO of the Twenty-seventh Marines, the Marine Corps's most decorated regiment. More recently, he was at Quantico and had been selected for promotion to brigadier general when he was assigned to come out here to take over the First Marines. Now we hear that his promotion has come through and that he will be leaving soon. Wornham is a short, rugged looking fellow who smokes cigars and looks like he might be an outdoor guide or a professional hunter. I suppose, in a way, that's what he is. He has not been here long enough to make a real impression on the regiment, but he is professionally distinguished; and he inspires confidence.

August 6. Baker Company is changing fast. This morning, the second rotation group leaves. It includes Bill Landon, my first-platoon sergeant; Howard Allmain, my second platoon sergeant; and Rudolph Hravatic, the company top sergeant and perhaps the ablest man in the company.

I've been out here now for a few months, and I've seen some outstanding Marines, real men. But Hravatic, or Top as he is called, is as good as anybody I've seen. He was here while Jim Cowan had the company, and now he's heading home on rotation. He is thirty-one, but in 1942, he was for a time the youngest master sergeant in the Marine Corps. He's from Detroit where he has a highly paid job in labor relations with Ford. He also has a wife and infant son to whom he's devoted with the same drive that he brings to everything important. I'd very much like to see him again, back in the States.

We have plenty of time now, and I drift over to the Second Battalion area to see my friend Stan Olson, the Old Swede. I just happen to be there during the twelve-hour period when Stan is the company commander. After I leave, a first lieutenant arrives to take over the company, and Stan becomes the company exec. again.

August 7. This morning, someone gave me a snapshot of Tex and Tom Parsons taken at the Jack Benny show on July 4. They are with Generals Thomas and Whaling, the division commander and ADC. To me it represents today's Marine Corps, the new and the old, in the field in combat gear. I like the picture.

There's currently much talk about faster rotation of officers out of rifle companies, but I like it here; and I'm not in any hurry to leave. I haven't been here long enough, anyhow. Both Tex and Tom who got here a month before I did would be rotated first. Come to think of it, officer casualties from our class at TBS have been very light, thus, far, although most of those in rifle platoons seem to have gotten hit.

The weather here in the Hongchon area is miserable, about as bad as it can be. The temperature and humidity both seem to hover consistently in the high nineties, and the mornings are wet and heavy with fog. By this time, we're all sick of reserve and ready to go anywhere to do anything else.

August 8. Still in reserve. Today though, we have a chance to watch Tex's platoon run a demonstration attack on a fortified position, a spectacular performance. Blocks of TNT simulate artillery prep fires. Brilliantly colored flares flame out overhead, and machine gun tracers arch into the fortified position. Then the Marines swarm up and over the objective. Tex does a superb job. No one would ever have known that he was suffering from a fever, stomach cramps, headache, and other symptoms of the flu that many here now have. General Thomas and Colonel Wornham are here to watch the demonstration.

August 9. It has rained hard all night, and the rain continues into this morning. Our field exercises for today are cancelled, so we stay in our racks to 0800. Bob Work is doing a good job as company commander. I don't think that just because he lets his platoon leaders run their platoons, or even because he calls on us for suggestions from time to time. But that does help. He's good to work with.

Last night we had another show here, our second in this reserve. It was an Army special services group called *Take Ten*. They are all men, and their featured performer is someone called Frankie D'Amour (if you can believe that name) from Los Angeles. They were obviously professional and versatile, each one taking a turn with the vocals or in the band when he was not working as a standup comic, singing barbershop, tap dancing, or taking part in one of the variety numbers. I thought it much better than the Jack Benny show. From that, I'd conclude that talent is more important than being famous.

August 10. Another steamy morning after an all-night rain. We run our troops and ourselves into the ground on a company attack exercise in the surrounding hills. The exercise is tough, but the weather is worse. We sweat like pigs and lose all our body salt fast. We have salt tablets, and they are essential, but you have to take them carefully and start before losing body salt. Otherwise, they make you sick.

John Breckinridge, our new company exec., seems to be working out very well. He's a very senior first lieutenant and may soon to be up for promotion to captain. At twenty-five, he's already had eight years in the Marine Corps. Part of that was service in Puerto Rico, and just before coming out here, he was an aide to General Seldon at Camp Lejeune. He's a solid addition to the company.

August 14. Today I had a chance to go to Japan for three weeks for radiological defense school. Baker Company is supposed to send one lieutenant who has been with the company for four months. Both Tex and I qualify, but neither of us wants to go, so they'll have to get someone from Charlie Company. There isn't anything in Japan that I want, and I simply don't want to miss anything here. The stream of replacement officers coming in here continues, with today a first lieutenant named Frank (called Tank, he's hefty) Brady. From Fall River, Massachusetts, and the Yale class of 1947.

Today Tex and I talked with Lieutenant Colonel Schmuck, now the regimental exec. From what he said, when we do leave Baker Company, we'll probably stay in the battalion, either in weapons company or as something on the battalion staff. That sounds fine to me.

August 15. Tank Brady is fine, but not all replacement officers are that good. At about the same time Tank came in, we got another senior first lieutenant, an unlikely looking Marine, slight, pale, and bespectacled. But that doesn't make any difference, his real problem is attitude. This guy is morbidly pessimistic. No matter the subject, the present is always bad enough, but the future is sure to be worse. Through several years he's been in the Marine Corps, he's never served with troops before, and now he's out here, the most senior officer in the company, senior even to Bob Work, the company commander. This fellow is unassigned so far, no specific responsibility.

August 18. Sometime in the next few days, Bob Work will head back to the States, and a new company commander will take over. He arrived at Baker Company yesterday. His name is Dick Kitchen, and he is generally called Kitch.

Kitchen is about thirty and newly promoted to captain. He was in the Marine Corps in WWII and managed to get to Iwo just as the war was ending. He graduated from Yale, where he was the leader of the Whiffenpoofs, and was practicing law in Greeley, Colorado, when he was called up for Korea and assigned to the junior course at Quantico. There he graduated first in his class and had been assigned to duty as the legal officer at Pearl Harbor. With a wife and two kids, he regarded that as a plum assignment. But a funny thing happened to him on his way to Hawaii.

At the junior course graduation party, Kitchen and a classmate, one James Parnell Egan, got swacked. Before leaving the party, they happened to see Colonel Wornham, their old regimental commander from Iwo, who was then on his way out to Korea to take command of the First Marines. Kitchen and Egan, with a bravado fueled by bourbon, approached him and—when he told them what he was going to do—volunteered to accompany him into this foreign war. Sentimental and boozy, their expressed desire to serve with him may have been even stronger than that. They may even have sworn that they'd do anything to serve with him again, that they wished there was something he could do to take them with him, etc.

Well, as it turned out, he could do something. And he did. About the time Kitchen and Egan must have been sobering up, their orders were being changed, and new orders were cut transferring them to the First Marines, on the line in Korea. By that time, of course, they had forgotten all about volunteering for combat duty with their old regimental commander, but obviously Colonel Wornham hadn't. The Marine Corps takes care of its own. Both Kitchen and Egan reported to Baker Company, First Marines, yesterday, shortly after Col. Wornham's arrival.

Kitchen is friendly, relaxed, and direct in manner and speech. In musing about civilian life, he says he starved for two years trying to set up a law practice in Greeley, Colorado. Clients were scarce. Then in February—just when two of his few clients had died, leaving large estates that he would probate—he was called up in the Marine Corps Reserve. Driving to Quantico in a station wagon with his wife, his infant daughter, and everything that they owned, they had a head-on collision with a large semi. The top was sheared off the station wagon, and both vehicles were totaled. So they were lucky to live through it. Kitchen ended up under the dashboard and had to be cut out of the wreck with an acetylene torch, but he and his family were able to walk away. Now he's out here. He may be a little reluctant, but he looks like a natural.

August 19. This climate is sweltering. It's about as hot here as I've ever been, but today Tex and I found a place in the river to swim. Cool relief for a time, probably the best escape from the heat since we arrived in Hongchon.

Another visit to the Third Battalion where they have built, of all things, an officers' club. The structure is made of rough-hewn timbers with a ceiling of parachute canopies. Camouflaged mosquito netting covers the walk at the entrance. The main feature, naturally, is a bar and bar stools. It's not the Stork Club, but Oliver, Marsh, and Reed take great pride in it. And I visited with them there today.

Our talk is what the division will do if there is a cease-fire, and the speculation is that we go to Japan or Okinawa to be in blocking position or available for an amphibious landing if there's another threat or emergency in the Far East. As we talk, I realize how much I like being with the platoon. I've got no interest in moving back to battalion or in any other position. Tex feels the same way, so we may both be here for a while.

Today I got a new MOS (military occupational specialty) a number that all Marines have to indicate what it is that they do. My MOS has been 0301, meaning basic infantry officer. From now on, it will be 0302, which I guess means working infantry officer. In peacetime, it takes six months' service in the FMF (Fleet Marine Force) to achieve this status. It is, oddly enough, the preferred MOS in the Marine Corps, and it doesn't change for years, all the way from lieutenant to colonel.

August 20. This morning on returning from a field exercise, I come into a tent filled with staff and line officers, all looking serious. The first thing I hear is that we are to draw a normal load of ammo, and I immediately think that the North Koreans have broken through somewhere, and we're headed back up to the line. But it's just another regimental field problem. First, we were on standby to move out on thirty minutes' notice. Later, this was cancelled. Now we are to move out at 0400 tomorrow morning and expect to be gone for the rest of the week

August 21. The first day of our regimental field problem. We're on the road marching briskly forward by 0500. Back at X Corps, apparently, they are planning for their next moves, including some that may involve us. A recurrent rumor has it that the First Marines may be sent on an end run, racing up the coast road, along the east coast of Korea, to engage the enemy farther north. Possibly thinking of something like that, X Corps sent First Marine Division the following inquiry this morning: "HOW LONG WILL IT TAKE THE 1st MARINES TO GET ON THE ROAD?"

The division's immediate response, supposedly transmitted by Brute Krulak, division chief of staff, was "THE 1st MARINES ARE ALREADY ON THE ROAD; WHICH DIRECTION DO YOU WANT THEM TO MOVE?"

Sometime later this morning, we do get off the road to begin a long, hard climb to the top of the highest mountain around. We—Baker Company's first platoon—are in the lead. For the problem, we are to take and hold the high ground. When we get there, we fall into defensive positions and settle down to wait. The peak we're on is really up there, maybe two thousand feet above the road in the valley below. By the time we reach the top, the rain has stopped, and the sun is bearing down. It is searingly hot.

As I settle down on this aerie with a pair of binoculars, I notice another battalion of our regiment moving along the road far below. They stop just past our position, at the point where the trail we have climbed leaves the road. After a short pause, they pull off the road on to the trail and start up. I think that looks a little odd, but I don't know what their orders may be, and I think they must know what they are doing. I continue to watch them until the entire battalion, some 1,200 men, is off the road and out of sight as they climb.

Time passes, first one hour and then second, until the head of this gigantic column comes into view again, this time much closer but still far below us. Leading the column is the battalion commander himself, a large man poling his way up the trail with a long wooden staff. By now, it is really hot. I watch as they draw closer, all of them breathing heavily, sweat pouring off them.

Finally, the column comes to a halt. They are at the top of the mountain, on the trail directly opposite where I'm sitting and only a few feet away. The battalion commander gives me a brief nod which I return, I hope courteously. They are like visitors coming into our area, and we are respectful.

With the long column halted behind him, the battalion commander turns outward to view the surrounding peaks. None is very close, and none is quite as high as we are. After a full minute, he looks puzzled as he reaches into his dungaree jacket and pulls out his map. He studies the map carefully then turns to look out first to one peak and then another. He's comparing each of his sightings with another hasty glance at the map. He is a study in intense concentration, but he finally has the answer. And he says it right out:

"Jesus Christ! The wrong fucking hill!"

By the time, he said it, I was beginning to suspect that might be it. And his verdict rang out, loud and clear. Maybe it was my imagination, but I thought I could hear a low groan, barely audible, start from the battalion commander and race on back and down through several hundred yards of the column behind him. Again, maybe my imagination, but I thought this wordless sound may have traveled with the speed of light from the head of the column to the last man in line.

Then, with the battalion commander still leading, the long column doubled back on itself and headed silently back down the trail they had just come up. We didn't see them again.

August 24. Here we are, back from the problem. We headed out again today at 0500 and marched ten miles to an assembly area in the drizzling rain. From there, I led a platoon patrol to another mountain peak where we spent the rest of the day. In late afternoon, we're ordered back to the assembly area, where we arrive about nightfall. We bolt down some C-rations and fall asleep.

Up at first light, we "attack" three ridgelines to our front, the area we had patrolled the day before, and tie in our lines on the final objective. It's then about 2300. The rain is back, and we're there on the line in a driving rain until noon yesterday when we pull out to march back here along the road. Now we're here on cots, air mattresses, and we have hot chow. I'm actually disappointed at how good it feels. I must have gotten soft in this reserve.

Today we have a critique of the problem, and everybody bitches about the officers on the battalion staff. They really are a bunch of pogues, young, fatheaded, and lacking in either experience or common sense. By contrast, we think that line officers—those of us in the rifle companies—function pretty well under any circumstances, including this problem. It seems to us that the problem just proved that.

August 26. We've now been in reserve for a month and a half. And we hate it. It may not be too much longer, as we're slated to go back on the line near the coast looking out on the Sea of Japan. Because we're restless and antsy, they give us a double feature every night. Last night was *Barrow of Arizona* (only fair) and *Ace in the Hole* with Kirk Douglas (great!). It must be that movies are getting better, or I need them more over here.

Today I get a letter from Wes Noren, a former Baker Company commander, now a major. He's one of my heroes, so I get a big honk out of hearing from him. With typical candor though, he notes that he addressed the letter to me because I am the only one he knew who would still be here. He's right. By now everyone who served in Baker Company under him is gone.

August 30-September 10. This period is really the dregs of Korea so far, a time when we're standing by with all our gear packed and ready to go. But we don't move out. Twice we've loaded everything but our shelter halves and sleeping bags and waited to board the trucks, only to be ordered to stand down. Also during this time, X Corps, the headquarters we are assigned to guard, does pack up and move out. Now we are here all alone. We are the guard that has nothing left to guard. Some say that we are now the southernmost unit—that is, the unit farthest to the rear—in the entire Eighth Army.

Generally, we run field problems during the day. They've brought back our movie screens, and we watch movies at night. The weather has changed. It's now much cooler, really cold at night, and we stay on. At one point, we got forty cases of beer for the company, and we organized a songfest (influence of a company commander who's a former Whiffenpoof). We drank beer and sang until 0200 and had a swell time. But reserve is still a drag.

Jim Egan, the other officer who came in with Kitchen, had graduated from Dennison College and stayed in the Marine Corps Reserve. When the reserves were called up, Egan was back on active duty and also sent to the junior course at Quantico. Now he's here, but temporarily without assignment in the company. Fortunately, Kitchen and Egan's chronically worried classmate has been reassigned to a supply job on the battalion staff. I'm sure he likes that better, and I feel certain it's better for us.

Just for the record, before we clear out of here, I'd like to note an assessment: Baker Company is really in great shape now. There are a lot of reasons, but the main one is leadership. Kitchen and Breckinridge are a good team. Kitchen is smart, perceptive, and focused. He's interested in outstanding performance, doing everything better than anyone thought it could be done, and interested in doing it with minimum of casualties. He has a natural talent for getting the most out of everyone, officers and men alike. Breck complements him in many ways, filling in what Kitchen may not get to or what he may not know about how the Marine Corps works. Together, they are very effective.

Another advantage of a company commander who's a former Whiffenpoof is that he has a lot of songs. An example is something supposedly drawn from the ditties of the Royal Marines. It's called "I Don't Want to Join the Army" and should be sung with a cockney accent. The lyrics go something like this:

> I don't want to be a soldier.
> I don't want to go to war.
> I'd rather hang around Picadilly Underground
> Livin' off the wages of a . . . high-brow lady

I don't want no bayonet up me arse 'ole.
I don't want me buttocks shot away.
I'd rather live in England, in jolly jolly England,
And roger all me bloody days away, Gar Bligh me.

So call out the Army and the Navy.
Call out the rank and file.
Call out the members of the Old Brigade,
They'll face danger with a smile. Gar Bligh me.

Call out the Royal Territorials.
They'll keep England free.
Call out your mothers, your sisters and your brothers,
But, for Christ's sake, don't call me.

The first platoon is a good example of high morale in the company now, and it's the one I'm most familiar with. After spending a lot of time with them here in reserve, I think I know them pretty well, as men and as individuals. And because morale is so high, I decided to try something I'd never heard of, just because I think it makes sense.

In a recap session, at the end of our last all-day field exercise, I said that I thought we could try out our own mini-rotation policy from the platoon. If anybody wanted to leave the platoon—presumably to move to the rear—all he had to do was ask. Of course, everybody understood that I had no authority to transfer anyone, but I would receive any such request in confidence and consider it in good faith. And if I thought it had merit, I'd try to make it happen.

My sense is that no one wants to leave the platoon, or that no one wants to leave bad enough to admit it to me, or maybe even to himself. I don't know that, and I haven't discussed it with anyone. But I think that if someone who deserved a chance to be rotated asked me to help him, I would. So I decided I might as well say that.

So far I've gotten zero reaction from anyone. Nothing from J. J. or the squad leaders, nothing from any of the men. We'll see.

Current policy on rotation out of rifle companies is four months for officers and eleven months for enlisted men. The policy is based mainly on availability and the desirability of qualifying officers as infantry troop leaders. It may seem unfair, but it's probably necessary, although there should be exceptions. In fact, I may have become one.

Major Edgar Carney, our battalion exec. officer is a serious, taciturn man. Redheaded with freckles and a broken nose, he looks tough, and he probably is. I've not had much direct contact with him, but he seems to be doing a good job. A couple of days before we were to leave reserve, I got a message to report to his tent. What could this be about?

When I got to his tent, I pulled the flap back and went in. I saluted and said that I understood he wanted to see me. He was sitting there in semidarkness at a field desk with a lantern on it. The light in the tent was very dim. As usual, he didn't waste words.

"Nolan, how long have you been in Baker Company?"

"I joined on May 7, sir. So I guess that's about four months."

"Okay, Nolan. That'll be all."

With that, I saluted again, turned around, and left. It occurred to me that in the course of that remarkably short meeting, Major Carney had done nothing to blow his reputation for terse comment.

At first, I didn't understand, but then I thought about it. The battalion was going back on the attack at the Punch Bowl, and Tex and I were the only two officers who'd been in Baker Company before we came into reserve; the others had all joined us here. Carney should want us to stay with the company at this time, no matter what. There was no need to say anything more. So it seemed to me that Carney had it right, and it was fine with me. Someone else was keeping track of my time, and I didn't want to leave the platoon anyway.

As our last frolic in reserve, Kitchen, Breckinridge, and I got a jeep and driver to take us about ten miles up the river, the Hongchon Gang, so we could float back down on air mattresses. The driver then brought our boots and other clothes back in the jeep, and my friend Parks was assigned to keep an eye on the stuff back in the company area. Our great outdoor adventure began on a warm, sunny day in early fall and at first was a lot of fun. But we had to haul the air mattresses over sharp rocks during several portages, and when our feet started bleeding, we realized we might not have been as tough as we thought. The trek also lasted much longer than we'd expected, and the wind was freezing after sundown. But this experience was far better than sitting around the reserve area for that last afternoon.

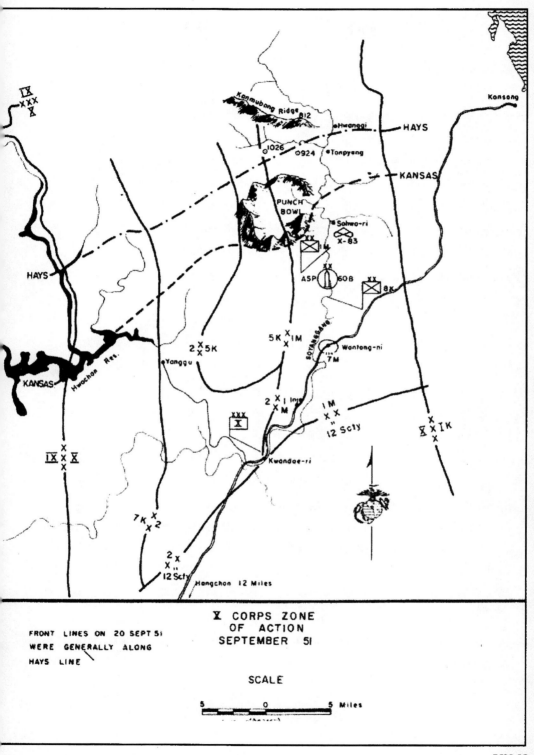

Kansong

Kanmubong Ridge 812
●Hwanggi — HAYS

○1026 ⊙924 ●Tonpyong

— KANSAS

PUNCH
BOWL

●Sohwa-ri
X-83

XX
IM

HAYS

KANSAS

ASP X
X 60B

XX
8K

Hwachon Res.

●Yanggu

2 X 5K
X

5K X IM
X

SOYANG-GANG

Wontong-ni
X
7M

2 X | Inf
X M

IM
X X
"
12 Scty

XXX
X

X
XX IK

IX X X
X X
X

7K X
X 2

2 X
X "
12 Scty

Kwandae-ri

Hongchon 12 Miles

FRONT LINES ON 20 SEPT 51
WERE GENERALLY ALONG
HAYS LINE

X CORPS ZONE
OF ACTION
SEPTEMBER 51

SCALE

5   0   5 Miles

Chapter 16

PARKS

What really counted out there was a
handlebar mustache, a Korean boy to
take care of your gear, and a rifle platoon.

Anonymous Lieutenant
Korea, 1951

If a handlebar mustache was the first thing that counted, it was obvious that I was going to start one down. But from sometime in the late spring, when I was still with the 60 mm mortars, we had picked up the Korean boy. His name was Pak Yon Kun, but we always called him Parks.

I first saw Parks one steamy morning when our counteroffensive was rolling ahead, and we needed bearers to carry mortar rounds. He came to us in a gang of replacement bearers, one of five assigned to the mortar section. I wanted to find a boss, one who understood enough English to run the other four, and when that question was put to them by an interpreter, they immediately agreed on Parks.

This surprised me because, standing about five feet, draped in dungarees several sizes too large, Parks was the smallest and looked to be the youngest of the group. He seemed agreeable, and his easy smile showed teeth that were clean, even and impressively white. But I was looking for a driver rather than a personality, and I wasn't sure that a Korean-English dictionary and a smile would do it. The others were inscrutable, though, and Parks looked like he wanted to help. He got the job.

We were moving every day then, and I hardly noticed him for the first week. But he seemed to get along well, and when I moved up to take over the first platoon, Parks came with me. Generally, platoon leaders had somebody like that around, and Parks took over that role for me and for the first platoon.

He passed his first test under fire with credit, but without distinction. In the chaotic maelstrom of screaming, shouting, and explosions that was a firefight, he wasn't much more confused than everyone else. I saw him dive to the ground once as a burst of machine-gun fire hit the tree next to him. But he came up grinning when he saw that I was watching.

On that day, he was still wearing the oversized dungarees, and he carried an M-1 rifle almost as long as he was tall. With Korean flat-soled shoes, a sagging cartridge belt, and tufts of black hair sticking out from under a battered helmet, he could have played the title role in a Korean version of *The Kid*.

Parks was bright, and he quickly learned how to heat C-rations, clean weapons, wash clothes, and carry messages. But we wanted to set him apart from other Korean helpers, and his training soon began. His principal tutor was Butch, Pfc. Milas F. Butcher, the platoon runner and also Parks's bunkmate, who took on the role with enthusiasm. Butch was from Kentucky, and when I'd hear them repeating the same English phrases over and over again, sometimes far into the night, I'd wonder if Parks would end up speaking English with the salty twang of Harlan County.

The rest of Parks's learning was fairly practical: the Marine Corps T/O (tables of organization)—the number of Marines in a squad, squads in a platoon, platoons in a company, etc., the rank of the Marine in charge of each of these units, and related USMC common knowledge. Then he learned who had each of these jobs in the company, and finally, we took him around and introduced him to the Marines whose names he'd learned. Parks was good on handshake and eye contact, and he was naturally courteous. From then on, he was recognized and trusted by everybody in the company likely to send or receive messages.

Next it was time to do something about Parks's appearance, and Sergeant Hunt, our ageless platoon guide who had every kind of clothes and equipment at hand, agreed to outfit him. First, he replaced Parks's M-1 with a carbine, lighter and obviously a better fit. Clothes and boots were more of a problem. Standard issue combat gear is made for the average-size American, not a five-foot Korean who wouldn't weigh 120 pounds with his pockets full of grenades. But Hunt got some dungarees that fit and a pair of Army-combat boots, size 5, and Parks was outfitted.

That was the last thought anyone gave to Parks's appearance. His carbine was always clean and well oiled, the stock gleaming (and he kept mine in the same condition). After that, he replaced anything needed on his own. And he always had a natty, freshly scrubbed look of a squared-away Marine. He would have starred in boot camp.

Parks had a quiet courage that was more impressive when you understood his temperament. He was not overly aggressive and definitely not a killer. When he threw grenades or charged bunkers, it looked like he just didn't want to miss what the rest of us were doing. But over time, I noticed that he always stayed close to the action, the head of the column going out and with the rear guard coming back. Some manage to do this, and in a rifle platoon, you notice who they are. He was one of them.

I gave Parks a few dollars a month, and some of the men gave him money or token gifts from time to time, but except for this, he was unpaid. He was there as a volunteer doing something that was extremely dangerous, but he could have walked away at any time. We did trust him completely, and he seemed to appreciate that. But there was nothing else holding him with us.

As Parks learned more English, he could do more and more in the platoon. Soon he was taking a turn on the sound power telephone at night, and it was no longer possible to fool him on C-ration trades. When he first joined us, the cans all looked alike because he couldn't read English. Because there were always preferences, there was a brisk trade in C-rations among the Marines, and in the beginning, Parks would sometimes end up with three cans of the *same* kind of food, whatever was temporarily out of favor in the platoon. After he learned how to read the labels on the cans, he knew what he liked, and he was no longer a patsy.

A high point for Parks was the first time a package arrived addressed to him. My wife, Joan, had sent it after reading about what he was doing for us. At first, he couldn't believe that it was actually intended for *him*, but when he finally got over that, he carefully unwrapped the layers of brown paper around the package. It contained the usual delicatessen foods, candies, and pocket books that came in regularly for others. It wasn't that these things counted so much—he gave most of them away anyhow—but this was *his*, and it gave him a chance to offer something to friends who had treated him earlier. It was the happiest time I'd ever seen him, and his thank you note to Joan was a classic.

When I left the platoon to go back to battalion as the S-2, Parks came with me. His English was vastly improved by then, and he went on the battalion payroll as a qualified interpreter. That meant hot food, three squares every day, and the job of interrogating prisoners. It was also a lot safer. Before I returned to the States, I heard that Parks had volunteered to go back up on the lines with another rifle company in the battalion. That was the last I heard of him until after the war ended, when I talked with several Marines who had served with him in that company.

For a year and a half, he'd stayed there, on the front lines, as desertions, strain, and casualties reduced the number of qualified interpreters. On a place called Bunker Hill, his good friend, Packy, the other interpreter in his company, was killed. After that, Parks carried on alone. That meant every ambush and every patrol, without relief. Where the regular Marines were drawing these hazardous assignments one night in six—or at most one night in three—Parks was going out every night. Then during the day, he was working with yobos. The men I talked with said the strain was beginning to tell. He was twice wounded and was plainly well past his limit. He had seen more war by the age of sixteen than many career military see in a lifetime.

I heard from Parks twice after that. The war was over, and South Korea was trying to rebuild. He had returned to school and was hoping to study medicine. His letter showed no trace of bitterness or cynicism.

Later, after the government of Syngman Rhee fell in a fresh outbreak of violence, I received another letter, lengthy and written in English that could never be imitated, a language he probably hadn't used much since his days with the Marines. Its concluding lines were:

> I really hope that God will bless you everlasting adorned with glorious and You might have lovely Your life. I'll always pray for your all family. Good luck forever.
>
> /s/ Parks

Chapter 17

LEBARON AT THE PUNCH BOWL

When the division came out of reserve, the Seventh Marine Regiment led off, straight to the Punch Bowl. Eddie LeBaron was by then one of the regiment's seasoned rifle platoon leaders, wounded, decorated, and revered by his men. Here, Eddie picks up the story, in his words:

"In early September, we moved into positions farther to the east, a few miles from the coast, close enough for battleships offshore to fire big 16" guns over our heads into North Korean targets. Our company, Baker Company, was on a position looking up to Hill 673, about one thousand yards away, over a small river and up a steep ridge. My platoon was on the far-left flank tied in with the First Marines, our positions separated by a river. The two sides exchanged artillery daily. We could see the enemy building up on Hill 673, and our patrols found that they were dug in, in great strength with minefields in front and artillery and mortars in support.

"At one point, my platoon was ordered to seek to recover a Marine from another platoon believed to have been lost on patrol. We headed down into the valley that ran parallel to the river and close to Hill 673, and about a mile out, we ran into an ambush and were hit by artillery fire. We were able to call in our own artillery firing WP (white phosphorous) between us and Hill 673, and under that cover, we were able to pull back without casualties. But from then on, we took incoming mortar and artillery fire every day we were up there as we watched the continuing buildup on Hill 673.

"Right after that, I was called to the company CP and told that sometime in the next few days my platoon was scheduled to make a helicopter landing behind enemy lines in order to take 673. Later that plan was changed, and we were to follow another platoon in our company. It was just as well that the plan was changed. That first helicopter landing site would have been on the CP of the North Korean battalion defending Hill 673, probably not the best place to try to come down.

"When we did jump off, my platoon followed the other two platoons in the company in order to be ready to exploit any break in the lines after they had taken out the initial defensive positions. But the other platoons hit the minefields raked by machine gun fire with live grenades rolling down toward them. The NKs' interlocking fields of fire gave them complete control of the top of Hill 673, and the result was a very tough firefight.

"We ended up hanging on at the end of the day, trying to sleep on the ground we still held just below the NK bunkers. The lead platoon had been pretty well shot up, and in the morning, we moved through them to attack over a minefield covered by fire. As we were going over, the Marine immediately next to me stepped on a mine which took off his leg. While I was carrying him back to get a corpsman, he was shot in my arms.

"Going back across the minefield was very scary, and I tried to step lightly. When I got far enough ahead to be able to see the bunker complex, I was able to call in 155 mm howitzer fire, and after that, we attacked from two different directions, straight up the hill against the enemy bunkers.

"One of the men in my platoon was later awarded the Medal of Honor for his actions on Hill 673. In grenading bunkers at the very top, he succeeded in taking out a key enemy position, but he lost his life to another grenade in that valiant effort. We had other casualties, killed and wounded, but finally, we were able to roll over the bunkers and on down the ridge, cleaning up as we went. Of the several months I spent on the front lines, this was far and away the toughest fighting I was involved in. In the end, we did have them on the run, but our losses were very high. Then the battle of the Punch Bowl ended. We were relieved by the Fifth Marines, and both our lines and the enemy's were stationary from then on. After that, the peace talks took over."

Chapter 18

JOE REED, TAKE IT
"IF NOT IN FRIENDLY HANDS"

On September 20, 1951, Third Battalion, First Marines, had been ordered to relieve two ROK battalions on the line. The place was a large hill mass, Hill 854, northeast of the Punch Bowl. And those writing the order must have known what lay ahead. The order provided that the Marines should take "such offensive action as might be necessary to complete securing of Hill 854, if not in friendly hands at the time of relief."

Apparently, the ROKs had gotten the summit of 854, leaving angry, belligerent gooks swarming all over the rest of the hill. This bothered the ROKs, so they laid a minefield around the summit and buttoned up, waiting to be relieved by the Marines. Not all of this—especially the part about the angry gooks and the minefield—was known to the Third Battalion when they arrived on site ready to carry out their relief. They found out pretty quickly though when they had to climb up the reverse slope to get to the ridge (the gooks commanded a clear view of all other approaches). And when they got there, it was plain

154

that they would have to fight to stay. Again, the call went out for Joe Reed.

When Joe got to the company commander, Captain Herb Anderson, the CO told him, "I need you to take the assault." The lead platoon could not be ready on time. Joe said he tried diplomatically to decline the honor on the ground that he and his platoon had led the last three assaults. But then the CO told him that was the very experience that was needed to get the job done. It was plain there was no way out. So Joe and his company commander huddled with the very shaken ROK officer whose company was being relieved. Plainly, all he wanted to do was get the hell outa' Dodge.

The rest of the story is better in Joe's own words:

"From the bunker, we had a good view of the ridge running out from where we were. Looking that way, I could see sections of white tape barely visible along the route we would have to follow in our attack. When I asked about the white tape, the ROK officer admitted they had laid mines out there two nights before. He said they expected an NK counterattack. But when I asked for a schematic or a map of the field, he only shrugged.

"We had about a half hour left before we were going to jump off, and he didn't look like he was going to respond. It was at that point that I took out my bayonet and told him he could either draw me an accurate sketch of the minefield, or he could personally lead me through it with my bayonet rammed firmly up his ass. I got the sketch.

"Obviously, this was an important negotiation with an ally. And it was helped greatly when our assault was delayed for two hours for an air strike. This gave us more time to get ready. But the delay meant that we wouldn't jump off until 1730 and would be attacking directly into the setting September sun. By this time, also the platoon leader of what should have been the lead platoon had been sent to the rear, and John Harper and his platoon had been moved up to follow us.

"The first enemy bunkers were about one hundred yards away with the path that led down to them no more than seven yards wide for the first fifty yards through the minefield. Then the ridgeline broadened to maybe twenty or twenty-five yards.

"The Corsairs, of course, were great. Napalm and all! When they'd finished, I jumped up on the bunker to rev things up. I fired off a full carbine magazine and headed down the path. That felt like a good start until I realized that the front hand guard on the carbine had come off, and the barrel was loose and ready to fall out. I still had a WWII Luger in my shoulder holster and all the grenades I could carry.

"We were lucky enough to get all of my platoon through the mines. But Harper, following, had one Marine KIA and another WIA there after the shooting started. Once through the minefield, we were able to spread out a little. But by that time, the enemy had come alive. And when they were able to build up a volume of fire, we started taking casualties. Just past the first four bunkers, the leader of the first squad and my platoon sergeant were both killed, and we had six more wounded.

"At that point, I held up. We set up a skirmish line and a machine gun with covering fire, so we could get our dead and wounded out. Apparently, the fires converging on us were part of a determined effort to cut us off from our base. And at about this time, the company commander, Herb Anderson, watching the action through a port in the command bunker, was killed by a sniper's bullet.

"We were ordered to dig in and hold where we were, with Harper's platoon to pass through us and continue the attack at 0700 the next morning. Everyone expected a counterattack that night, so we kept the star shells going all night long. About midnight, I was pulled back to become the How Company XO. Apparently, we had a standoff on the hill because there were only a few grenade exchanges. The expected counterattack never happened.

"The next morning, the company held up for the air strike which was late. Harper finally jumped off at about 1220 and was able to gain another two hundred yards against stiff opposition, but in the afternoon, air support was no longer available. With heavy artillery and mortar support, they were able to secure the last section of the ridge by about 1745.

"For us this was more than a skirmish. Third Battalion's casualties for the two days were 9 KIA and 55 WIA, and the NK casualties were much higher. For us, it had started out to be just a relief of lines, but then I remembered the order. Clearly, we were to attack if the hill was '*not in friendly hands at the time of relief.*' It wasn't. And those words had more meaning for all of us after the experience than they did when we first saw them."

Chapter 19

THE PUNCH BOWL AND FOLLOW-UP, SEPTEMBER 11-30

September 11. A word of explanation about what has happened while we have been sitting out the war in reserve here in Hongchon. After relieving us on the line, the Second Army Division tried for a week to capture Hill 1179, called Fool's Ridge, at the southwest edge of the Punch Bowl. They finally got it, and from there, they were able to fire artillery on an enemy stronghold on Hill 983, their primary objective.

They pounded 983 with air and artillery for weeks. Then a ROK regiment did capture it but couldn't hang on. The position changed hands six times in two weeks as the ROKs were pushed off again and again by determined enemy counterattacks. Finally, the Second Division flanked 983 and captured it from the rear. In this fighting, it came to be known as Bloody Ridge.

This cleared the way for our offensive coming out of reserve, with the Seventh Marines and the KMC regiment attacking on the high ground northeast of the Punch Bowl.

The Punch Bowl is an ancient volcanic crater about twenty miles north of the 38th parallel and fifteen miles in from the coast of the Sea of Japan. It is an oval four to five miles in diameter with the longer axis running north to south. Within the oval is flatland of no military significance, but the oval itself is made up of granite ridges jutting several thousand feet into the sky, and from these ridges, the North Koreans could control a vast surrounding area by fire. Initially, the Seventh Marines and KMCs captured their first objectives, but the NKs poured reinforcements into the area and clawed their way back to much of the ground they had lost.

While all of this was going on, our regiment was still in Corps reserve at Hongchon. It was here we kept hearing rumors that we'd be ordered to an end run up the coastal highway, but we never did. Instead, today, September 11, we boarded trucks at Hongchon and were moved into position behind the Seventh Marines, who were trying desperately to hang on to the precarious positions they had taken northeast of the Punch Bowl.

September 12-13. The Seventh Marines have been furiously engaged here, and for the last two days, we've been strung out along the trail behind them, waiting to move up. The Seventh is attacking Hill 749, the main enemy position to our front. Their battle is raging, and the trail we're on is a busy thoroughfare with heavy traffic in both directions—supply trains of yobos hauling ammunition and supplies forward and carrying stretchers of wounded Marines back down to be evacuated.

The gooks are plastering this area—including the part where we are—with their heaviest artillery and mortar barrage of the war. Big artillery shells roar in without letup, and everything around us is pockmarked with large shell craters. We use those holes for cover. They are deep enough to protect against everything but a shell landing right in the hole with you. But of course, at a time like this, that's what you think of. It can happen. Our close air support, Corsairs flown by Marine and Navy pilots, swing in low overhead before swooping down for their strafing and napalm runs on the enemy just to our front.

The Corsairs are a great help, but sitting here getting pasted is very hard on the nerves, harder than anything else so far. Maybe it's because we're not doing anything, but the strain builds hour after hour and now day after day. During this period, I don't sleep or eat. Even thinking about eating nauseates me, and a small sip of water from my canteen brings me to the edge of throwing up.

During this period, we've moved up a couple of times. And as we've gotten closer to the fighting, we've had to move through the bodies of the dead, Marines stacked along both sides of the trail. In the valley below us, the road was jammed with 6xs, trucks used as ambulances for wounded Marines or loaded with more of the dead wrapped in ponchos.

Finally, our regiment does relieve the Seventh Marines, and the battle is carried forward by 2/1 and 3/1, the Second and Third Battalions of the First Marines. Our First Battalion is still in reserve behind 2/1.

September 14. For us, the bombardment continues without letup all through this long and bloody night. Just ahead of us, the Second and Third Battalions fight tenaciously in the face of intermittent gook counterattacks. And, somehow, they hold on. The Second Battalion alone has 17 Marines killed in action (KIA) and 109 wounded (WIA) before sunup. Those who died include one Pfc. Edward Gomez, called Lefty by his fellow Marines in Easy Company. Gomez, from the time he arrived in Korea, had yearned for the Medal of Honor. As he said to some of the others in his platoon, "I sure hope they don't run out of those things before I have a chance to get one." His chance came last night.

During the frenzied peak of the fighting in this long, hot night, Gomez pulled a live gook grenade to his body and dived into an adjoining ditch. Of course, a second later when the grenade exploded, it took out Gomez, but his comrades survived. Apparently, Gomez had been no Boy Scout in his home town, and one of his friends from Omaha, on hearing of his death, remarked that "the cops in Omaha will be glad to hear that Lefty Gomez is dead." But out here, that was not the feeling. Some of his mates in Easy Company surely owed their lives to him, and they knew it. And in saving his comrades, he died a hero and earned the medal he'd dreamed of.

Without even being engaged last night, the First Battalion had eight Marines wounded, including Tom Parsons, a platoon leader in Charlie Company and Tex's best friend. And today, we lost our battalion commander.

Early this morning, he was striding along the trail that headed back down to the road. He was moving at the head of a small party, his radioman and others from the battalion staff. By the account I heard, the battalion commander kicked the wire of a booby-trapped grenade, apparently without noticing it. When the spoon flew off, it pinged with a sound that the others recognized instantly. With a single reflex, they dived to the ground on both sides of the trail. Some of them were wounded also, but the battalion commander only had time enough to turn halfway around. He was still standing when the grenade detonated just below him, and he took the full force of the blast in his chest and lower body. That could be a very serious injury. He was carried to the road and evacuated immediately. We hope and pray for his recovery.

September 15. We're still right behind the Second Battalion. They are attacking against withering fire, and they are taking heavy losses. We can't do anything but watch their casualties come back through our lines and try to stay out of the way of incoming artillery and mortar rounds.

There is a small helicopter pad just to our rear, and some of the Second Battalion wounded are carried back there to be flown out. This afternoon, Second Battalion makes its last try for a foothold on Hill 749 when Fox Company jumps off at 1600. The platoon that led the final assault had only about sixteen men when they started and half that number left when they finished. They did capture Hill 749, briefly, but then they didn't have enough men or ammo to hold it, and they were forced to pull back.

September 15 is an important date in Korea. It was just a year ago today that the Marines stormed ashore at Inchon to blow the war wide open. Now it is the third day of the First Marines' assault on Hill 749, and the seesaw battle rages on.

September 16. Right after midnight, we heard the stepped-up volume of gook artillery and the swelling roar of battle on the Second Battalion positions a hundred yards to our front. What we didn't know at the time is that this was the climax, the tipping point.

Hill 749 was the North Korean's key position, the anchor of their Punch Bowl defenses. They intended to hold it forever. Their bunkers were deep and solidly built of massive logs under several feet of earth. They could withstand anything but a direct hit. They were so strong that when Marines got in close, the gooks could fire mortars directly on top of their own bunkers. Even our close air support was less effective than it had been a few months earlier, because the bunkers were nearly impregnable.

Further, Hill 749 was surrounded by ridges so thin and spidery, and it was hard to get even a second squad up in position to attack. The Second Battalion had to take on the bunkers frontally and then try to flank them. With a BAR firing into the bunker through the opening, it was sometimes possible to move close enough to throw in a grenade and then rush the position.

Plainly, in the early hours of September 16, the gooks were out to take it all back, to recapture everything they had lost in the last few days. They came at the Marine positions over and over again, wave after wave coming out of the night.

It was here, in the first few hours of September 16, that Cpl. Joe Vittori, Fox Company, Second Battalion earned his place on the roll of heroes of the Korean War. Vittori was all over, fighting from different holes, firing at various times a BAR or a machine gun into the waves of oncoming attackers. Through the night, he was hit repeatedly and finally killed in the closing minutes of the battle. When morning came, there were more than two hundred enemy bodies piled up in front of his last position.

For this, Vittori was awarded the Medal of Honor, the battalion's second in forty-eight hours. And when the night was over, the Second Battalion was still holding on. They hadn't been able to capture all of Hill 749, but they were still there, intact and in force. Their casualties had been horrific, some 450 Marines out of the 700 or so in the battalion's rifle companies wounded, and an additional 31 KIA over a five-day period.

We began relief of Second Battalion at 0830 this morning to continue the attack along the ridges leading to Hill 749, the same ridges the Seventh Marines were on last week. Able Company was leading for the First Battalion against continuing, stiff resistance. During the day they had heavy casualties, but they were finally on the approaches to the last objective about 1700 this afternoon.

Around midday, our new battalion commander arrived, looking from the very beginning like he belongs here, like he's just coming home. He is John Evans Gorman, thirty-six, a reserve officer from Southern California with extensive combat service on Iwo Jima in World War II. He is a rangy, athletic-looking man who seems naturally comfortable and at ease here.

Shortly after1700, we pull up alongside Able Company to take on the final objective. This is Dick Kitchen's first time running an assault. He calls for an air strike and, somewhat to our surprise, manages to get the planes without delay. Four Corsairs come screaming in to pound the hill we're facing. They strafe it with .50 caliber machine gun fire and pound it with bombs, and napalm. We can never get enough of this, of course, although this one does look pretty good to us.

But it's not good enough for Kitchen. He looks it over coolly and calls for a second air strike. No delay. A second flight of four Corsairs arrives to rework the gook position. And when they finish, the artillery caps it with a final barrage. Now we're really ready. Baker Company moves out in the assault.

This is the end of the line for us, the final objective for the First Marines. It is the high ground across a saddle from the hill Able Company has just captured. In an earlier op plan, this was to have been a jumping-off place for our assault. But this entire operation has been much tougher than anyone expected. The plans have been revised, and for now, this is it.

It's a big hill, and we spread out across it—three platoons abreast, bayonets fixed. We start up. The artillery and big mortars have finished. Now the heavy machine guns are firing just in front of us and our company; 60 mm mortars are landing about fifty yards out and moving ahead as we advance. On this hill, it works. Before we get to the top, everyone is firing, moving on up the hill and over the enemy positions. We pick up a few wounded NKs on the way, but otherwise, we roll over the top. It may be anticlimactic, but Hill 749 is finally ours.

We hurriedly lock in defensive positions and prepare for a counterattack that night. But it never came. The night was strangely quiet. For now, the North Koreans seem to have shot their wad in this area.

September 17. We hold up here on the line, strengthening our defenses and sending patrols out to the front. During the day, we have an occasional gook sniper firing into the line, and there are a few casualties on the patrols. But it's not too bad except for the 76s. There are several of them, high velocity 76 mm antitank rifles, that the gooks have across the way. They fire intermittently, usually at any movement on the line or other activity that catches their eye. You worry about them because there's no advance warning. They hit before you hear them. *Bang!* Just knowing that the 76s are there cuts down on our unnecessary movement, and when they do open up, everyone dives for cover.

September 18. By now I have concluded that men get along better in rifle platoons than they do anywhere else. A sage Army corporal in the Fifth Cavalry is supposed to have said that this is so because teamwork is essential. Everyone shares the good and the bad. In other words, as the corporal put it, "If a guy did not have the backing of his squad, he was very much up shit creek." That's why I was so surprised today when three Marines came to me to complain about another Marine in their squad.

"Lieutenant, we'd like to talk to you."

"Sure," as we stepped over on to the reverse slope, just off the trail. "What's up?"

"Sir, we're having a problem with Tilt. He's dogging it. Whenever we have work details—laying barbed wire or cutting fields of fire—he claims he's sick or doesn't feel good. He goes back to his hole whenever the squad has to turn to. The squad leader has talked to him, but that hasn't done any good."

Not only had I never heard of anything like this, but it didn't sound like something I'd want to get into. That's what we have squad leaders for. But I told them that I'd keep an eye out for it. That ended our talk.

I scarcely knew who Tilt was. I knew he was a pfc. replacement who'd joined the platoon recently, shortly before we came out of reserve, but I'd seen very little of him. He was slender, of medium height, and he'd apparently had acne when he was younger. He had the look of someone who'd spent more time under fluorescent lights than outdoors.

I had talked with him briefly when he first joined the platoon. He told me that he had grown up around racetracks in Northern New Jersey, and I gathered that he'd lived with his father and that his father worked at something around the tracks. When I asked him where he'd gotten the name Tilt, he said that it had come from playing pinball machines, apparently a sport that he'd excelled at before coming into the Marine Corps.

I had plenty of other things to do, and I was inclined to let this slide, but later today, Tilt himself came to see me.

"Lieutenant, I need to talk with you."

"Sure, Tilt. What's up?"

"You know, you said if anyone in the platoon wanted to transfer out—wanted to get to the rear—all they had to do was ask, and you'd do what you could to help them?"

"Ugh . . . yeah."

"Well, I want to get out. I want to get to the rear. My nerves are killing me, especially at night. I can't get to sleep. I haven't been able to sleep since I got here. So I can't keep up during the day, and I'm gradually wearing down."

"How long have you been here, Tilt?"

"This is my third week. In another few days, it'll be three weeks."

I nearly gagged at that. We still had Marines in the platoon who had been in Baker Company through the toughest fighting of the war, for nine, ten, and eleven *months*. What I'd intended was only to make it easier for those who'd been there a long time to move a little out of harm's way near the end of their tour. And so far, *no one* had asked to get out. None of the Marines that I would consider eligible had even asked for what Tilt was now asking for!

If the policy was going to make any sense, it had to be fair. And two and a half weeks in a rifle company wasn't going to cut it.

Of course, that was not what Tilt wanted to hear. But as we talked, he seemed to calm down, maybe even to understand. I told him he was just going to have to hang in there. He was a Marine. There was a lot of work to be done. As long as we were in a defensive position, we'd have to build bunkers and strengthen them. We'd have to put out barbed wire, cut fields of fire, and lay out trip flares. And if he wasn't wounded or on patrol, he was going to have to take on his share of that work.

I may even have said that if he got tired enough, he *would* sleep at night. In wrapping it up, I said that he could always talk to me, about this problem, or anything else. I'd always be there. I'd always be willing to talk with him, and we left it at that. We'll see.

September 19. Today my classmate and friend, Bill Rockey, came through leading *his* company, Easy Company, First Marines. He's the only second lieutenant I know of who has command of a rifle company. Bill, of course, takes it in stride. No big deal. But it is a big deal. I think it's sensational! And I'd guess that the Marines of Easy Company probably think it's okay too.

This is our last day up here in the hills, on the highest ground for miles around. We are being relieved by the First Battalion, Fifth Marines, a unit that includes Jim Breckinridge, Breck's brother. They are almost the same age, and both first lieutenants only a few numbers apart. They are close friends, but competitive, each striving to outdo the other. This was their first meeting here in Korea, an important family event even if they didn't have much time to talk. The relief was completed, and we moved off the hill in the early afternoon.

When Tex talked to me earlier about my taking J. J. Morrow as our platoon sergeant, I recognized it as a good thing. But at that time, I just didn't know how good it would be.

J. J. is clearly the best thing that's happened to the first platoon since I've been here. It isn't just that he gets along well with the platoon and with me. It's mainly that he enjoys their total respect. The Marines in the platoon jump to do what he says, even what he might suggest, sometimes even what they might *think* he wants them to do.

J. J. smokes Tampa Nugget cigars. He has an easy manner, but he doesn't talk much, and he laughs even less. He doesn't fool around; he's all business all the time. For a while after he came over here, I wondered if he had a sense of humor. But I don't wonder about that anymore, after hearing a few of his stories.

In real life, as he puts it, J. J. drove a Trailways bus. He tells stories well, and many of his stories start right there in the driver's seat of the bus. One day, he said, he was waiting to start a scheduled run when two rather officious looking older ladies got on and sat down in the seat directly behind him. They were talking almost at his ear, and he couldn't help overhearing their comments as they looked around the bus, minutely scrutinizing the interior and commenting on its condition. One noted some dust on the floor; the other mentioned that running her finger over the window left a streak, etc. J.J., of course, listened without comment. Finally, one of the ladies leaned forward and tapped him on the shoulder to ask a more important question:

"Driver, are you sure you can drive this bus safely over the twisting mountain road between here and our destination at Black Rock?"

In situations like this, J. J. is always gravely courteous, and I'm sure he was then as he turned around to reply, "Yes, ma'am. You see this is my second try at it. And they told me that if I didn't make it this time, I was going to lose my job."

Whatever that might have done for the confidence of those passengers, J. J. is superb at maintaining the confidence of younger Marines in the platoon. This is a business where whatever the leader feels those around him will sense, right off; whether it's confidence or fear, the troops will get it at a glance, and that's where J. J.'s manner is so helpful. To any suggestion of worry or even uncertainty, he is likely to come back with his stock response, "Now don't you worry 'bout the mule being po'. You just hitch up the wagon. When you ready to go, he'll move." It may not sound like much, but it works for J. J. And now it's working for the platoon as well.

September 20. After coming off line yesterday, we settled into a reserve assembly area close to the front. We had quick showers and a hot meal there with How Company, Third Battalion, and I had a chance to talk briefly with Joe Reed.

This morning at 0600, we are off again, headed back to the line. We are all day on the road and on the long climb up to relieve a unit of the Eighth ROK Division, a truly surreal relief of lines.

Given that the road was approximately at sea level, and we were to relieve the ROK unit on Hill 854 (854 meters), that meant a climb of some 2,800 feet. But that was only part of our difficulties. Another part was continuing uncertainty about where the various ROK units actually were. We can't take anything for granted.

Of more serious concern were the mines, both friendly and enemy, planted all over the area we were moving through. Where mines had been laid by the ROKs, they were supposed to know where they were. But in many instances, they had no map or overlay that could be relied on. In other cases, they just didn't know. Then they'd simply shrug their shoulders.

Our move into their positions was held up frequently by long delays when we had no idea why we were stopped. And seeing the ROKs up close in their own military environment was not reassuring.

There was a randomness to what they did—firing rifles or throwing grenades—that defied any rational explanation. They like to shoot, and in the morning, many of their positions are surrounded by shell casings with no enemy bodies or evidence of any enemy having been there. And they love grenades. One Marine told me that he had seen a ROK soldier rise in the morning, stand up, stretch, yawn, pull the pin on a grenade, and lob the grenade straight out from his position without looking, before or after.

With all our delays en route, the relief that we had started at 0600 in the morning stretched through the entire day and well into the night. It was finally carried out in total darkness when we settled in here around 0200. By that time, all we could do was find a hole to rest in and wait for daylight. When J. J. and I awoke with the first streaks of light, we saw that we were only a couple feet away from another hole occupied by two ROK soldiers. At least, we thought there were two.

Actually, there were. But, as it turned out, only one was alive. Shortly after daybreak, the live one arose, stretched, yawned, nodded to us, and proceeded to pull his gear together, preparing to leave. We thought it better not to interfere with his preparations, but we watched, mildly interested. When he had his gear in order, he placed it on the ground just outside their hole, and he turned to his comrade who, by this time, we realized, was *not* alive. The live ROK solider took out his entrenching tool, and with several hard, clean strokes, whacked off his comrade's head. Then, after strapping on his pack, he reached down and picked up the head by its long black hair and, swinging it up over his shoulder, marched off.

Later, when I asked someone about this, the answer was that the dead comrade was probably a relative or a friend from the same village, and the carrier was probably bringing the head back to the family. What remained of the body was buried later in our general cleanup of the area. Throughout the day, the rest of the ROK soldiers drifted off, and by the time they were gone, we very much appreciated having the area to ourselves.

September 22. Here I am, grimy and unshaven, sitting near the peak of a tremendous, war-scarred mountain looking out on the Sea of Japan. Because the first platoon has the high ground again, rockets, machine guns, and all of the forward observers are attached to our platoon, a total of 103 Marines. After last week's push, we were pulled off the line and shifted eastward, toward the coast. Supposedly, this is the Eighth Army's winter defensive line. We are about twenty-five miles above the 38th parallel and ten miles inland from Korea's east coast. The terrain here is rugged and very steep. Hauling up supplies is a backbreaking trek. But we're so high that everything is relatively quiet here. We patrol to the front, and we have some incoming, but casualties have been low for the last week.

September 23. Over the past week or so, I have kept an eye out for Tilt, and from what I've seen of him, he's looked okay. The times that I've noticed him he has been with other Marines in his squad, and it looked like he was working. That is, he seemed to be shaping up.

But late this afternoon, Tilt showed up back at my hole. I was writing a letter, and I put down the tablet and invited him in.

"Hey, Tilt, how's it going?"

"Lieutenant, I've gotta talk to you. It's not goin' very good."

"Well, Tilt, I've seen you a few times out there, and it looked to me like you were really carrying your weight. What's the problem?"

"It's the same thing, Lieutenant. I keep hearing noises all night, and I can't get any sleep. When I can't sleep at night, I can hardly stay awake the next day. And then the guys get down on me. It's not any better. It's getting worse."

We had another session, not that much different from the first. I explained that nobody—or hardly anybody—would ever feel comfortable doing what we're doing. Everybody's scared, but how scared anybody is might vary from one Marine to another and from time to time. We're all scared sometimes, if we have any sense. That's only natural. The trick is to deal with it. And I said that, from what I'd seen, he seemed to be dealing with it very well, much better than before. He just had to keep it up. He was getting there, etc.

Once again, Tilt seemed to settle down in the course of our exchange. At any rate, he went away assuring me that he'd be okay, that he'd get back on track and continue to do his job.

I was left thinking that this is probably what being an AA counselor is like. Maybe I'd missed my calling.

September 25. This has been a day to remember. I first heard about it last night when I came in from inspecting the lines. Frank Wakeland, a company runner, was on phone watch, sitting there in the darkness.

"Lieutenant, we just got a message from battalion. Here it is."

The message, directed to Baker Company, was simple enough. "One reinforced rifle platoon . . . Hill 467 . . . leave at first light . . . kill or capture." That meant a combat patrol—not reconnaissance. We needed intelligence, and getting prisoners was one way to get it.

Today was our turn for the patrol, so I knew the order meant us. Wakeland had an interest in it too; he would be going along as our radioman. First light was less than eight hours away.

Hill 467 was an ugly twisting ridge running directly across our front. It was connected to Hill 802, a massive, natural stronghold, further to the northwest, to our left. At times, we could see the enemy swarming like ants on Hill 802, but we didn't know what was on Hill 467. We had kept it under surveillance with binoculars, but it was mostly covered with trees, and we couldn't see much. Now the patrol would find out.

Kitchen was catching a nap when I first talked with Wakeland. But by the time I got to my bunker, he was on watch in the company CP. He called me on the sound power phone, and we went over the order briefly. I talked with J. J. and called the squad leaders, asking them to have everything ready to go and to be at my bunker fifteen minutes early. With that, I crawled into my sleeping bag and started to try to think it through. First light would come soon enough.

Patrols like this are what platoon leaders do. But still, I was always anxious at the first word. With every new patrol order, I'd try to think of all the contingencies. What could go wrong? How could we get the advantage? How could we break through? Once you're in it, there's no time, so you better have thought about it before. Sometimes I was able to think of things that did happen, but usually not.

So last night, I started thinking about Hill 467. On the map, it was about 1,300 yards away. More important was the topography. Between us and 467, the mountain plunged into a deep ravine, more than a thousand feet below us, with a stream coursing through it. The route down was steep and rocky, and when we'd got across the stream we'd be right on the approaches to 467. Just going down there and then climbing back up to 467 would be enough of a problem. But I wanted to see if we could do it with some kind of cover, out of sight of the gooks on top who might just be waiting for a visit from us.

I didn't think this would be easy, and I knew it would take longer to get there without being spotted. But I thought we should be able to do it—out and back—in about six hours. So we ought to be able to get back around noon, and we wouldn't have to carry rations. That, as it turned out, was wrong.

I figured we would be most vulnerable on the approach. If Hill 467 was fortified and the gooks were able to watch us climbing down and then coming up toward them, they could simply wait until we got close and blow us away. Maintaining our cover on the approach phase would be critical, if we wanted to stay alive.

But if we could get up on 467 without having been spotted, we could probably do all right. With the advantage of surprise, we should be in control, at least for a while. And then, after that, it would take the main NK force on Hill 802 still more time to react. That was about as much as I could think of before we got out there.

I was up a few hours later, and when dawn broke, the platoon was strung out in a column along the trail on the reverse slope of our position. We were at full strength with a light machine gun section and a forward observer from the battalion's 81 mm mortar platoon. Wakeland was there with his SCR 300 radio. We checked weapons and equipment. Each Marine, in addition to his weapon and ammo, carried three grenades and two canteens of water. I felt okay, but I thought the men looked a little tense. Maybe it was just too early in the morning. I headed over for a last word from the skipper.

Kitchen, as always, was calm, organized, and thoughtful. "We'll be able to see all of the objective from here," he said, "and we can cover you all the way out and back. We can give you artillery or whatever kind of support you need.

"You may step in it on this patrol. Remember that your radio is your link with us and with everything we might be able to do for you. If you lose radio contact, you lose all of that. Then you're on your own. It's going to be up to you. You know when to come back, and we'll always be glad to see you. Good luck."

I led out through the trip flares and barbed wire rigged in front of our position. Starting down was easy, and as we moved, we loosened up, and we all felt better. After we were underway, I dropped back behind the lead fire team in the column. I could still direct our route from there, and the fire team leader became the leadman. He was Pfc. Donald Miles, a slender quiet veteran of eight months in the company. He picked his way down the steep slope like a mountain goat.

Going down was slower than I'd thought, and it was taking a long time. It wasn't a trail, or even a path. No one, surely, had gone that way before, and we were only doing it because we had to. We took a lot of detours, sometimes dropping to all fours to work our way around jagged rocks or to skirt points where the hill dropped off in a cliff face. At one point, we stopped to hang for the moment from the overhead branches of a tree and drop to a narrow shelf below. The bottom of the ravine below was shrouded in fog, and from where we were, well above it, the surrounding peaks stood out like islands. By the time the morning sun got high enough to reach in where we were, we were sweating freely. We continued on down through the trees, moving slowly and quietly.

At the end of the first hour, it seemed we had not made much progress. When we came to a short ledge nestled into a corner of the cliff face, I halted the column to look around. The ledge, obscured from view by rock, scrub growth, and entwined branches, was a natural crow's nest with a clear view of the objective. I called up one of our two machine gun squads and set them up there on the ledge. From that position, they could cover us on Hill 467, lower and about eight hundred yards away.

Over the past months, we had learned to use supporting machine gun fire much closer than the prescribed safety limits. From doing this, we had gained confidence in the gunners attached to our platoon, and the gunners had gotten sure of themselves. Our point men wore bright yellow air panels. In sunlight, their brilliant reflection could be seen for miles. We relied on the machine gunners not to shoot into those panels, and they never had.

Before leaving the ledge, I thought to tell the gunners, "If you see us flash a red air panel, it'll mean we're going back another way. Cover us until we get off the ridge. Then get back on your own." That, as it turned out, was a useful instruction.

I was ready to rotate the lead, but Miles insisted on staying on the point. We moved out again. When I looked at my watch, it was 0900. Half the morning shot and we were still not even close to the streambed. Then I knew we'd never be back at noon. We could be out there all day, maybe into the darkness.

At that moment, I didn't think our chances looked so great. The sun was bearing down, and sweat was draining out of all of us. I figured we could reach the stream by noon. But that was only the beginning. We'd still have a hard climb to the opposite ridge, and that's where our real problems could start.

If there were no gooks there, the patrol would have been a tough hike for nothing, basically a big yawn. But if they were there, everything was up for grabs. We could have a real firefight on our hands, and with any dead or wounded Marines, we'd be right under the gooks' strength on Hill 802 and a long way from home. It could be hard to get back.

Then . . . this reverie was broken by a volley of explosions crashing into the gorge below. It sounded like artillery, and it sounded big. But because of our position, we'd heard nothing coming in. Worse, we couldn't tell whether it was ours or theirs, and we still had no clue whether we had been seen. I held up the column in place.

"Wakeland, crank it up and find out what the hell that was."

Whatever it was, it wasn't good. If enemy fire, it meant we'd been spotted. If ours, that was different. But we'd be down there shortly, and we sure didn't want anything like that coming in then.

Wakeland was a good operator. He got everything right. And I liked hearing him on the radio.

"Windstorm Baker. Windstorm Baker, this is Windstorm Baker X-ray. Over."

We waited while he repeated the call sign several times. There was a long pause, and finally, they acknowledged. Then Wakeland again.

"Windstorm Baker, this is Windstorm Baker X-ray. Has Fox 2 been firing? Over."

The company had to relay his question back to the artillery battery, so it took a little time. It seemed long, but finally, the response was coming back. I watched Wakeland's face. His expression never changed, but somehow, I knew it when he did. It had been ours.

I asked for a complete cease-fire of all friendly, supporting arms until further notice from us. *Only* from us! We held up until we'd gotten their affirmative reply. Then we started to move on down again.

When we arrived at the stream, we were able to look up at Hill 467 from directly below. It looked different, higher and more imposing. Still straining to see through the trees, I had a much better view of the route I'd earlier thought about taking up. It was a humped spur covered with trees and bordered on both sides by shale slides. We couldn't climb through the shale, but the enemy couldn't stay in position on it either. We could climb through the trees on the hump. That route offered some cover, and it looked even better up close than it had from our lines.

By then it was noon. Still thinking about the time, I realized we couldn't go back the way we'd come. It had taken us all morning just to climb down, and it would take us much longer going back. Because we'd taken no rations, we should try to get back by nightfall. There was a draw running alongside of the company position, and we'd have to duck into that draw and climb back to the company from there. I was glad our machine gunners could get back on their own.

Meanwhile, we had to deal with the stream. We worked our way along it for some distance, looking for a covered place to ford. There was none. And the farther along we went, the closer we came to the enemy stronghold at Hill 802. It was well ahead of us, but looming above. And Hill 802 had a clear view of the entire gorge, like looking down the lane of a bowling alley. It couldn't have been more open, and we felt naked just looking up at it.

It was about that time that Wakeland told me that we'd lost all radio contact with the company. Our radio was being filled with a babble of Korean voices. And we had no idea whether that was jamming or whether it was even related to us.

Here, we were most vulnerable. If the gooks discovered us in this position, we'd have little chance of ever getting on top of Hill

467. We couldn't safely get any closer to Hill 802, and we sure couldn't stay where we were. We had to cross the stream. So we moved into the water, starting to cross as fast and as carefully as possible.

We had crossed streams like this a lot. Staying low, leaning into the current, moving singly and in pairs, always moving, now up to our waists, then chests; no talk, no more noise than the fish, we'd like to think. It's not so hard to do. But all I could think of was, "Have we been seen? Are we being watched?"

Finally, we're all across and spread out on the Hill 467 side of the stream. We start to move slowly up through the trees. Three rifle squads in wedge formation, one behind the other. We're spread out to the limit of covering trees on the humped back of the spur. We feel like the hunter stalking game, or maybe the stalking hunter who is being stalked at the same time. There is tension now, and the fatigue slips away. We're no longer tired. We're moving slowly, peering intently to the front. Trying to see through the foliage. As we move up, the tension builds. We're getting close.

Finally, we come through the trees into daylight on the narrow crest of the ridgeline, near the top of Hill 467. This was it. And there's no trace of the enemy. Maybe they weren't even there.

I felt something like relief, and I could see it in the others. But this is no time to feel like that. It's always dangerous to feel relieved, maybe *most* dangerous at a time like that.

We were then near the middle of the ridge. To our right, it extended several hundred yards before dropping off sharply into the valley below. To our left, it ran on into the approaches to Hill 802. Also to our left, and closer to us, was a large knob, the highest point on the ridge, the point designated on maps as Hill 467.

By this time, I'd decided that one squad should go to the right to clear out whatever might be out there. After they'd started, I'd go with a second squad to the high knob to our left. We'd take care of that and set up a covering force with our remaining machine-gun squad there. Then I'd move in with the rest of the platoon toward Hill 802. When we'd finished that sweep, we'd regroup by the knob and head back together. That plan was all right. The question was how it would work.

Our deliberate, stealthy approach carried through in the minutes that followed. The first squad moved off to the right, and I swung around with the rest of the platoon and headed for the knob. Just short of the knob, we ran across our first clue.

We were not alone out there on the hill!

At our feet, running along the ground in a slight depression, was a telltale sign—communication wires. They weren't ours. They had to be gook. But they looked weathered, might have been used earlier, and abandoned. We couldn't tell. We cut them and moved on. Our point fire team, led by Cpl. Bill Fralic, was just coming up to the top of the knob when we heard the first sound. Thinking of it later, it sounded like a death rattle. But there on the knob, it was familiar, the first burst of a North Korean burp gun. It broke through the quiet around us as a string of bullets snapped into the branches over our heads. Okay. This was it!

Maybe we were just lucky. The NK sentry we had surprised had fired in haste, and wildly. He missed. And he could not have lived long enough to release the trigger, as Fralic's BAR man, George Grubisha, gunned most of a full magazine into him. Grubisha, a pfc., husky enough to handle the BAR but still looking too young to shave, swung his BAR to the right and pumped the last burst into another NK a few yards away. By this time, we were so close that a third enemy just had time to throw up his hands and be grabbed as a prisoner as we swept over him.

All of this happened in the seconds it took for me to get to the head of the column. So far, so good. It had started off well. We were moving ahead—fast.

Just beyond the knob, a low saddle extended for some fifty yards. We couldn't have seen it from our lines or from our climb to the top, but we could see it here. Both sides of the saddle were studded with enemy bunkers. And racing out of them and, in some cases, diving back into them, were more gooks than I had ever seen this close before—more than I'd ever want to see running loose again.

Miles's fire team and the fire team led by Cpl. Gary Boutwell of Bellingham, Washington, swung up alongside us as we started receiving fire. With the first enemy rounds zinging past us, two NKs just to our front swung their heavy Russian Maxim machine gun around to face us. But they never got off the first round. One had the top of his head blown away, and the second was slammed backward into a tree as a fusillade of BAR rounds converged on them.

Another NK was cut down as he ran from his noon rice bowl to a second machine gun. So far, we still had the jump on them. I called over my shoulder for the squad behind to cover us, and we moved down into the nest of bunkers.

This was really what the first platoon did well, maybe as well as it could be done. They'd had all the practice they needed and a lot of experience. By staying low and working fast, we could concentrate on the bunkers. We were getting some fire from the far end of the saddle, toward Hill 802. But that was returned by our covering force and the machine gun back on the knob.

As we approached the first bunker, one of the NKs inside jumped up and out through the entrance. It looked like a jump shot as he released two potato masher grenades that he must have held to the last second. They exploded instantly.

As I dived to the ground, something—I suppose a chunk of metal—whanged past my head into the tree next to me, and I saw Grubisha crumple in a cloud of black smoke.

After his spectacular leap, the NK spun, twisted, and tried to roll over the side of the ridge. He got over all right, but he caught on a tree on the way down, and by this time, everyone was up and firing again. His body was riddled, still hanging on a branch, until it finally dropped over.

Strangely enough, through all the fire, smoke, and exploding grenades, two other NKs managed to come out of the same bunker with their hands up. We grabbed them and hustled them back to where our first prisoner was being held.

While this was going on, the fire team to my left had blown up two bunkers and captured a fourth prisoner. We found that Boutwell had been hit with Grubisha, neither seriously. They stayed on their feet and refused to go back. They kept up with us as we ran forward.

From the apertures of the next bunker, two automatic weapons managed to set up a killing zone that no one could enter. We flanked it rapidly after one Marine was knocked down with several rounds stitched into his left side and shoulder. The first two grenades thrown into the bunker were pitched back out like they'd rebounded. But a third exploded inside with a splintering crash. We waited briefly to see black smoke drift out of the entrance and then shoveled in more grenades to finish off the bunker.

I shifted then to another fire team just as two NKs jumped out several yards ahead of it. When one was cut down in a hail of automatic weapons' fire, the other threw up his hands in surrender. An NK charged out of a bunker to hose down the area with his burp gun, and another Marine was hit before the gook was felled.

So it went. Moving, firing, grenading, moving again until we'd reached the end of their built-up positions. We had taken out the last bunker and just begun a hasty search of the dead NKs when we heard a burst of firing well behind us, from the area the first squad had gone out to, on the far-right end of the ridge.

That startled me, but there was no time to deal with it.

When we reached the end of the ridge, all firing died down as we scooped up enemy papers and insignia from the bodies. We grabbed any enemy weapons we could carry and broke up the rest, including the two Maxim machine guns that we threw with other wreckage into the gorge below.

It was a lucky break that our few wounded could walk. With them and our prisoners in tow, we hustled back to the knob. There Wakeland told me that Captain Kitchen had been trying to get me on the radio.

I took the receiver and heard his voice, "Come on, Nolan. Get your ass back here! We'll cover you as well as we can. But they're going to plaster you now. Get in here on the double!"

Kitchen wasn't telling me anything I didn't know, and I didn't need to be urged to pull down off Hill 467. But we still had to pick up the first squad. I had sent a runner out to get them, and he met them already on their way back. They arrived in the next couple of minutes. From the squad leader, Bobbie Bradford's, grin, I could see they were in good shape. They had no casualties. They'd killed five of the enemy, and they were pushing and dragging three more prisoners along with them.

From that point on, everything broke right. Our wounded could walk. Our prisoners scuttled along, eager to keep up. We flashed the red air panel to send our machine gunners back, and we headed straight down near the same route we had climbed up a few hours before. Moving fast, the platoon stirred up a great cloud of dust.

About half way down, the NK mortars started. Whoomph! . . . whoomph! . . . whoomph! Not unexpected, really, but not something we wanted to hear. Ever. Luckily, the first rounds were wide of their mark, and by the time the gooks adjusted, we were nearly down and back to the stream.

Then we were far enough away for the heavy fire support Kitchen had standing by to open up. They rapidly covered us with an umbrella of overhead fire, WP (white phosphorous) and HE (high explosive) slamming into Hill 802 and the 467 ridgeline. By the time we ducked into the draw running back toward our lines, the enemy mortars were trailing off. We knew we were safe.

Our arrival back on the line was a ball. Because the rest of the front was quiet that day, and because our patrol had attracted attention, there was a crowd there to receive us. The intelligence people from regiment and division were there for our prisoners. Correspondents from *Stars and Stripes* and the news services were there for the story. Various observers from division and X Corps were there, I guess to observe.

For the first platoon, it was a real kick. We'd gone out to get prisoners, and we'd hauled back eight, more than we had seen in a long time. We'd pulled additional papers and maps from the twenty or so enemy dead we'd searched, and we knew we'd left more dead NKs back there in the bunkers. Just that seemed like a pretty good score, but the totals ballooned overnight when enemy casualties from artillery estimates were added. The *Stars and Stripes* story a couple days later had 160 enemy dead from our artillery alone!

We really liked the idea that our platoon had pulled this off with only scratch casualties. And everyone was back now, within our lines and in good shape.

After watching the prisoner interrogations for a few minutes, I headed away toward my bunker. Despite the excitement still in the air, I felt drained, deflated, and very tired. And (maybe this is an excuse) I must have had a momentary lapse of attention as well.

As I was striding along through the company area, picking my way around bunkers and gun emplacements, I absentmindedly started to clear the chamber of my carbine, something I'd done again and again, dozens of times. For me, it was reflex action, automatic without thinking.

This time was no different. After a lot of firing, a single round remained in the chamber of my M-2 carbine. As I walked, still holding the weapon in my right hand, pointed down, I reached across with my left hand to push back the slide and eject the round. My left hand was cupped, and I caught the round as it came out of the chamber. Then, lowering the muzzle as I walked, I pulled the trigger, expecting to hear a click—the bolt going forward on the empty chamber.

Instead, this time, to my total shock, I heard the sharp report of the weapon discharging and a *wham* as the bullet fired into the ground. The impact could not have been more than an inch from my right foot, swinging along in full stride. It may have been closer than any of the gook bullets earlier on Hill 467.

Of course, I knew immediately what had happened. Unconsciously, I had pushed the slide back farther than necessary to eject the chambered round. And, on its return, the slide had picked up and chambered the next round. That had never happened to me before, but it was a simple enough mistake. It was also dumb, inexcusable, and it would have been impossible to explain. But—because it didn't hit my foot—I've never had to explain it.

I also realized immediately how close I'd come to total embarrassment. Shooting yourself in the foot is a figure of speech for any self-inflicted gaffe. But actually doing it in a Marine rifle company, on the line, facing the enemy, has a significance immediately apparent to anyone who hears of it. It ain't good. And it would be almost impossible to explain, even to yourself.

After the discharge, I simply continued walking, without breaking stride, without even looking around. To this day, I have no idea whether anyone saw it happen or even heard it. Because of the general commotion and high noise level there, with mortars and artillery going by overhead, no one may have noticed. No one has ever mentioned it to me, and I have never brought it up. I used to have disturbing dreams about it, and sometimes it still bothers me. I know I'll never forget it.

September 26. I would have to say that if there are any perfect days on the line in a rifle company, we are probably enjoying them now. There's still a glow—a feeling of satisfaction—from yesterday's patrol action, now called a raid. There is much talk about it among ourselves, of course. We like to go over something like that while it's still fresh in our minds. That's how you find out what happened, maybe right under your nose, when you are totally concentrated on dealing with something right in front of your rifle.

But today there is a follow-up from outside the platoon. There are staff officers and intelligence personnel here trying to put together the total picture from our reports and from the prisoners we took yesterday.

Also on this position, we are again very far to the north and about as high as it's possible to get in this area. We have an excellent view of the surrounding peaks to the north and west and to the Sea of Japan to the east. The weather every day is perfect, clear, and sunny during the day and cool at night.

When it's quiet like this, regular everyday things get noticed more, our C-ration dump, for example. Maybe every platoon has a C-ration dump, but I'm only familiar with ours. It is simply a cardboard box conveniently located in the platoon area, where anyone can throw in anything from his C-ration carton that he doesn't want for that day. Into the box go all brands of cigarettes, cans of main meals that any Marine might not feel like eating that day, and anything else from the carton. Then anyone can go to the box and take whatever he likes.

For example, I smoke Philip Morris cigarettes, far and away the least popular brand in the platoon generally. On any given day, there are always extra packs of Philip Morris there. So I could smoke six packs a day and never have to worry about supply.

Another aspect of the C-ration dump is that it may encourage fad eating. And I may have become a fad eater, i.e., one who stays with a particular C-ration delicacy for several days or as much as a week at a time. The C-ration entrees are packed in clearly labeled cans: ground meat and spaghetti, ham and lima beans, hamburger patties, etc. I simply take whatever I might have gotten in my C-ration package and toss it into the cardboard box. Then I select from the box whatever my current fad preference might be. There is always a surfeit of supply, more than enough of everything to go around. It would be unheard of to have a dispute over something in (or not in) the C-ration dump.

Interestingly enough, similar tastes even affect who your companions are and how you make friends. Take cocoa, for example. John Breckinridge and I both like cocoa. For us, this taste or craving is certainly stronger than it is for others here. Maybe it's excessive. Because of this, we've started getting together for cocoa in the late afternoon, much as others might for tea. At first, we each made our own cocoa and heated it in canteen cups over a Coleman stove while discussing events of the day. Then, with my father's idea that "anything worth doing, is worth doing to excess," we started using more cocoa. We could pig out on cocoa because there is always an available supply at the C-ration dump.

As we used more and more pads, the cocoa was more concentrated, and we found that we liked it better. At some point, we switched from using two canteen cups to a single one—loaded. By then, we may have been using six to eight pads to the cup, so there was not much room left for water. The "drink" was a semisolid. It may sound goofy, but that's what we did.

We would usually sit facing each other over the Coleman stove, drinking from opposite ends of the canteen cup, warming the cocoa as we talked. I suppose this was something like a poor man's hunt cup. I looked forward to these sessions, and as September slid into October, we were meeting for cocoa every day. Anything we were interested in got threshed out at the cocoa hour.

At one of these sessions, Breck raised the subject of what he'd do next. He'd been the exec. officer of Baker Company since he arrived. That might have seemed a good experience, but he was tired of it. In truth, it wasn't his kind of job. He wanted something more active, something that involved direct command of troops. Because I would be leaving the first platoon soon, there would be an opening there for someone to take over an outstanding platoon and still stay in Baker Company. And having J. J. as the platoon sergeant would be a big plus.

When Breck asked what I thought, I told him I thought it was great. I was enthusiastic. I couldn't have thought of anything better for the platoon. Further, I thought it would be good for J. J., and it would be an ideal, if slightly irregular, career move for Breck himself.

We were sure that Kitchen, the company commander would agree, as he did. So from that point on, the switch was a done deal.

September 27. The First Marine Division is now stretched out over an enormous line, some 23,000 yards from one end to the other. We, First Marines, are on the extreme right, the eastern end of that line. And, with control of the highest and most difficult terrain, we're in good shape. The same cannot be said for the division's far left flank, where the line is split by extremely rugged terrain, but there are no roads. It was concern about how to meet an emergency on the far left flank that led to the development of Operation Blackbird, so called because it was thought that any emergency was likely to come at night, and the response would have to be carried out in darkness. Thus, Operation Blackbird was a plan to helicopter lift one company from the reserve battalion into position in the Punch Bowl to respond to an attack there on the extreme western end.

The company selected for this pioneering operation was Easy Company, First Marines, commanded by my friend, Bill Rockey. There was a daylight rehearsal and then the operation itself, both completed today. The rehearsal was terminated by the battalion commander after one of the Marines hit a land mine. But the operation in darkness ran off without a hitch. It was the only night helicopter lift of the Korean War, and Rockey and his men completed it in 140 minutes, rather than the nine hours it would have taken on foot. Despite the mines and technical difficulties noted in the operation reports, Operation Blackbird was a singular achievement, "the only night helicopter troop lift during the war in Korea."

September 28. At least conceptually, optimism can be a problem. I recognize that, and I think that usually it's better to worry. Better to assume that if anything can go wrong, it will, and think about how to right it. Nonetheless, optimism sometimes gets the better of me. It did with Tilt.

I had thought that Tilt was generally making it these days. Then, during our firefight on Hill 467, it seemed to me he'd come all the way home. There, he was a hard charger, a combat Marine. In the few glimpses I'd had of him, he looked as aggressive as any rifleman on the hill, firing at anything that moved, throwing grenades into bunkers, and howling like a banshee. I didn't say anything. But I did note it, and I thought his problem with nerves might be over.

So it was a downer today when Tilt showed up at my hole with his characteristic, melancholy expression.

"Hey, Tilt. How's it going?"

"It's not good, Lieutenant. It's the same problem. I can't get to sleep. I hear too many sounds at night."

"But, Tilt. I saw you the other day in that firefight on our patrol. I thought you were great, and I said to myself, 'Tilt really gets it now. He's here with us!' If you can handle that part of it, you shouldn't have a problem getting to sleep and getting your work done."

"I know, Lieutenant. That felt good, and I thought it might be over too. But it's not. It's just the same."

Without saying anything new—either of us—the conversation was simply a rerun of what we'd said before. It may have lasted ten minutes. I was beginning to get a little tired of these exchanges, although this talk seemed to have the same effect on Tilt that the earlier sessions had. He looked relieved.

When he left, I thought to myself, "He's still getting by. Maybe he just has to keep working at it."

September 30. The view from our position here on the top of this mountain is extraordinary, maybe the best of any place I've been. During the day, we work at improving our defenses. Baker Company sends patrols out to the front every day, but contacts are light. We are still in the war, and we have scattered incoming from time to time. There are still a few casualties. But generally, this is about as quiet as it can ever get on the line.

The naval gunfire control party is here with us. And the USS *New Jersey* is just offshore in the Sea of Japan. We can see her sail by from time to time, a standout against the deep blue water. It's also comforting to think that the *New Jersey* is on call for us and can fire gigantic 16-inch shells into any target the control party designates. But we don't need it now.

Those 16-inch guns are unquestionably great assets. The projectiles weigh two thousand pounds and are big enough to be seen with the naked eye. They look like boxcars going by overhead. Last week, with the aid of Marine forward observers in advanced positions, *New Jersey* fired one hundred rounds of these gigantic warheads into North Korean ammunition dumps and artillery positions near Hill 951, due west of here, with devastating impact. The Fourth of July in late September.

The war has been easy for Baker Company this month, especially at the end. But it hasn't been easy for the First Marine Division. The division has had nearly 2,500 casualties this month. September has registered more casualties than any month except December at the Chosin Reservoir and this past June during the counterattack after the Chinese offensive. How tough it is, though, depends on where you happen to be.

Chapter 20

OCTOBER IS AN ACTIVE MONTH, AND SAD

*O*ctober 1. Our combat patrol to Hill 467 last week was so satisfying (at least to the members of first platoon) that we've tended to forget all those truisms from sports: "It ain't over 'til it's over, 'til the fat lady sings," etc. The thing is, they also apply in war. We went out to 467. There was a firefight where we had the advantage of surprise, and we handled all the gooks that were there. The hill was ours, and we occupied it—albeit briefly—but we had taken it fair and square. It was ours, right?

No. Not so. If you want to hold something, it's not enough just to capture it. You have to occupy it, stay there, and defend it. Otherwise, if the other side wants to take it back, they take it.

Now there is unmistakable evidence that the gooks are back on Hill 467, in force. It is directly to the front of our positions, and all we have to do is to look down and see them there.

Knowing that they are there doesn't necessarily mean that we'll go out there to take it back from them again. Hill 467 is directly attached to Hill 802, which the gooks also have. And it probably would not be possible to maintain a force on 467 without also taking 802. Besides, Hill 467 is not much of a threat to us, or even an annoyance. We look right down on it and can control it by fire without going out there. So we'll see how the rest of this plays out. It will be interesting.

October 5. For the past few days, we've watched the gooks moving around on Hill 467. It looks like they're restoring the bunkers they had there before our raid and digging in further. Intelligence estimates that there are forty gooks on the hill now. Today for the first time, we received small arms fire from Hill 467 which we returned from our positions. We called in artillery fire as well, and the artillery is now registered directly on the crest of 467. We also received several barrages of 82 mm mortars incoming that landed in back of our position. It is thought to have come from the vicinity of Hill 802. These rounds are all wide of the mark. We have no casualties for the day.

October 6. This morning again, we received small arms fire from the vicinity of Hill 467. No one here is hurt, but this is annoying. We fire back, a concerted effort, and artillery plasters the hill again. But the real response comes in the middle of the afternoon when Kitchen's request for an air strike is finally granted. Four Corsairs come over for about a half hour of serious work. It's all there. Bombs, napalm, and .50 caliber machine guns firing into the ridge from one end to the other. When that's over, they claim 100 percent coverage on the target and many gook casualties.

Maybe that will cool the gooks' interest in that particular hill. It's dumb really. Anything on Hill 467 is easy, a sitting duck for either side, whichever side is shooting at it. They could make it pretty hot for us if we were out there too.

October 7. Today was relatively quiet through the daylight hours. The air strike has given us a respite. Understandably, there was not much action on Hill 467 today. But, in contrast, the night was fairly active.

I was on the sound power telephones in the company CP all night talking with Marines in the three platoons on the line. We've been accumulating sound power phones forever, and we now have a lot of them, maybe one for every fire team. So what I was doing was like running a switchboard in a small town in the country where everyone has a party line. Last night, there was a little action and much anxiety, enough to keep everybody up.

It started shortly after midnight. Out in the darkness, in fighting holes along the ridgeline, Marines were peering into the night so intently that they were seeing all kinds of things, some real, some imaginary. After a while, it gets hard to tell which is which. Everything blended together, sights and sounds. It's all in the dark; it's all scary, and it's very hard to stay inactive. The urge, sometimes overwhelming, is to fire a weapon or at least throw a grenade. Neither action is likely to do much good in the darkness, and either can be harmful if nothing is there, maybe more harmful if something is.

There was *something* there last night, at different times and different points along the line. But I was never able to tell how serious it was. It was plainly not as serious as some of those closest to it thought that it was at the time. Their comments came through to me in whispers or strained, hushed voices behind hands cupped over the mouthpieces of their phones as they tried to describe what they were seeing, or thought they were seeing.

My role in this was to try to provide some balance or restraint for them as they worked through what was obviously a difficult experience. It wasn't perfect. There were some grenades thrown out into the barbed wire we'd laid in, and there were a couple instances of firing. But, essentially, we got through the night with no casualties and nothing more than a bad case of nerves.

Of the dozen or so Marines I was in voice contact with through the night, there was only one exception to the high anxiety level and generally rattled reports I was getting. Of course, that voice stood out like a clarion call. As the night wore on, I became progressively more impressed with the calm, sensible reactions of a squad leader in the third platoon on our right flank, the flash point on the line for most of the night.

When it was over, I learned that the voice I'd come to regard highly belonged to Bart Bartholomew, the same squad leader whose heroics I'd seen back in May in the first firefight I'd watched. Since then, his outstanding performance under fire had continued, and he had just been awarded the Distinguished Service Cross when an Army general visited our regiment. I knew that Bartholomew had been here longer than anyone around, and I marveled that he had never seemed to tire or even slow up. I decided that he must be an iron man, a superior being without nerves. Some people just have it.

October 9. The hole that J. J. and I sleep in is right next to the trail leading out of the platoon area. Early this morning, shortly before sunrise, I was awakened by Breck on the trail outside. He was fully loaded, pack and all, and with two of the company runners, he was headed back to set up the reserve assembly area for our arrival later in the day. We chatted for a few minutes, mostly about what we'd be doing in reserve. For me, it was a pleasant wakeup call. We expected to be meeting again around midday. As I last saw him, he was striding off trailed by the runners, moving forward at a good clip. He seemed to be almost propelling himself forward with the large staff he used as a walking stick. Later this morning, we were relieved on the line by the Second Battalion of our regiment, and Baker Company moved out along the same trail with the first platoon leading. I was at the head of the column. It was a clear day and comfortably cool. We were going back for a rest, swinging along, carefree and easy.

About a half mile back, as we rounded a bend, I saw something on the trail ahead, maybe one hundred yards or so away. I couldn't tell what it was, but we were moving toward it at a steady pace, so I didn't strain to see it. We'd be there soon.

As we drew closer, I could see that there were actually two things, both on the trail, maybe a couple of yards apart. I continued to look as we approached. First, I recognized what looked like field packs, maybe clothes. Then I think, maybe *bodies.* Maybe even Marines!

With this awareness, we break into a trot toward the objects. We see that they are Marines. The first we come upon is Corporal Moore, one of the company runners. He is dead, and the body is cold. A couple of yards ahead is the body of the second Marine, Breck, pitched forward on his side, that formidable staff still clutched in his right hand. Breck had a line of small bullet holes—the marks typically left by a burst of burp-gun rounds—stitched up the left side of his head. Apparently, they had been ambushed there, probably at least two hours before.

That would have been enough time for them to have covered the distance from our platoon area to the site where we found them.

Kitchen arrived within minutes. We looked over everything carefully, and it was easy enough to see what must have happened. Breck and his party must have gotten to this spot still in the half light around dawn. At that time, gooks waiting along the trail must have shot the first and last men in line, Breck and Corporal Moore, and grabbed the man in the middle, Pfc. B. A. Brown. Brown, nowhere to be found, was missing and presumed a prisoner.

The only question was where were Brown and his captors could be by that time. Had they been able to get down into the draw below us and through the gook lines with their prisoner? Or were they still somewhere behind our lines where we could get them? Was there any chance that Brown had not been captured or had managed to escape? Was Brown wounded? And, even if wounded, had he been able to get away? If so, was he still in the area? Or, was he at any place where we might find him?

We radioed back to the Second Battalion on the line. Kitchen explained everything we knew about the ambush to the company commander who'd relieved him. Could they send a patrol down immediately to the mouth of the draw to block escape of anyone still behind our lines? Of course! It was on the way!

Baker Company left one of its platoons there to search the area around the site of the ambush. The rest of us moved ahead with the bodies down to the assembly area, one of the saddest trips I've ever made.

From the assembly area, we returned immediately to the site of the ambush. We fanned out according to the search plan we developed with Captain Kitchen, and for the rest of a very long day, we combed all of the area from the ambush site back to the draw leading out of the UN lines. We were reasonably familiar with this area, especially around the draw. That was where we had come in, returning from the raid on Hill 467 two weeks earlier. But we found nothing. Not a trace, not a clue, nothing.

We continued searching up to darkness, and we hated to stop, even then. But we had scrubbed the entire area, much of it several times. All to no avail. It was a bitterly disappointing effort, with an unsatisfactory end, when we finally dragged our way back to the assembly area. Later that night, we moved out again to march farther south to the reserve area.

October 11. Here we are in reserve again, memories of the last reserve still fresh enough so that even the things that are supposed to be good for us, the things we are supposed to enjoy, seem flat. I get no kick out of hot food, even hot showers. We get a change of dungarees, not new dungarees of course, but ones that some other troops had peeled off earlier and then had passed through the steam laundry. They're okay. I clearly needed the change, and I have no objection to the procedure. But it's a drag.

Last night, I had an extraordinary experience. After the evening meal, I drifted over to the officers' tent for beer drinking and singing. The songs are loud and off key, some bawdy. The fellowship is great, and the beer lasts. Several hours go by, and sometime after midnight with the singing still rolling along, I go outside to relieve myself. It's a cool fall night, pitch black, moonless, but with the stars brilliant against their deep background. For just a moment, I revel in the feeling of being out there under the stars, utterly alone. Or so I thought.

Suddenly, I heard or sensed something. *I was not alone!*

People in our business are probably more sensitive to things like that, and the reaction is totally reflexive. I whirled around to grab a man close behind and stepping toward me. His hands flew up as I lunged toward him, and I heard a hoarse voice, *"Lieutenant, it's me, Bartholomew. Hold up!"*

Especially after our last night on the line, I knew who Bartholomew was, although I don't think I had ever talked with him before. But I could tell this was another Marine, and somehow, I took him at his word.

The voice said, "I've got to talk to you, Lieutenant. I need help."

"Okay, Bartholomew, I'll try to help you. What do you need?"

"I have to get out of here, Lieutenant. I've been in this company for eleven months now, and I've used up all my chances. I can't take any more of it. I've got to get out."

Of course, I thought immediately of the comparison with my friend Tilt. And then I thought how astonishing it was to be standing here under the stars having this conversation with Bartholomew, of all people.

"You came in right after Inchon, Bartholomew?"

"Yes, sir. I joined up at Yongdongpo, and I've been in the company ever since. Every day, and every night."

"Well I know what kind of a job you've been doing. I would think that you're eligible for rotation now, and I'll look into it. I'll see what can be done."

That was the end of our conversation. He thanked me and left, backing away into the night, leaving me to wonder about this strange encounter.

I thought he must have waited to see me because he'd heard that I had offered to help Marines with creditable service rotate out of our platoon. He may not have known that, except for Tilt, no one had asked. I wondered how long he'd waited there in the darkness before I came out. It may have been several hours. Most of all, I wondered how he'd arrived at his decision and when. It seemed to me that the hardest part of it may have been admitting it to himself, and maybe it was easier for him to do that there in the darkness. When he'd reached that point, I was just an available means to the end he'd decided to seek. I wondered how long he would have waited in the shadows if I had not come out when I did. I wondered who else knew. Surely, there were a lot of questions. But that's the way it happened.

As far as qualifying to get off the front line, Bartholomew had it all. He had time in the rifle company, the action, and distinguished combat service, all in spades. He was more than qualified by every standard there was. I talked with Kitchen when the singing broke up, and Bartholomew was on his way out before noon today.

October 12. Several days ago, I wrote a letter to Joan in LaJolla, California. Today the letter came back to me here, in a Marine rifle company, just off the line in Korea. The letter was marked *"Return to sender. 12 cents postage due."* I was impressed. Really. I like to know that not only is the mail being delivered, but the vigilance of our postal service is maintained, that such letters are returned, even to a serviceman with a franking privilege ten thousand miles away in wartime. I'm sure that this illustrates the evenhanded administration of our postal laws. That is good. But I really don't know why.

Tex is gone. He was rotated out of Baker Company to the 81 mm mortars at battalion, which he didn't like. Now, somehow, he has now been transferred to operations as an assistant G-3 on the division staff. That does sound like a much better job, and it should be good experience, a good place to learn what's going on in the war. He may be the lowest-ranking officer on the division staff, but that shouldn't bother him.

Today I heard that I'll be leaving Baker Company next week, on the seventeenth. The battalion S-2 (intelligence officer) is going home, and I've been assigned to be the S-2. I hate to leave the company, but I'm glad to not be going too far away. In addition, I'm told that the S-2 has a tent, a cot, and a jeep. These are not necessities, of course; I've hardly seen any of them since coming to Korea. But I should be able to struggle along with them. This S-2 business may be okay.

October 16. This is a cold, damp fall day. With the present battalion intelligence officer, the fellow I am to relieve, I go up on the line for a reconnaissance of the area where Third Battalion is now. This is where we, First Battalion, will be going when we come out of reserve. Fall is clearly in the air here. I can feel it, and it reminds me of football season. Riding up in the jeep, if I closed my eyes, I could almost imagine I was heading for a Navy game at Babe Ruth Stadium in Baltimore. Almost, but not quite.

These reconnaissances are an important part of the S-2's duties, I'm told, and my reconnaissance of the Third Battalion positions is very thorough. It consists of awakening one Joseph Dues Reed, now the company commander of Third Battalion's H&S Company, who is sleeping soundly in his tent when I arrive. Joe gradually pulls himself together. I sit on the edge of his cot. And we talk the rest of the morning.

In his swan song as a rifle platoon leader, Joe had yet another tough firefight, actually on the hill next to the one we were on. He lost five Marines from his platoon and had an additional twenty wounded, not an easy encounter. As usual, Joe came through without getting hit. Somebody up there must like him, or he must have used up some more of his chances in this one.

Later, I noticed that this platoon action was scarcely mentioned in the division operations report for the day. On the same date, though, the division recon company landed from helicopters *unopposed* on another hill about two thousand yards away. The recon company action was written up everywhere from *Stars & Stripes* to Stateside newspapers. This comparison is mine. Joe didn't mention it, and I suppose it happens all the time. Still, I find it ironic.

By now, I think everyone from our replacement draft is out of rifle companies with the sole exception of Jim Marsh. Always the individual, Jimmy must have found some way to stay with his platoon, now six and a half months after taking it over.

Bob Oliver is in operations at regiment as an assistant S-3. That should be good experience and an excellent job for him. John Olterman and Eddie LeBaron are both back with the Seventh Marines as liaison officers. And tomorrow, I take over as the First Battalion, First Marines, S-2. Time marches on.

October 17. I'm the S-2, here in reserve. Big deal. Or as we say in the Marines, big fucking deal. I haven't really gotten into the job yet. What I've done so far has consisted of filling in on reconnaissance teams that go around to check out various locations that we are going to move into, or that we're thinking about doing something in. When we do this, I mainly visit with my buddies, now roosting around here in other staff jobs in the First Marines. It's not exciting, but it offers a chance to learn more about the war. And I'm learning.

Also, I heard today that I may have worms. Yikes! I'm told that 90 percent of the men returning from Korea do have them. If you do, you have to be "dewormed." That takes about a week, and it can be done either in Japan or back in the States at Camp Pendleton. You take one pill a day and rest. That sounds tough. But I should be able to stand it.

October 18. I heard from Tex today. He's at division, but now he's moaning that he may be stuck there and may not get rotated as fast as the rest of us. Tex is essentially a man of action. He's fine on the football field or in the boxing ring. He's also fine leading a rifle platoon in the attack. But when everything is quiet, he can get lost within himself. He was frustrated for a year at Quantico until he was finally able to get out here. When he did get to Baker Company, he thought the company commander was not sufficiently aggressive (Tex referred to him as "Barbed Wire John"), so he simply stayed with his platoon and stayed away from the company CP.

But he had some difficulties with his platoon as well. When he started off with an exceedingly rigorous, stateside inspection, his seasoned and weathered combat Marines may have gotten the wrong idea. Or, as they would put it, they thought he was "stateside and chicken shit." Later, when they understood how eager he was to close with the enemy and slug it out, they had a different concern, i.e., that his obviously *gung ho* attitude might put them unnecessarily at risk.

There was never any question about his personal courage. Tex just radiates that. The concern was that he had too much, rather than too little. Of course, they admired him for that, but at the same time, they worried.

Tex is also a perfectionist. After a year with schools troops at Quantico, he knows more about small-unit tactics than anyone around here. But when he can't get something done the way he wants it done—which is always exactly the right way—he's inclined to go ahead and do it himself. As a result, whatever it is, gets done right, but Tex may end up pulling the whole load.

He is totally and selflessly devoted to duty. Not a bad characteristic anywhere, but especially valuable out here.

For sometime, Tex was underappreciated in Baker Company. This began to change when Jim Cowan took over the company, and the first time Jim called the company officers together, he started to work on it. Tex came out of his shell, and from June on, when Tex, Ike Cronin, and I had the three platoons, the company worked together as a team. Then Ike lost a leg in the minefield in July, and Tex was approaching the time when he'd leave the platoon on rotation. Tex hated to leave the platoon, actually more than they hated to see him go. I've always thought that was just a matter of time. Given a few more months, the platoon would have known him better and would have appreciated him more, as the company officers did, without exception.

I'll be interested to see how the Marine Corps works out for Tex. If there's fighting and he's involved in it, I think he has a great future. But if he's stuck in staff work and administrative duties, he may find that he's running into a lot of walls. I think that is really too bad. War fighting is the main reason for the Marine Corps's existence. Those who know what war fighting is and are willing to take it on, totally and selflessly with all that entails, are not as common as we'd like to think. Tex will always be in that small group. He is totally dedicated. He'll always be ready; he'll see to that. And that counts for a lot.

October 22. The ambush in which Breck was killed hit the First Marine Division like a bomb. For some time before, the division policy was to rotate officers out of rifle companies after four months. The policy was generally followed, but it was not inflexible, and whenever it made sense to extend, individual officers stayed on. Then, after the ambush, when the division looked at the rifle companies and how long the officers had been there, they were startled. At that time, there were fourteen sons and sons-in-law of Marine Corps general officers in the companies. Not all of them had been there for more than four months, but several had. And, not surprisingly, the division saw merit in enforcing the policy. The immediate impact for Baker Company was to rotate Tex out. And I heard that Breck's brother, Jim Breckinridge, was pulled out of a rifle company in the Fifth Marines as well. In these cases, and others, I know, the changes were made over protest. But now the policy is enforced.

Another reaction to the ambush was an acute concern at the division about who else might be here behind our front lines. Are there other gook guerrillas back here where we're supposed to be secure? So on this date, October 22, two companies of our battalion lifted off in the guerilla sweep, only the third tactical use of helicopters in Korea or any other war.

The operation was carried out at the direction of Lieutenant Colonel Gorman, the battalion commander. It was planned and executed by my new tent mates, Major Ray Luckel, the battalion S-3, and Captain Cal Baker, assistant S-3 and former Able Company commander. I helped with some of the planning.

The operation order for the guerilla sweep noted that although the targeted area "had been reported cleared of enemy," there had recently been "reports of enemy activity behind our lines." Further, the order noted that reconnaissance teams of the "1st Recon Bn, 11 NK Division have succeeded in penetrating our lines and are reported engaging in guerilla and sabotage activity in this vicinity." The order also warned of both friendly and enemy mines and cautioned that "the utmost care must be exercised . . . when searching bunkers, houses, or moving through the area."

In carrying out the order, we had about forty-eight hours from start of the planning to liftoff. That seemed too fast when we started, but it turned out to be enough time. The plan was that two companies, Able and Baker, would be lifted by helicopter from a field in our reserve area and dropped on designated landing sites running along the division's right flank on the east. Then, in a coordinated sweep, they would move directly west to the MSR, the road running through our reserve area. Their mission was to "destroy enemy and enemy materiel and apprehend all unidentified persons in the assigned area." In other words, Able and Baker companies were to flush out and eliminate any NKs or other guerrillas who might have gotten through the line and be lurking under cover in the densely forested area to be covered.

The sweep involved lifting some two hundred Marines, generally six to a helicopter, in thirty-six flights from landing strips on our field. Amazingly, to me, of the ten helicopters from HMR, 161 were able to load and be ready for takeoff in about a half minute each. We had built a control tower from fresh-cut logs, and Ray Luckel directed the operation from that tower.

The loading and liftoffs came off without a hitch. It was only when the helicopters arrived at the line of departure, and Marines started down the ropes that the operation encountered problems.

The drill was that each helicopter would hover some ten to twelve feet over its designated drop site. Then the Marines would go, one after the other, hand over hand, down a rope to the ground. In theory, it's simple. And at sea level, it works. But some of the drop sites were high enough so that thinner air made a difference, and at those sites, the rotor blades could not hold the helicopters steady at that altitude.

When a helicopter could not stay up in the air, it had to bank and swoop down into an adjacent ravine until it reached air dense enough to support it. This happened three times. And, on two of the three swoops, there was a Marine still clinging to the line when the copter had to peel off.

This, of course, is unsettling if you're on the rope. One minute you're rappelling easily down a line to the ground a few feet below. And the next, you may be swinging out on the same rope, several hundred feet over the valley floor, hanging on for your life.

Two helicopters crashed in this way, and a Marine and a corpsman were injured, neither seriously. There were two additional casualties from a booby-trapped fragmentation grenade, also not serious. Crews later came back in to the crash sites to cannibalize the helicopters, taking out radios, instruments, and other sensitive equipment before blowing the copters up.

In evaluating the operation, the patrol report stated simply that "enemy contact . . . for the operation was negative." So no guerillas were sighted. None killed or captured. On the other hand, a large and difficult area to cover—all behind our lines—was searched out, closely and effectively. Now we know, I guess, that there are no guerillas living among us, at least not at this time between the line of departure and the MLR. And we pioneered a new means of moving and landing Marines by helicopter for this type of mission. It can be done, and it can be done at a speed never before approached. In light of this experience, the cost is not unreasonable, and the next operation like this will be better. We learned something.

October 27. Here we are, out of reserve and back on the line. The First Battalion came back up here on the 24th, but for me now, the battalion's being on the line is not the same as it was. Here I'm only working at a desk in the operations tent of the battalion CP. It's a different life. And there's no real punch in it. It's a drag.

General Cates, Commandant of the Marine Corps, is here in Korea. And Bernie Hletko, my top squad leader, was called to a ceremony at the division today where the Commandant is to award him the Silver Star for his heroic actions in our firefight on June 9.

Yesterday, I did actually go up on the line to look around. While I was there, the battalion called to say they were sending up an AP correspondent who wanted to talk with me. When he arrived on the line, Kitchen met him first and pointed out Hill 467 to him but apparently did nothing to relieve the fellow of the exaggerated stories he'd heard. I hope I was able to straighten him out, but I'm not at all sure that I did. He's writing a wire story that may run later in some newspaper in the States.

Interestingly, this fellow also said that our raid last month was a determining factor in the division's holding up on the line we're now on. Some of the information from the raid confirmed that the enemy MLR (main line of resistance) was directly to our front. When this information was conveyed to X Corps by General Thomas, they decided to establish our line here, where we now are. I liked hearing that, but it's impossible to tell how accurate it is.

One feature of this job that I do like is that I have great tent mates. They include Maj. Ray Luckel, S-3 (operations officer), a 47-year-old former master sergeant with 23 years in the Corps. In World War II, he was a company commander in the Second Raider Battalion, Carlson's Raiders, where he received a field promotion to captain on the recommendation of Jimmy Roosevelt, then XO of the battalion. Ray Luckel is the greatest, and living with him here is like living with the Old Corps. He's seen it all. The others are Maj. Don Wykoff, a quiet, gentlemanly fellow who works harder than the rest of us at keeping the tent in shape, and Cal Baker, a captain who had Able Company before coming back here to the battalion staff. Baker, a reserve officer, was a jeweler in Las Vegas, New Mexico, before being called up to come out here. They couldn't be any better to live with.

A minor health note: It's very cold here now, and the other three in the tent all have terrible head colds. I don't. We all wonder why that is. The only difference we know of is that they sleep with their faces sticking out of their sleeping bags, breathing air that is very cold—sometimes below zero—all night. In contrast, I pull my head into the bag like a turtle, and then I reach up and pull the sides of the opening in the bag together, over my face. I only do this to keep out the cold. But it may mean that I'm breathing stale air while they're breathing fresh air. However, I don't have a cold, and we can't figure any other explanation.

The other Marines I work with—work for, really—are Lt. Col. John Gorman, the battalion commander, and Maj. Edgar Carney, the battalion XO.

As the battalion intelligence officer, my job includes keeping Colonel Gorman up to date on everything that can be known about the enemy, where they are and what they are capable of doing. Of course, I view the job as much broader than that. I should keep him informed about everything that could bear on whatever decisions he might have to make, sometimes very fast. So I think I have the right perspective for the job; I know what I should be doing. But that's different from being able to do it well. And as far as performance is concerned, I still have a long way to go.

Gorman is an outstanding battalion commander. He obviously loves doing this, and he is well suited for it by temperament and experience. He's worked a lot with aerial photographs, and he seems to get a lot of information from them. He always wants to see more, and I'm on the phone every day, ordering additional photo runs over an area that he has fresh curiosity about. I get the pictures and go over them first in detail with the stereo vision magnifier. This enlarges the impressions and gives them a 3D effect that makes any installation or new construction stand out. Then I bring them to him, and we go over them together. This is not a confidence-enhancing experience for me.

Gorman, like Ted Williams, has eyes that are set far apart. Ted Williams was supposed to have one pair of eyes in a hundred thousand, and he had extraordinary depth perception. His advantage was that he could see the ball from the moment it left the pitcher's hand and could tell exactly when it would be coming over the plate. Similarly, Colonel Gorman can see 3D without the stereo glasses. He just holds out any two offset aerial photos and moves them back and forth. Details of any buildup emerge for him in 3D. They just pop up. He can see more this way than I can with the magnifier, or he claims that he can at any rate. These sessions always range from outer limits of my perception to sightings that are well beyond it. Our conversations are challenging, indeed. Maybe Gorman couldn't have hit over four hundred, but I don't know how well Ted Williams could have seen stereo without a glass.

Major Carney is a very different cup of tea. He's serious and conscientious to a fault. He works hard and works everyone around him hard and grinds out everything he's responsible for, all the day-to-day operations of the battalion. I don't see him much, but I think he's probably an okay guy. When we do run into each other and he glowers at me, I grin. And he grins back.

All in all, being an S-2 has some advantages, mainly that here I know more about what's going on. Nonetheless, it's less than being a rifle platoon leader, in almost every way.

October 28. This assignment is beginning to look up. Now one of my responsibilities is broadcasting propaganda across lines to the gooks. We work out the text of the message here: "Come on over to surrender, and we'll treat you well, good food, warm clothing, etc." Then the message is broadcast by an interpreter through a PA system that can project his voice over a mile under the right conditions. It actually works. Today we got the first prisoner drawn into our lines by the broadcasts. I'm to interrogate him later this afternoon.

Chapter 21

JIM MARSH OUTLASTS US ALL

If length of service in a line company of the First Marines were a game of *Last Man Standing*, Jim Marsh would have won the game—going away. Last spring, a number of us got to rifle companies at about the same time. There was a lot going on then, a lot of stuff flying around, so some left early, on stretchers. And over time, the rest of us all shifted, by regular reassignment, through the summer and early fall. When I left Baker Company last week, Jimmy was the only member of our class still in a rifle company. He continues as a rifle platoon leader in George Company, First Marines, and now I don't know if he'll ever leave. He's still going strong.

At the Naval Academy, Jim starred in academics and was a crack runner, as he had been earlier at high school in Clovis, New Mexico. He was always totally focused on the Marine Corps, and he barely tolerated everything else, sometimes with a wry, irreverent sense of humor that was his mark.

On arrival in Korea, he went straight to George Company, more than six months ago. And, except for a brief interval after he'd been wounded and evacuated, he's been there ever since. He's had a lot of close calls. In his first days as a platoon leader, a Bouncing

Betty that another Marine kicked off exploded, wounding him seriously on the side of the head. Later, a canteen was shot out of his hand. His wristwatch was shot off. Another time, a round went through his pants' leg just behind the knee.

Nobody thinks this rifle platoon business is a piece of cake, but still there are different ways to look at incidents like this. To some, they might even be cause for concern. Not to Jimmy. To him, they proved irrefutably that he was going to last. As he put it, "Those sons-a-bitches can't kill me." That attitude and enough time to work at it are what legends are built on. And while still in Korea, Jim was well on his way to becoming a legend. I know I've heard more stories about him out here than I've heard about anyone else.

The point is, he's still in action, still at it. In late October, he led his platoon in a patrol forward of the lines in an effort to capture enemy prisoners for information. When they hit a built-up NK outpost, they were catapulted into a firefight that they couldn't withdraw from. They had to slug it out there and then go on to take the enemy position. That took a while, and it resulted in casualties, and of course, Jimmy was right in the thick of it. By instinct, he moved toward wherever shots were being fired. As one of the Marines in his platoon said, "His leadership style was always simply 'get up here with me!'"

When this particular fracas was winding down, George Company still had not got its prisoners. So Jim called out to the NKs still firing and *in Korean* called for them to surrender. Some did. So the patrol did accomplish its mission before running over the last holdouts. The next day, Jim went out with his platoon again to destroy weapons the NKs had left on the site and to blow up remaining bunkers. He just doesn't stop.

Chapter 22

NOVEMBER, DECEMBER, AND THE WINDUP

November 3. Seintan-ni, Korea. I'm beginning to see now; the possibilities of this job are quite broad. We have developed a new technique to mess around with the gooks' heads, popularly referred to here as "rat fucking." We borrowed a bugler named Hays from the division for a couple of days. He has patiently learned to blow the North Korean bugle calls, and we are setting him up with the PA system. The idea is to get them all stirred up and milling around, and when any number of NKs is seen to be gathering in one place, their gathering can be celebrated with artillery fire and rocket barrages. This started out first as a gag but will now be operational, and there's a lively interest in it here.

We are now on the line here, very far to the north. I have just seen a recent issue of *Newsweek* with a map showing the UN line in Korea, supposedly with the frontline units identified. But it's like we're not even here; there's no reference to the First Marine Division. This is hard to explain, unless it's another instance of the Army's tight censorship of all news relating to Marines.

November 12. Well, it's over. What has been recently the longest tenure as a rifle platoon leader in the First Marines is coming to an end. Jim Marsh is leaving George Company to take command of the regimental tank platoon. That's not exactly the rear, of course. It may actually be more active and more dangerous than a rifle platoon, and that's probably how they presented it to Jim to increase his interest in doing it. He was wounded again slightly in that last fracas but has not been evacuated. He had a great run with the rifle platoon, but on balance, I can't help thinking it's a good thing that he's out.

We are now back in division reserve at a place called Injie, twenty miles behind the lines, and we may be here through the end of the month. This is really the rear, actually eight miles south of the division CP where Tex is. This is the farthest out of it I've been since arriving in Korea, and I feel uncomfortable, antsy for some reason. So I went out with Dick Kitchen and Tank Brady and got mildly drunk a couple of nights ago. That really didn't help much, and I had a helluva hangover the next day, enough to give me definite assurance that I'll never become an alcoholic. Now I know why.

In the course of that evening, we started at the division and later stopped at the Third Battalion where I visited with Joe Reed. He asked to talk privately with me and then told me that he is thinking of converting to Catholicism. He seems to have read a lot and done a lot of thinking about it, and he's coming over here to see the Catholic chaplain tomorrow.

November 18. It's cold here, very cold. At night, the sleeping bags are warm, but the only way I can stay warm during the day is by moving right up next to the stove. There is a stove in each tent, and the area for a foot or so around the stove is warm, but the rest of space in the tent is freezing. So like everyone else here, I'm always moving from the stove in one tent to the stove in the next tent. And even at the stoves, there's much huffing and blowing and stomping of feet. It really is cold!

We have a new form of prime time entertainment here. Clem Vaughan, a classmate of Kitchen's from the first special junior school class, Quantico, is from a small town in Virginia that has a weekly newspaper. Vaughan also has a thoughtful, serious manner concealing a sense of humor as wicked as it is keen. Whenever his weekly paper arrives, we gather in someone's tent for a reading that may last anywhere from a half hour to an hour. Selectively and seriously, he reads the items that he knows will crack us up, and his judgment in that regard is flawless. He never misses, despite the fact that every item was written seriously, and he reads them all straight. I've always known there was great humor in country newspapers, but I never imagined they could be this funny.

The First Marine Division is now filled with officers from this special junior school class. They are all reserves, and most of them are now here in Korea. They are commanding 19 of the 27 rifle companies in the division, and there are dozens more in the motor transport and service battalions. They had a wild class reunion party here last night that I went to with Kitchen, Tank Brady, Jim Egan, and Clem Vaughan, at their invitation. There were probably fifty to sixty of their classmates there. They seemed to be mostly former college football players, now ten years or so after their graduation, so they've had time to put on a little extra weight. At any rate, on an individual basis, they are huge, the biggest guys I've seen ever seen together. Fortunately, they were all good-natured, cordial, friendly, even after working most of their way through forty-five fifths of whiskey and more cases of beer than could be counted. I didn't have much to drink, and as I looked around, I couldn't help thinking how wild it would be if these behemoths ever started swinging at each other. They could do real damage to any normal-sized person caught in their melee, but they stayed happy to the end.

November 19. Still in reserve and by now it's obvious that we've been here too long. The rest and relative comforts of this area are not worth it, and inactivity is creating a host of small problems, some relating to the battalion commander.

Colonel Gorman, superb battalion commander that he is, as it turns out, is not good at being in reserve. This may seem like a small thing. You might think, what the hell? Here's a guy who knows it all because he's done it all before. He was a Marine paratrooper, a judo instructor, rifle platoon leader, company commander, and intelligence officer, on Iwo in WWII. He's excelled all along the way, and in addition, he's knowledgeable, confident, and very strong, a natural leader who even looks the part. Why bother about what he's like in reserve? Who the hell cares?

Well, that's a point. But the problem is that now we *are* in reserve. And here if the battalion commander is out of sorts, after a while it gets around, and then everybody cares. I don't know how many people see Gorman in a typical day. Major Carney does. I do. There may be a few others that he sees. But the ones I hear about are mainly the ones that he calls to his tent to chew out. I see him every day under circumstances that are interesting, even stimulating. I would guess the same is true of Major Carney who runs the battalion day to day under Gorman's direction. For the rest of the time, as nearly as I can tell, the colonel sits in his tent, almost in darkness, brooding. When he does ask somebody in for the kind of exchange a battalion commander would usually have with his officers, he may end up by stomping his visitor. Within the last few days, he shredded a perfectly adequate lieutenant, told him he was yellow, and threatened to transfer him out of the battalion. And his exchanges with his company commanders have been little better. They respect and fear him, but tensions within the battalion have been building daily since we've been back here. Of course, there's no possibility of a revolt, but there is too much drinking and bitching about battalion leadership. And all of this is unnecessary. Maybe it will turn around when we get back on the line.

November 20. I got a long letter from Jim Cowan today. He's back in Los Angeles, and it sounds like he's readjusted to civilian life which I'm sure was not difficult for him. He says he's really enjoying himself, although his girlfriend did marry someone else while he was over here.

November 24. Today was by far the coldest day with a hard Siberian wind whipping across the parade ground and everything frozen solid. Perhaps to get us through this frigid period, our whiskey ration came in today. This is a boon to many, including my friends Kitchen and Egan who are in high spirits. (Or should I say they have high spirits in them?) Thus, fortified to go out into the cold, they traveled through officers' country from tent to tent, performing a song-and-dance routine in each one. For amateurs, they're not bad. The first heavy snow of the year is now pouring down outside.

November 25. Sad news. I had two friends from St. Paul in the class of 1950 at West Point. Bill Bonfoy was a classmate from a preparatory school we attended in Minnesota, and I spent time with him and his friend, Goozie Michaels, when I was at West Point on an exchange weekend from the Naval Academy. We went to the Army-Williams hockey game together. Today I learned that they were both killed leading rifle platoons over here.

November 27. I'm here at the division for a few days going to an intelligence school. It is cloudy weather here and very cold, five degrees above, this morning. It is so cold that the canteen cup of boiling water that I carried out of the mess hall this morning had almost frozen by the time I got it to Tex's tent where I'm staying. The school is not exciting, but for the moment, it may be better than sitting around at battalion and listening to all the dissension that hangs over that place like a fog. I know quite a few of the officers here, and I keep running into them on the paths around the division area. I stand watch in the intelligence section here as well as going to classes. It's cold here, to be sure, but it must be really cold up on the line at this time.

November 28. The time is not very productive for me here at the division, but I have been able to talk at length with Tex and also with Eddie LeBaron and Colonel Davenport, my old battalion commander from the Naval Academy. At last, it looks like this may be the beginning of the end of the Korean War. Last night, they decided on the exact location of the cease-fire line if talks are concluded in the next thirty days. That is interpreted here as a sign that the end is in sight. For the past ten days, the division has been pushing patrols out two thousand meters forward of the MLR in an effort to make contact with the enemy because the cease-fire line was to have been determined by reported "points of contact." Today, the order came down from X Corps to limit patrols to local security requirements, a short distance in front of the lines. All air strikes have been cancelled as have all artillery except for defensive missions. Two additional lines have been drawn in front of our positions. The one farther out is the line beyond which our patrols will not go; the closer line is the one beyond which the enemy may not come without being fired on. North of the closer line, they can move around freely, and we don't fire on them. Today was the quietest day on the line since last August. It's like a cease-fire, with your guard up.

There was also an interesting meeting today on the line in front of the Third Battalion, Seventh Marines positions. At one point, they are within one hundred yards of the gook lines, well within hearing distance. The Marines got an interpreter up there with a loud speaker to call over to the gooks and ask what they thought about the cease-fire developments. The response was to call for a meeting, and at 1415 the two groups carrying white flags met on neutral ground to talk the situation over. I don't know what the discussion covered, but both parties returned safely to their own lines. The whole event seems ludicrous to me, but it actually happened.

At another point on the line last night, a Marine fell asleep on watch, and four gooks came into his bunker. They picked up two pair of winter boots, an M-1 rifle, and a BAR. Before leaving, they awakened the Marine and in English asked him to come with them. At this, he bolted, and they threw a grenade which wounded him. By that time, the rest of the line was alerted. They fired on the gooks, driving them away. Obviously, this could have been much more serious. For some reason, the gooks were fooling around. If they had grenaded the bunker in the first place, they could have killed all of those Marines before anyone knew they were there.

December 2. Today, great mail delivery from Joan. A fifth of Old Parr scotch. Joe Reed came by last night with exquisite timing, and we dealt with the scotch, quietly and totally. You can really appreciate good whiskey under those circumstances. You have someone to share it with; there are no interruptions, and you have enough. I have a new favorite brand of scotch.

Rotation continues to occupy most of our thoughts and almost all of our conversation here. There are always more rumors. Drafts of a certain size are coming in or going out, or they are cancelled; or they have a different number of Marines in them. It's exasperating to think about it. I'm beginning to hate it, and I know we'd all be better off if we lived entirely in the present, rather than trying to live some two months in the future. But I can't help myself.

Currently, it seems that most Marines are leaving Korea after about nine months. For me, that would mean sometime around February 5. But who the hell knows? Parks, the Korean boy who accompanies our platoon, got a package of small gifts from Joan today and is delighted with it. I want to be sure that I don't get any Christmas gifts now. Nothing except cookies and booze, that is. I may not be here that long, and I don't want to have to think about gifts being here or drifting in over time.

December 4. Still in reserve. Tonight, we head out on an all-night problem that looks like a long and cold affair and not very interesting. In a week or so, we're scheduled to go back up on the line to relieve the Seventh Marines in their defensive positions. Now the line is solidly built up, especially battalion CPs. Heavy log construction, various kinds of heat, and electric lights. The line now is going to be pretty much like reserve, a few more reports to fill out and maybe less detail about regulations and training. Reserve may offer the line companies a chance to rest. But for us pogues on the battalion staff—a group that now includes me—it's pretty much same same, whether we're here or back on the line.

The November 19 issue of *Newsweek* that we got today has a good story on Korea, not melodramatic, as most of the articles we see are. Kitchen is now coming to the end of his fourth month here, the time that officers are to be rotated out of rifle companies. He's had enough of Korea, and now, for the second time, he thinks he will receive orders to Pearl Harbor to be the legal officer there. He's had an outstanding tour as a company commander here, and he deserves the best.

December 6. Now that I'm getting close to end here, I'm getting a lot of advice. Good friends, and even some I don't know so well, coming to tell me what I should do next. They all mean well, and some of them are even well informed. The trouble is, their advice is conflicting. About half of them explain why I should stay in the Marine Corps, and the other half explain why I should get out. I suppose I can figure this out for myself when the time comes, but I haven't figured it out yet.

I think I really do understand the battalion now. There are now only two officers in the entire battalion who were here when I joined last May, which seems like a lifetime ago. Because I don't have an agenda, I hear things from a lot of different sources, and I can now appreciate this outfit in depth.

Our night problem a couple of nights ago was simple. It consisted of marching from 10:30 PM to 1:30 AM, freezing in place until 5:00 AM, and then climbing up and down hills, not getting back until 11:00 that morning. It was a tryout for our new thermal boots. They are very warm, and that's a gain. But they also hold moisture within the boot itself, and everyone had blisters by the time we got back. Then we had a hot meal, and the rest of the day was clear. Good thing.

December 8. Saturday night. Quiet in reserve. I have a couple of beers and stay back in the tent pulling stuff together to go back up on the line on Monday. During the day, I talk with Joe Reed and with Bob Oliver on the phone. We're all ready to get back to the business.

December 10. Here we are, all set to move out. It may not sound like much, but it means moving 1,200 men with all their weapons and personal equipment, all of the battalion's supporting arms and organizational gear a distance of some fifteen miles. Then we relieve another unit of the same size and about the same equipment on the line in total darkness. We had a battalion briefing on the move yesterday. It was in the theatre here. Colonel Gorman, Major Luckel, and I each talked to the troops about the aspects of the move we were responsible for. Generally, it was a lot more information than is usually provided to troops before a move like that. I think that kind of briefing makes a lot of sense, and it seems to have gone over well.

There is now a replacement captain here for Baker Company, and Kitchen will be leaving soon. Tank Brady has already left to become a personnel officer at our battalion rear echelon. Surprisingly enough, Kitchen is now the last officer who was in Baker Company while I was there. When he leaves, the entire officer complement will have turned over in the short time since I left the company.

I finally got together last night with Stan Olson, Joe Reed, Bob Oliver, and Jimmy Marsh. We were in Joe Reed's tent, and he had the recent *Life Magazine* article that his wife Marilyn had sent him.

Joe's platoon, the second platoon of How Company, is mentioned in the article in connection with an action on the night of September 20-21. That was the night that we passed through the rear of the Third Battalion, First Marines, on our way to relieve an ROK unit on the line. It was also the night that the division reconnaissance company was airlifted to an adjoining hill that they took without firing a shot at the same time Joe was taking casualties against stiff opposition. The recon company "action" was fully reported in the press, and until now, there was nothing about Joe's firefight.

December 12. Back on the line. I'm on watch in the battalion CP, midnight to 4:00 AM. We moved out of division reserve and came up here, starting around 11:00 on the night of the tenth. We made the move in truck convoys, relieving the Third Battalion, Seventh Marines in darkness. Relief of lines is always tricky, especially with the enemy this close. But this time, it was done fast without incident. Everyone feels good about that. Last night and again tonight, there is a full moon, and the snow-covered hills stand out in sharp relief. A moment of rare beauty in Korea. Colonel Gorman is a changed man up here, no more brooding in the darkness of his tent. He's great when there's something going on, or even when there's the prospect of action ahead. Everything else is better now too.

December 16. We had several probes on the line last night, and there was a patrol skirmish today.

Kitchen leaves tomorrow, headed for Marine Barracks, Pearl Harbor. His timing could hardly be improved. He gets over here in the summer and gets a company right away. That's an outstanding tour for him and for the company as well. Then, just when the cold has really set in, he finishes up here and heads off to the beaches of Hawaii where he'll be for the next year or so, and where his wife and family will be able to join him. I wish him well.

December 18. Everything here is quiet, that is, no enemy action. But if there is no enemy to bother us, somehow we can manage to bother ourselves. Over the last week, we've had a rash of accidents, mostly accidental discharges of personal handguns, but some involving grenades as well. Two nights ago, a Marine rolled over in his sleeping bag, and his pistol discharged. The round went through his wrist. Last night one of the platoon leaders went out to check the line, and on approaching his bunker in returning, his platoon sergeant shot him three times in the leg with a .45 automatic. Whether he didn't hear the challenge or didn't know the password, the shooting was an accident. The platoon leader is a husky fellow, and all three rounds went through the upper part of his right thigh without hitting the bone. We've had several other accidents like this, mostly involving personal handguns and grenades. In the course of the last week, this battalion on the line has had seven casualties, all accidental, without enemy action or an enemy shot being fired.

December 20. News. First Battalion is supposed to go into regimental reserve on the 25th, Christmas night. Then if the cease-fire does go into effect on the 27th as planned, our battalion is to go out to an outpost on what is called Line Peak. That is to the rear of where we are now, but in front of the line that the rest of the division is to take up positions on. We—our battalion—will be spread over a series of outposts across the entire division front to provide warning and delay any advance in case of an enemy violation of the truce. There is to be a two-and-a-half-mile buffer zone between us and the NKs, and no one is to be allowed in that zone. This is actually a considerable improvement over the present lines where in a couple of places they are within one hundred yards of each other. Still, this won't be easy. The battalion will be so spread out that communications and logistics will be challenging, but it should be workable. We're making detailed plans for it now. I'm very glad to be leaving. I can't think it would be much fun to be here after the cease-fire.

December 22. Joe Reed called tonight with fast-breaking news. Apparently, two planeloads of Marine officers have just arrived in Korea, and the planes are ready to haul two loads back to the States. That means that with what is already scheduled, they are ready to start taking out the 8th replacement draft, the group we came over with. When they called Joe, they told him to be ready to leave at 11:00 tomorrow morning.

Then they realized that schedule would not be fair; it would mean that some who got out here later would fly and be home for New Year's Eve, while men on earlier drafts would take the slower ocean route and get home later. When they got all of that straightened out, the result is that everybody ahead of us will be cleared out, probably by the end of this month, and we should be close to being next, whenever that is. They are supposed to have some kind of a point system based on combat time, wounds, decorations, dependents, etc., but so far, they have not started using it. To the extent possible, they are trying to send Marines in the same replacement draft home at the same time.

I haven't heard anything from Tex, but he should be gone in a matter of days.

December 28. Finally. The word. I'm to leave Korea on December 31 and return to the States by ship. Joe Reed is to leave at the same time. Maybe Tex is too, but I still haven't heard from him.

Jan. 5, 1952. Osaka, Japan. We were picked up by an LST on the east coast of Korea last week and delivered here to Osaka. This is our last night before sailing. We leave port at 0700 tomorrow on the USS *General William Weigel*. We don't know the destination yet, but it will be either San Diego or San Francisco. Bill Rockey, Joe Reed, and I are on board.

There's plenty of room, and Joe and I share a junior officers' compartment with four bunks. We have drawn stacks of paperback books from the ship's library, and that's all we need for the trip. We are ready to sleep and read our way across the Pacific. We only leave the compartment to get food in the galley, which is open twenty-four hours a day, and we usually go there at odd times of the day and night, sometimes singly and sometimes together. In a little over two weeks, we arrive in San Francisco where our wives have traveled together to meet us, that is Joan to meet me, and Marilyn, who had brought their infant son with her to California from Ohio, to meet Joe.

That was, to be sure, the end of the voyage. And also the end of an era.

Chapter 23

MUSINGS

Musings: thoughts, especially when
aimless and unsystematic. (Encarta, 1999.)

War is an important subject. And it may be that musings about it, if they are to ring true, have to come from actual experience. Maybe war is a place you can't visit by reading about it.

Since Korea, I have done some reading about war. I've also thought about it a good deal, and I saw another war up close for a few weeks in Vietnam, just before the Tet offensive. But the reading and thinking, and even the trip to Vietnam, haven't really had much impact on these impressions. What I think now is based almost entirely on the experience of leading a rifle platoon in Korea—my own experience and some others'—although our impressions may well be similar to the impressions anyone might have, fighting in a war anywhere.

War compresses and focuses a combatant's attention to a remarkable degree. It is often said that closeness of death, or even extreme danger, concentrates one's attention. But I mean something more than that. Men under fire, it seems to me, are living in their own world, isolated from the rest of the universe. Time there is reckoned differently. So is space: their attention is concentrated on a small area. And they are strongly bound to those who share that area with them—in Col. John Thomason's immortal phrase " . . . a Few Marines." Everything else is extraneous. And they don't think much about it.

A few examples:

In Korea, time existed mostly in the present. Yesterday was history, not important enough to keep track of. Tomorrow was too uncertain to think about. We did keep track of today—at least morning and afternoon, maybe all night if something was going on. We might have in mind a date somewhere in the future, but that was only a kind of marking stake, not significant to what we were actually doing. Anything beyond today was remote, and we were hardly aware of it.

Of course, there was planning at higher levels, and there were certainly advance schedules. It was just that in a rifle platoon we didn't know anything about them, and it wouldn't have made any difference if we did. We knew that schedules were only tentative: they could change from hour to hour, and sometimes from minute to minute. Reacting fast, being able to turn on a dime, was essential. That's war. So we could get along fine with only a wristwatch; we didn't need a calendar.

Similarly, our attention was always focused on a very small area, generally what we could see to our direct front, or that fold of the map that showed where we were and where we were going. The maps were drawn by Army Map Service to a scale of 1:50,000. They were based on earlier Japanese Imperial Land Surveys, and each covered an area of about 150 square miles. When we moved out of the area covered by one map, we'd get another for where we were going. Depending on where we were, sometimes we could see enough on the ground, but often we had to rely on the map. And beyond that single map, there was nothing, only a void at the end of the landscape. We might have been using one of those antique maps with sea monsters at the edges to indicate dangers in the unknown.

And in Korea, our attention was concentrated on a limited number of other Marines. For me, it was the men in my platoon, the other officers in the company, and the two young Koreans, Parks and Butch, who worked with us. The total might be between 50 and 75. In the ranks, men knew the others in their squad and, if they had been there for a while, the rest of the platoon.

For everyone, there was little contact with battalion. If we were on the line, we knew that the battalion headquarters would be at the battalion CP—wherever that was. But if we were moving, or in the attack, battalion might be anywhere, as might the other companies. Of course, everybody knew who the battalion commander was, but we only saw him intermittently, and we saw even less of other battalion officers. Beyond that, the larger units— regiment, division, Corps, Army, and the UN command—all were abstractions.

The contacts we did have were strong. There may not be stronger bonds anywhere than those among Marines in a rifle platoon on the line. Everything is done for the welfare of the group, whether it's clearing fields of fire and putting out trip flares or covering another's advance in a firefight. Total strangers rapidly come to rely on each other. Whether you call it a band of brothers, comradeship, or a buddy system, the individual Marine is tightly bound into his outfit. As Eugene Sledge, a Marine who fought through Peleliu and Okinawa in World War II, put it, "I really had no desire to leave company K. It was home to me, and I had strong feelings of belonging to the company, no matter how miserable or dangerous conditions might be."

In Korea, this concentration was enhanced by our limited communication with the outside. It is surely different now, but in 1951, there was no television, no radio (except an SCR 300 from battalion), and little else. Irregular mail deliveries might bring only clippings or newsmagazines from home. The Marine rifle company on the line was a self-contained unit; its attention was concentrated on the urgent matters of life and death before it. The unit talked to itself.

So, in the summer of 1951, when I got a letter from my friend Whizzer asking if I knew what I was fighting for, I was startled. From New Haven, it may have been a perfectly reasonable question, but to me, it didn't seem reasonable at all. I thought it was ridiculous. (Whizzer himself was later commissioned in the

Marine Corps, in time to get to Korea while the war was still going on. My wife and I worried about him, with his gung ho attitude, but he came through all right.)

Now I think I understand why his question seemed ridiculous to me then: my view of the war was so tightly focused that he seemed to be calling in from another planet.

And I'd guess that my reaction was typical of others in Korea then, and of those fighting in other wars at other times. There may be exceptions, but by the time someone gets into a rifle platoon in a shooting war, he'd better have gotten past the question of why he's there. There's no time for pondering that or anything else in a firefight.

Looking back over the remove of a half century, I am impressed with how few our requirements were. We needed weapons: usually, a rifle or carbine, ammunition, and grenades. We needed helmets and some kind of cover or protection, a fighting hole, or bunker on the line. We needed water and C-rations, clothing adequate for the weather, and something to sleep on. That was about it. Occasionally, we had more, but we could go for long stretches with much less. This spartan lifestyle may have contributed to the feeling of separateness as well; certainly, very few of us lived this way either before we got to Korea or after we got home.

And that simple life had its simple pleasures, simple jokes. Sledge captures the mood, describing a USO show on the Pacific island of Pavuvu (where they were then staging for Peleliu). Bob Hope asks Jerry Colonna how he liked the trip over, and Jerry replies that it was "tough sledding." When asked why, Colonna replies, "No snow." That really cracked them up, Sledge says, "It was the funniest thing we had ever heard." We might have had the same reaction in Korea.

Another observation: perhaps in no other human activity can very slight differences lead to such radically different results. That's not an original thought, I know, at least since someone suggested that the battle of Waterloo was lost "for want of a nail."

But if baseball is the game of inches, events in war may turn on millimeters. And in baseball, it's usually only a matter of scoring a run or winning the game; in war, it may be who lives or dies—or, ultimately, who wins the war. In Korea, if you were out there very long, in combat or on combat patrols, you were going to have a lot of close calls. And close calls didn't count, because they were really a lift. As Winston Churchill noted after the Boer War, "Nothing in life is so exhilarating as to be shot at without result."

So, as rifle platoon leaders, we had plenty of exhilaration. Jim Marsh had his helmet banged in from a Bouncing Betty, had a canteen shot out of his hand, had his wristwatch shot off, and his pants' leg shot through. Of course, from all these incidents, he simply concluded that "those sons-a-bitches can't kill me," though they came very close. Bill Rockey took two concussion grenades and two bullet creases in his helmet, had his chinstrap shot off and a couple of rounds go through the blanket on the pack strapped to his back. Walter Murphy also was lucky to be helmeted on his way up Hill 676, where his helmet took a beating that would otherwise have taken him out several times. My sleeping bag was shredded—while I was in it—and just to make the point, the front of my dungaree jacket was shredded through the folds at the same time. And even that hardly counted as close: the T-shirt I had on was untouched.

There were incidents like this without number. And these were only the misses, the everyday events that mercifully did not result in casualties. Where wounds were involved—bullets or shrapnel tearing into flesh—some negligible shift in point of entry or direction might be critical. Charlie Cooper is a good example.

Charlie had been dropped on Hill 907 when an enemy machine gun stitched up the left side of his body. With a broken back, paralysis, and massive blood loss, he was not expected to survive, but somehow he did. If that gook gunner's aim had been slightly higher, or if his machine gun had just elevated in firing, Charlie would have taken one through the heart, and no emergency care would have helped him.

Of course, if you'd had a number of close calls, you might begin to think about what might have been. I sometimes think of going up the hill with Sims Morse. We were too close together as it was. But if our positions had had been reversed, Sims might be writing this memoir now, and my service would have ended suddenly, as his did.

And another "what if" that I find disturbing is the time, a few months later, when I unintentionally discharged my carbine into the ground, barely missing my own foot. If I had actually shot myself in the foot, the foot probably would have recovered. But it would have taken me a long time to straighten out my head.

Well, so what? Stuff happens. There are close calls in everyone's life, some good and some bad. What's the big deal?

I guess I think that close calls in war are a big deal. They are closer. They happen faster, and there is more riding on them. They often mean the difference between living and dying. And they can make the difference between being a hero and being a goat; the line that divides is often paper thin. Thinking seriously about those experiences, those close calls, should make anyone humble. It has had that effect on me.

There are different ways of thinking about these things when you are out there. If you are religious, you might think that whatever happens is controlled by a Supreme Being: Christ, Allah, Buddha, Providence, or some other all-powerful entity. Or you may simply be fatalistic. What will happen will happen; there's no point in worrying about it. Or you may feel that it's all chaos anyhow, and it's impossible to tell what will happen or to have any effect on it. But whatever your answer, you are more likely to think about the question in some place like the Korean War, than if you are at home (say) driving a bus.

The poet John Donne wrote, many years ago, that "no man is an island." Nor is any man a rock, hard and unyielding. We are all human, and we have human limits. When we reach those limits, something may happen. We may become dysfunctional, physically or mentally, unable to go on. This is a fact of life for prisoners of war, recognized by General William Dean, John McCain, and others who have been there. It is also a fact of life in shooting wars, where men are under extreme stress for extended periods.

We all have different limits, and there is probably an infinite variety of conditions that push us out to those limits, through them and beyond. The differences showed up starkly in two Marines I served with in Korea, when each had reached his limit.

One, Corporal Bartholomew (called Bart), was a squad leader, pretty close to being the ideal Marine. He had gotten to Korea early, and he'd stayed on. In closing with the enemy, he was always superb, extraordinary in the attack. As a leader, he led by example and inspired an entire company. He was a scourge to every North Korean in his path, and if they weren't able to get their hands up fast enough, he'd drill them or blow them away. When not engaged in such violence, he was quiet, reserved, and controlled. He carried out all assignments well, and he didn't talk much. Bart was cool. He never rattled. He was in another platoon in Baker Company; I always wished he was in mine.

The second Marine, Tilt, was far from ideal. He was in Baker Company a relatively short time, and while he was there, he apparently hated every minute of it. He fretted and worried, and he didn't keep it to himself. I got accustomed to having Tilt in the platoon, but I would not have wanted to have many others like him. Because he worried, he'd hear strange sounds in the night and couldn't sleep. Then he'd be exhausted from lack of sleep and couldn't hold up his end of the work details during the day. Tilt did all right the one time I saw him in a firefight, but he required very high maintenance.

When Bartholomew decided he'd reached his limit, he may not have been able to admit it, even to himself. He waited in darkness outside the tent to approach me. He was by then more than qualified for relief from rifle company duty, and he was moved promptly to the rear until he went home. He rated it, no questions asked.

Tilt probably thought he'd reached his limit the day he arrived on the line at Baker Company. He came to see me shortly after and asked to be moved back. I denied that request, but I continued to talk with him whenever he came to see me, which was periodically. Each time, after we talked, he seemed to feel better, and he hung in there. He did everything I asked.

Now, the question that continues to intrigue me is which of these men was braver? Had more guts? Showed more courage?

I have no idea what Bartholomew was thinking about. He was cool and self-contained. Maybe it was hard for him to perform as he did, though I doubt it; my guess is that he was a natural and just didn't think much about it. Then, when his time was nearly up, and he'd been awarded the DSC, he decided it was time to cut out. He figured, correctly, that talking to me was the quietest way out. And he didn't want it known that he'd asked.

Poor old Tilt, on the other hand, couldn't help telling everybody exactly how he felt. He blabbed. He had no case, but he blabbed anyhow. But then, with only a little encouragement from me, he stayed on. He didn't walk away; he didn't shoot himself in the foot, and he didn't fall apart as some others did. It may have been a struggle for him, but if it was, he struggled; and he largely overcame his fears. He was never outstanding, but he stayed. Then, when there was an opportunity to take a job as a runner at battalion, a job that no one else wanted, Tilt jumped at it, and he was out of the company. I was not sorry to see him go, but I recognized that it must have been a challenge for him just to get up every day he'd been with us—and he always did get up. In the end, I had come to respect him for that.

So that's why the question continues to intrigue me: I don't know the answer. At one time I thought the answer was obvious, but I no longer do.

Finally, Korea left me with one overwhelming impression. It has to do with the awesome performance of young enlisted Marines in combat.

Just a couple of days after I took over the platoon, we were involved in a firefight. Thinking about it at the time, I marveled at the way it had all worked out, the way the men responded to me, a green second lieutenant, leading them through something most of them had done dozens of times before. But after talking with my friends in similar positions, I understood that my experience was no big deal. Rather, it was typical.

Joe Reed took over a rifle platoon in the *middle* of a firefight, thirty minutes before leading the final assault. So did Eddie LeBaron. The Marines in their platoons may not even have known who they were, at the moment they took over.

And one of the first things Joe and Eddie say, probably their strongest impressions, were how great the Marines they led performed. That would be one of my strongest impressions as well, as it would for everyone I've talked with, without exception. Jim Marsh *revered* the young Marines he led. There's no better word for it; he never stopped talking about them. The same is true for Charlie Cooper, who would become the Marine Corps' top inspirational speaker on the subject. Bill Rockey talked of his "wonderful young Marines" and how he would "never forget their calmness and their eyes on me, as I queried their readiness for the attack with an arm-and-hand signal." And Murph was just as emphatic, "I cannot find the words to describe the determined heroism of those other 75 young Marines. Commanding them was like leading a pack of ferocious wildcats. They were not going to let gooks stop them, no matter what the cost to themselves."

These are honest tributes, drawn from firsthand experience. The comments are spontaneous, and they confirm a judgment that is really extraordinary when you think about it.

Think what would happen if you approached any group of 18-to-19-year-old men anywhere in the world with the following proposition: "I would like you to join me in a challenging but dangerous effort. You won't get paid any more for it, and you might get wounded, maimed, maybe crippled for life, or even killed, because we're going up against the enemy, armed to the teeth, who will be trying to destroy you. You will have to crawl up a steep incline to get to them. They are in bunkers and heavily fortified emplacements. They have mortars, machine guns, grenades, and satchel charges, and they will use all of those, and anything else they can get their hands on, to kill you before you can even get to them. If you do get to their positions, you may have to kill them with bayonets or with your bare hands, or they will kill you there. Now, all of you who will join me in this, come on! Let's go!"

Any sensible group, of course, would think you were nuts. They would try to get as far away from you as possible. Unless, in contrast, they were Marines, in which case they would go with you. And if you were willing to lead, they would certainly follow you.

What's the difference? What makes young men who are Marines different from other young men?

Part of the answer is self-selection, and the Marine Corps pitches to that strike zone. All those recruiting posters—like, "We never promised you a rose garden"—are aimed at young men who will respond to that kind of challenge. Another part of the answer is training. It has always been excellent, and it's gotten better. (See Tom Ricks' *Making the Corps*, Scribner, New York, 1997.) But training can't do it all, and some of the best Marines I knew in Korea didn't have much. Bernie Hletko, for example, had never had a rifle on his shoulder when he arrived at Pendleton on his way to Korea and Baker Company's first platoon. And Eddie LeBaron had not fired a rifle on the range before he headed out to Korea.

More important, I think—really the essence of it—is what is usually called culture. And the Marine culture has a couple of outstanding features.

First is the relationship in the Corps between junior officers and enlisted men and women. The distinctive aspect of that is the officers' attitude. Deeply engrained, and to me thrilling, it's one of the few examples of working altruism I've encountered in modern life. The rule is simple: If the job is tough or dangerous, you don't ask your troops to do anything you wouldn't do yourself. You may be doing it with them—but whether you are or not, there's never any question about it; they always know you would.

And whenever there are benefits—anything that contributes to health or safety, any material advantage—you make sure that all your enlisted Marines have them before you draw them yourself. This goes for food in the chow line in the field, essentials like boots, flack jackets, and cold-weather gear, and especially anything in short supply. It also goes for medical treatment, as in Murph's account of the battalion commander who "went to the end of the line at the aid station and waited until all his men had been treated before letting a corpsman examine him." *The battalion commander!* It doesn't take long for that word to get around.

I was delighted to see this idea as the keynote of the program for the Marine Corps' 2003 Succession of Command ceremony:

> A king does not dine while his men go hungry, nor sleep when they stand watch upon the wall . . . . That which comprises the harshest burden, a king lifts first and sets down last. A king does not require service of those he leads but provides it to them. He serves them, not they him.

The quote is from Steven Pressfield's *Gates of Fire*. In flying that flag, General Mike Hagee got off to a great start as the Marine Corps' 33rd Commandant.

Second, perhaps even more important, has to do with what happens on the battlefield. It is simply the unvarying rule that *everybody who goes out comes back*. That is: all the wounded and, if humanly possible, all the dead. Nobody gets left behind. For Marines who might otherwise have qualms about jumping off in the attack, or heading out on a deadly combat patrol, that is the best insurance policy in the world. There were spectacular examples of it in Korea—and some striking contrasts between the way the Marines did it and what happened in other services.

That's a lot of it, but there is much more to be found in the lore and legends of the Marine Corps. As General Tony Zinni puts it, "We feel stronger about traditions than any other service." And the traditions include terrific stories about *characters*, Marines who are distinctively different. Zinni again, "We probably have the greatest tolerance for mavericks . . . In the Marines, you're much more likely to find people who succeed who don't fit the usual pattern." And, like members of the old brigade, these characters all "face danger with a smile." Their trademark is a kind of gallows humor, clipped, ironic phrases that ring down the years from war to war. "Come on, you, sons-of-bitches, do you want to live forever?" worked for Ken Bailey on Guadalcanal as it had for Gunnery Sergeant Dan Daly, in the Belleau Wood of World War I. Red Mike Edson rallied his Raiders with the taunt, "The only thing the Japs have that you don't have is guts!" There are scores of these famous challenges, and Marines hear them—actually inhale them—from boot camp on.

As Zinni sums it up, "We carry a sense of responsibility to those who went before us, which ends up meaning a lot to Marines who are in combat. We don't want to let our predecessors down, or taint our magnificent heritage."

The stories are carried forward in fiction as well as fact. Colonel John W. Thomason Jr. is the acknowledged dean of Marine Corps fiction. Thomason, a distinguished officer of Marines who served all over the globe for 27 years, was an artist and illustrator as well as a writer. His stories, initially carried in *The Saturday Evening Post*, were collected in several volumes, ending with "—and a Few Marines" (published in 1935). The same themes may be found today, in the fiction and nonfiction of Brig. Gen. Edwin Howard Simmons, USMC retired, and in novels of *The Corps* published under the pen name W.E.B. Griffin.

These themes and principles endure in the statements of Marines today. For Marines, the past is not prologue; it's always present, right there with you. Maj. Gen. James Mattis, CO of the First Marine Division, on the eve of the war in Iraq, concluded his message to the troops: "For the mission's sake, our country's sake, and the sake of the men who carried the division's colors in past battles—who fought for life and never lost their nerve—carry out your mission and keep your honor clean. Demonstrate to the world there is 'no better friend, no worse enemy' than a U.S. Marine."

And some of the real Marines have more smack than the fictional ones. Without peer at the pinnacle of real Marines, of course, is Chesty Puller. He fought in every war and skirmish from Haiti in 1919 to the breakout from the Chosin Reservoir at the end of 1950, and he was a legend for his phrases as well as his heroism.

Others, not well known outside the Corps, are legends within it. This group would include Smedley Butler, Dan Daly, and John Lejeune from the early days; Mike Edson, David Shoup, Lou Diamond, and Graves Erskine from World War II; and, more recently, Ray Davis, Lou Wilson, Bob Barrow, Bigfoot Brown, and John Ripley, among others. Today's Marines draw pride and inspiration from the yarns spun around these celebrated Marines who came before.

And within every battalion and regiment, stories are told about characters who served there in the past. In First Battalion, First Marines, I heard more about Buck Schmuck, Wes Noren, and Bobby Tobin, Baker Company's artillery FO, than I did about any of the Marines who were there in my time.

All this adds to the legend, of course. And it's an essential part of what makes young Marines ready to go up the hill.

Chapter 24

AFTERWORD

A t this writing, the events of 1951 all occurred more than a half century ago. And over that time, much has happened to the Marines of the Korean War referred to here. In an effort to bring some of their stories up to date, briefly, this *Afterword* is the kind of piece that Tom Lehrer called "one of those 'where are they now' columns, whatever happened to Deanna Durbin, etc."

Here's a partial update:

Howard Allmain. After his return to the States in late 1951, Allmain was released to inactive duty. While working in construction and on the railroad, he took a series of correspondence courses in bookkeeping and tax accounting. When his first marriage ended, he raised his three children for a number of years and in 1976 moved to Sandy, Oregon, a suburb of Portland, in the foothills of Mount Hood. There, now in his mid-70's, he is hearty, in good health, and happily remarried. He is the proprietor of Allmain Tax Services, serving the Sandy area.

Bobbie Bradford. After Korea, Bob returned to his native Arkansas and started with Frito Lay as a route salesman. He worked for the company for thirty-four years and was their sales manager in Little Rock at the time of his retirement in 1986. He and his wife had two sons, and the family later moved to Rogers, Arkansas, near the borders of Oklahoma and Missouri in the extreme northwestern corner of the state. There, Bob and one of his sons started a blueberry farm on thirty acres of undeveloped land. They managed the farm for twelve years and sold it only recently for residential development. Bob and his wife now have five grandchildren, all living nearby Rogers or in the Little Rock area.

Marvin Burnett. After Marv came back to the States in May, 1952, he finished college at Colorado A & M (now Colorado State) and entered medical school at the University of Colorado. He was an intern at Madigan Army Hospital in Tacoma, Washington, and a resident at Denver Presbyterian Hospital before entering medical practice as an oncologist in Denver in 1966. Interestingly enough (recruiting officers, attention), he told me that he acquired the discipline for medical school and advanced study from his time in a Marine rifle company in Korea. His career as an oncologist spanned thirty-two years to his retirement in 1998. He and his wife, Alison, have three grown daughters. They continue to live in Denver where Marv says he now has time for fishing and an occasional game of golf.

Charlie Cooper. Charlie has probably had the model Marine Corps career of our class. Over a long run, he stayed close to active operations in the FMF; he had most of the major commands, and he always delivered the mail. It's a good story, and Charlie has written it himself in *Cheers and Tears, A Marine's Story of Combat in Peace and War*. His heroism in Korea almost came at the cost of his life. But he survived, and everything must have seemed easier to him after that.

Back from Korea, Charlie faced a lengthy recovery period, hospitalization, and rehabilitation in military hospitals, but he drove himself back into active duty as fast as humanly possible. He was for a time the Marine aide to the chief of naval operations, and he commanded First Battalion, Seventh Marines in Vietnam. He was later legislative assistant to the Commandant. He was Commanding General of the First Marine Division and, finally, of the Fleet Marine Force, Pacific, the command he held at retirement in 1985 after thirty-five years of distinguished service.

Now active in his retirement, Charlie remains a constructive force in Marine Corps affairs. He and Carol, his wife, live in Falls Church, Virginia. They have a grown son and daughter.

Jim Cowan. In the fall of 1951, when Jim returned to the California he'd always talked about, he went back to the field of landscape architecture. In 1957, he moved to Malibu and started James H. Cowan & Associates, a landscape construction business. He was very successful. As the Los Angeles area mushroomed in size, the Cowan firm grew with it. In 1967, Jim came to Washington to receive the *Beautify America Award* at the White House from the hands of First Lady, Lady Bird Johnson. The award was for his outstanding work in the development of Busch Gardens at Van Nuys, California, a short time before. Later, his son Clark and his daughter Kendall joined him in the Cowan firm, and he found time for fishing at a camp that he owned in Alaska. After his first wife died, Jim remarried. He lived in Malibu and was active in the landscaping firm until shortly before his death on February 4, 2003.

Vic Heins. When he was released to inactive duty in the reserve, Vic returned to the University of Washington where he was majoring in physical education. But with marriage and the start of a family, he switched to a paying position, first with Boys' Clubs of America and later with the Seattle Police Department.

Over the twenty-year period from 1959 to 1979, Vic handled a range of assignments for the department. He worked in the central district of downtown Seattle, a transition neighborhood, and he worked for several years with the special squad, designed to defeat increased crime in particular areas of the city. He served in the burglary, homicide, and narcotic units, and, for the last three years of his law enforcement service, was in charge of tracking down forged prescriptions in the city of Seattle, an activity then focused on Pill Hill overlooking the downtown district. After his retirement from the force, he was a safety officer for a local school district.

Vic and his wife, Josie, now live in Paulsbo, outside of Seattle. They have two sons and two daughters and twelve grandchildren.

Bernie Hletko. While Hletko was in Korea, his father bought a resort property on a spectacular lake near Eagle River in Northern Wisconsin, and when Bernie was released to inactive duty, he headed for there. He graduated from the University of Wisconsin in 1956 and was married later that year. For a time, he had an accounting office in Rhineland, Wisconsin, and with his sister, he operated the resort until 1976. When we visited Eagle River in the summer of 1986 for a Baker Company reunion that Bernie had organized, he was the Prudential agent in Northern Wisconsin and an active civic leader in the area.

Before we got to Eagle River, Joan and I had learned that this remote town in northern Wisconsin is recognized as the muskie capital of the world. And Bernie was primed with muskie stories for our benefit. I had scarcely heard the name before, and I knew nothing of the muskellunge, or muskie, as it is usually called, a form of freshwater shark, stronger and more savage than all other fish. It is found only in lakes in the North Country. After hearing several of his stories, we recognized that they were all variations on the same theme:

An unsuspecting dude, typically an Easterner, comes to Eagle River to catch a muskie, a singular if not rare achievement. Properly outfitted at a local bait store, the dude goes out on the lake. Usually, nothing happens. The muskies are not biting (some locals have fished all their lives and never seen a muskie). But even if his cast should attract this most-feared fish, the thrill may be brief. Suddenly, the muskie dives to the lake's dark, unfathomed depths and races into the distance. The fisherman's line is ripped out of his rod. The reel is steaming, too hot to touch, as smoke drifts slowly upward from it. Ruefully, the dude shakes his head, wondering what happened. And at this point, the guide may tell him he's lucky he wasn't pulled out of the boat.

This local lore fascinated us, but needless to say, we did not get a muskie during our short stay in Eagle River.

We learned from a large billboard on entering the town that Eagle River is also the self-styled snowmobile capital of the world. Hletko had been the grand marshal at the first snowmobile *jumping* contest held in Eagle River the previous winter. It was a great event with the crowd overflowing the stadium on the outskirts of town. When Bernie dropped the starter's flag, the first contestant roared down the runway, up into the air and away. It was an impressive jump, but he landed hard; and before the ambulance was able to cart him off, they learned that he'd broken both legs.

The second contestant also got off a long jump. But he landed hard as well, breaking one leg. The only other ambulance carried him away, as the next contestant crowded the starting line, revving his engine impatiently. When the grand marshall (Hletko) told him the rest of the contest was cancelled, and he was not going to go, the contestant challenged that decision, insisting that he was. It was necessary for Bernie to reach into the vehicle and pull the keys out of the dashboard to stop the show. Such was life in Eagle River, Wisconsin's Lake Woebegone.

The Baker Company reunion was a great success drawing together some twenty-five grizzled former Marines whose only common experience had been in a rifle company in Korea thirty-five years before. Included in the group were Buck Schmuck, a retired general who'd commanded 1/1, the battalion that Baker Company was in; Wes Noren who had commanded the company; and Bobby Tobin who'd been the artillery FO coming out of the Chosin Reservoir. At the time there was great enthusiasm for doing another reunion, but that has not yet come about.

We may not have gathered together again because we no longer have Hletko. Tragically, he was killed in an automobile accident on the main street in Eagle River in the summer of 1994. There's never much traffic there, and it seemed ironic that someone who had repeatedly survived a hail of enemy fire in the frozen mountains of Korea should die on a quiet street in his own hometown.

Dick Kitchen. Kitch did go to sunny Hawaii as the legal officer at Pearl Harbor, the position he was supposed to have earlier when he'd finished the junior course at Quantico. After a year in Hawaii, he was released from active duty, and he returned to Colorado, this time to practice law in Denver. In time, he became a partner in Hughes and Dorsey, counsel for the bank that owned part of the Denver Broncos, and Kitch became general counsel of the team during the halcyon days when the Broncos were a perennial Super Bowl contender.

During this period, I went to Denver to speak to the local chapter of the Lawyers Committee for Civil Rights, and before going, I called Kitch to say I would be there and ask could we meet for a drink. He said that he would like to get together, but that was the day of the NFL draft, and he would have to be in the bunker all day. But if my son—then a student at the University of Colorado—and I had time to stop by, he would be delighted to see us, and we might even find it interesting to see how the draft worked.

At the time he suggested, we checked in at the bunker, a concrete blockhouse in an industrial section of the city. It had more security than Fort Knox. And inside, with an open line to New York where the draft was being conducted, the players the Broncos expected to draft were waiting. There were lights and television cameras, and as each player was drafted as a Bronco, he would step before the cameras to be interviewed. Kitch was right; this was an experience for our son Richard, as it was for me. And Kitch reveled in it, as he did in everything about the Broncos and the Super Bowl.

Throughout his life, Kitchen was no stranger to the pressed grape. He loved women and close-harmony singing, the latter a carryover from his days as a Whiff. One night around 1990, he called to say that his singing group would be in Washington to sing in a barbershop contest at Georgetown University. Could we join him and his then-wife for dinner and listen to the singing? Sure. We did, and after the dinner and singing, we ended up at our house near midnight having a nightcap around the kitchen table. One nightcap led to another. Kitch was drinking straight vodka, and about 4:00 AM, when he said he thought it was time to go, we asked what his hurry was. Then he mentioned that he had to sing again at nine o'clock that same morning. I could hardly believe it, but of course, I drove them to their hotel without delay. That was the last time we saw him.

Kitch was frequently married. He died in February 1994, and his obituary in the *Denver Post* noted that he was survived by eight children and nine grandchildren. He was a good friend and always fun to be with. And he was a superb company commander

Tex Lawrence. After Korea, Tex served in various infantry commands in the First and Second Marine Divisions. He was in the reconnaissance business for several years as a recon company commander and in various staff positions. From 1961-1964, he was assigned to Valparaiso, Chile, as an advisor to the Chilean government in establishing a Chilean Marine Corps.

He was later in the Dominican Republic as the United States naval attaché and Vietnam in 1965 working on arrangements for the Marines' arrival in force later that year. Along the way, he studied languages at Georgetown University in Washington, D.C. and attended the Naval War College in Newport. His final tour of duty for some seven years was with the Inspector General's Office at Headquarters Marine Corps, and from there, he traveled to Marine units and installations all over the world. Tex retired from the Marine Corps after thirty years in 1979. He now lives in San Diego.

Eddie LeBaron. When he came back from Korea in 1952, Eddie rejoined the Washington Redskins where he played from 1952 to 1960, except for a season in Canada. During his time with the Skins, he played in the Hula Bowl at the end of his first season and three times in Pro Bowls. He led the NFL in passing in 1958 and was second in 1957. He also went to law school at George Washington during his last three years in Washington, graduating in 1959 and taking the California bar that same year. Some of this involved fairly tight scheduling, like when he spent all day taking the bar exam in Los Angeles on a Wednesday and flew directly to Baltimore where he played the entire game against the Colts on Friday evening.

After the 1960 season, Eddie left Washington to go into the legal side of the oil and gas business in Midland, Texas. There, when he was about to enter a law firm, he got a call from Tex Schramm, general manager of the Dallas Cowboys, then a new expansion team in the NFL.

Schramm wanted to know if he'd be interested in playing for the Cowboys, and when Eddie agreed, they traded number 1 and number 5 draft choices for him. He played four years in Dallas and practiced law there in the off-season and when not on the field. During that period, he played in a fourth Pro Bowl. When he left Dallas, Eddie moved to Nevada to work first with a company owned by Clint Murchison, owner of the Cowboys, and later with law firms in Reno and Las Vegas. He was the managing partner of the law firm founded by Paul Laxalt, later governor of Nevada, when he was recruited as general manager of the Atlanta Falcons. That was 1977, and Eddie and his family moved to Atlanta where they lived for the next thirteen years and where two of their three sons still live. Eddie became a minority stockholder in the Falcons and after the 1980 season was named NFL Executive of the Year. He was appointed to the Competition Committee of the NFL where he served for five years with Pete Rozelle, Tex Schramm, Paul Brown, and Don Shula. He was inducted into the college football Hall of Fame in 1980. When he left the Falcons, he joined a large law firm in Atlanta and represented the NFL during the labor strife of the late 1980s.

Eddie and Doralee, his wife, returned to California in 1989, the year that Eddie opened the Sacramento office for the law firm of Pillsbury, Madison, and Sutro, where he still has an office. They live in Fair Oaks, California, and Eddie's time is now devoted to developing family properties with his son and serving on various boards of directors, one public, one golf, and a number of charitable boards.

Jim Marsh. Jimmy never slacked off. After Korea, he was stationed at the Naval Academy, and then he served with the Third Marines on Okinawa and in various billets with the Second Marine Division at Camp Lejeune. After taking graduate degrees at Stanford and George Washington, he worked at Headquarters Marine Corps developing databases and computer modeling for Marine personnel. In the late 1960s, he commanded the Third Battalion, Third Marines, in Vietnam and served as the exec. officer of the Fourth Marines and as the CO of the Second Marines, again at Lejeune.

As a rising star in the Marine Corps, Jim was deep-selected for lieutenant colonel and deep-selected again for colonel over the heads of others who later achieved three- and four-star rank. But when a serious health condition recurred in 1975, he retired from the Marine Corps, many thought prematurely. It wasn't Jim Marsh's way to wait around.

After a few years with a software company in suburban Maryland, he returned to Headquarters Marine Corps in 1981. Surprisingly enough, his greatest contribution to the Corps was to come there in the years ahead. Serving in the Senior Executive Service as the principal advisor to a series of lieutenant generals who headed Manpower and Reserve Affairs, Jim is generally credited with bringing Marine Corps personnel management into the twentieth century. As one of the lieutenant generals put it,

"We signed the papers, made the statements, and testified before the Congress. But it was Jim who provided the creativity and the impetus for dynamic change. He developed the computerized system for bringing our management into the modern era and the research system to keep it constantly on track." He retired a second time in 1994 and died early in 1996.

A few years later, the Marine Corps moved all of its personnel functions from headquarters to a large modern building, newly built at Quantico. Shortly before the building was to go into service, Chuck Krulak, then Commandant of the Marine Corps, called Dottie, Jim's wife, to ask if the building could be named for Jim.

So on a warm, sunny morning in 1998, before a large crowd of his friends, including many former Marines from the battalion he'd commanded in Vietnam, the James Wesley Marsh building was dedicated. Two years later, at a reunion of the Seventh Basic Class, an oil painting of Jim waving a red scarf to draw fire so that the enemy would disclose its positions was presented by the Marsh family to the Marine Corps.

Our class has had more than its share of officers who achieved high rank and great military distinction. But no one else has had a major Marine Corps facility named for him.

Walter Murphy. While stationed at the Naval Academy after Korea, Murph earned a master's degree at George Washington University. He resigned his regular commission in 1955 and entered the Marine Corps Reserve. In 1957, he received a Ph.D. from the University of Chicago and was a fellow at the Brookings Institution. He joined the Princeton faculty in 1958. He remained in the Marine Corps Reserve until 1974, when he retired as a colonel. His final Marine Corps assignment was as a member of the adjunct faculty of the Marine Corps Command and Staff School at Quantico. At Princeton, from 1965 until his retirement in 1995, he was the McCormick Professor of Jurisprudence, a chair originally established for Woodrow Wilson. Since 1995, he has been professor emeritus at Princeton.

Over the years, Murph has written a slew of books in the fields of American and comparative politics, constitutional interpretation, judicial strategy, and public opinion He has published more articles and received more awards and academic fellowships than could be recounted here. In 1979 he published a novel, *The Vicar of Christ*, in which the central character, a law professor, is called back to active duty in the Marine Corps during the Korean War. He commanded an infantry battalion in combat, served as a presidential advisor, became chief justice of the United States, then entered a monastery as a humble monk, and finally was elected pope. Murph has some knowledge of each of these fields and somehow he managed to make the transitions plausible. The book was on the *New York Times*'s bestseller list for more than three months and was translated into French, German, Spanish, and Italian, and even "pirated by our gallant Taiwanese allies." Nonetheless, he elected to continue teaching jurisprudence at Princeton rather than leaving to write screenplays for Hollywood.

In 1993, Murph came to Washington, D.C. for the funeral of Jack Frease, a friend who had been a platoon leader in Easy Company in 1951. On June 10, 1993, forty-two years to the day after their tussle on Hill 676, Murph found himself standing with Bill Rockey at the gravesite in Arlington Cemetery as Frease's casket was lowered into the ground. Murphy thought of the matching dates over the span of years in these words:

John Millard Frease: Easy Company, First Marines

June, 1951: Northeast of Yang-gu, Southwest of the Punch Bowl
Clear blue skies, the crash of gunfire
Easy Company, First Marines, bloodies its way ahead
Three young lieutenants lead their troops over Korean Hills
Death grips their throats in cold hands

June, 1993: Northeast of Lee's Mansion, Southwest of Washington
Clear blue skies, the crash of gunfire
A red-jacketed band dirges the Marine Corps Hymn
Two old colonels tearfully salute to taps
The caisson rolls away, empty as death's cold hands.

W. F. M.

Murph and Terry, his wife, have two grown daughters. After his retirement from the Princeton faculty, they moved to the mountains above Albuquerque, New Mexico, where they now live among coyotes, bobcats, bears, and cougars, whose deliberative gatherings remind Murphy of faculty meetings at Princeton.

John Nolan. From Korea, I was ordered to the Marine detachment at the Navy Yard in Washington, D.C. While stationed there, I started law school, evening classes at Georgetown, in the fall of 1952. I transferred to full-time day school after getting out of the Marine Corps and graduated in 1955. I was a law clerk for Justice Clark at the Supreme Court of the United States during the 1955 term, and in June of 1956, I started as an associate at the Washington law firm of Steptoe & Johnson, where I am currently a partner.

In John F. Kennedy's campaign for the presidency in 1960, I recruited and managed advance men and, for the last month of the campaign, handled scheduling for the candidate as well.

During 1961 and 1962, I was asked to take on a number of short-term assignments for the White House or the Democratic National Committee while I was still at the law firm trying to practice law. The last and most extensive of those stints involved working with Jim Donovan, a New York lawyer who had arranged the release of the Cuban Brigade, the men who had landed at the Bay of Pigs in April 1961. That came to be called the Cuban Prisoners Exchange, and it stretched over several months as Donovan and I made repeated trips to Havana to obtain the release of others, including three CIA agents that Castro was holding. It also involved extensive contact with Attorney General Robert Kennedy as well as Fidel Castro. And when the last of the prisoners was released, I went over to the Justice Department as the Administrative Assistant to the Attorney General.

That was April 1963, the height of civil rights activity and desegregation in the South and a time when the Cold War was pretty hot. Robert Kennedy was active in all of this, and from the time I started until late November of that year, we were always on a fast track. I spent most of the summer of 1963 in the South, in places like Birmingham, Gadsden, and Tuscaloosa, Alabama. We were trying to see that court orders were carried out or sometimes just trying to see that people didn't get hurt. Casualties were limited, but the atmosphere was electric. From time to time, it felt more like Korea than anything else I've done.

The other part of my job involved issues like counterinsurgency and international security, where Bob Kennedy's initiatives were driving the agencies in Washington and the country teams in emerging nations around the world. After President Kennedy was assassinated, in an effort to see how those programs were working, I traveled through Latin America, Africa, the Far East, and finally around the world.

When Bob Kennedy left the Justice Department to run for the Senate, I went up to New York with him and ran the scheduling and advance for that campaign. And when he came back to Washington as a Senator, I returned to the law firm.

For several years, I advanced Bob Kennedy's foreign trips. These included the trip to Germany and Poland in 1964, South America in 1965, and the following year to South Africa for the Day of Affirmation Address at the University of Capetown. In late 1967, I went to Vietnam as special counsel to the Senate Judiciary Committee, Subcommittee on Refugees, as part of a study of civilian casualties and refugees. For me, this was a fascinating experience. My pals from Marine Corps days were by then battalion commanders or ranking staff officers, and they were enormously helpful in digging out the facts the committee was seeking, as was Army General Creighton Abrams, a friend from the South in 1963 and Germany in 1964. While we were in Vietnam, General Westmoreland was on Christmas leave, and Abrams was the commanding officer in Vietnam.

In Vietnam, we flew around in military helicopters. Occasionally, the copters would have to take evasive action, and sometimes there would be holes in the body of the plane from ground fire. This was not particularly bothersome, but I was amused to learn later that the $100,000 life insurance policy purchased for me by the United States Senate, carried a premium of $5,000 a month, the same rate journalists were paying there at that time. My experience in Vietnam was more informative than what I had been doing in Korea in 1951 and far less dangerous. In addition, I was better insured. I left Vietnam near the end of 1967, about three weeks before the Tet offensive.

In 1968, I handled the advance and scheduling again for Bob Kennedy's presidential campaign until it ended with his tragic death in Los Angeles. Then there was the funeral Mass at St. Patrick's Cathedral in New York, and the long, somber train ride to Washington's Union Station and burial at Arlington Cemetery. Once more, I returned to the law firm. Shortly after that, Larry O'Brien talked to me about going out to Chicago to work with the mayor's office for the Humphrey campaign. I liked Humphrey, but I just didn't have the heart for it. And I haven't really done anything in politics since.

In 1970, NEPA, the National Environmental Policy Act, became law, and in the fall of that year, Steptoe & Johnson was retained by Alyeska, the consortium of major oil companies formed to build and operate the Trans-Alaska Pipeline. Construction of the pipeline had been stopped cold by an injunction, and Alyeska was mired down in environmental litigation. We spent the next three years litigating that case from the Department of Interior through the Supreme Court. And with that experience as a base, I represented the automobile and coal industries in major environmental cases over the next ten years.

In 1981, I represented Ernie Fitzgerald, first of the great whistle-blowers, in two cases in the Supreme Court, and later I argued other cases in the Court on behalf of the insurance industry.

In 1987 and again in 1992, Joan and I were at Cambridge University in England where I was a Visiting Fellow for one term each time. We've had five children, four of whom are still living and married, each with two children of their own. We live in a Maryland suburb, just outside Washington, D.C.

Bob Oliver. After Korea, and two years in Hawaii, Bob was assigned to I&I duty with a Marine reserve unit in Dearborn, Michigan. I&I officers are sometimes drawn into the life of the communities where their units are located, and that was true of Bob in Dearborn.

When the Marine reserve unit picked William Ford, (now chairman of the Ford Motor Company, but then running the Lincoln Continental Division) as their chairman for Armed Forces Day, the Marines' performance knocked his socks off. Ford thought that if Oliver could do that with a reserve unit, he might be able to help the company and tried to sign him on as his administrative assistant. The job would have involved a lot more money, a new Lincoln every year, and a promising future. But Bob elected to stay with the Corps.

More intriguing was his encounter with Orville Hubbard, then the flamboyant mayor of Dearborn. At the time of the Ribbon Creek disaster in 1956, Mayor Hubbard announced that if the Marine Corps whitewashed Staff Sergeant McKeon, he—the mayor—would personally drive the Marines out of town. Since the only Marines then in town were the ones in Bob's unit, the Detroit papers sought to portray this as a clash between the mayor and the unit. The mayor was also feuding with the Episcopal Bishop of Michigan then, and he ultimately called Bob to propose a truce. He said that he couldn't fight on two fronts at the same time, and if Bob would accept the job as his chief of police, he would leave the Marine Corps alone.

But Oliver didn't go for that one either. Instead, he went to sea as the CO of the Marine detachment on the USS *Hornet*, then operating out of San Diego. Various command and staff and school assignments followed, including a tour in Vietnam where I met him in December 1967. Bob retired in 1971. After retirement, he served as a consultant for the Naval Electronics Command and worked for some ten years with the pharmaceutical industry.

Bob and Mary, his wife, had a son and a daughter and have four grandchildren. They now live in Annandale, Virginia.

Stan Olson. The Old Swede came back from Korea in early 1952 and for the next couple of years taught marine engineering at the Naval Academy at the same time that Jim Marsh and Walter Murphy were there. He admits that he actually spent most of his time then at the Officers' Club relaxing and "looking for a date." Later he resigned from the Marine Corps to enter the MBA program at the University of North Carolina. Swede says that, at that time, he was bent on self-improvement and firmly intended to spend his mornings in class and his afternoons in the library studying. But with his fly rod in the car and the waters of North Carolina so enticing, somehow classes faded into the background. Even the library was not what it cracked up to be; Stan found that he really owed it to himself to go into the stacks and read the

London Times from cover to cover each day. This may have contributed more to his understanding of world issues, and maybe even life itself, than it did to his pursuit of the MBA, and in time, Florida beckoned. Stan checked out of the school, stashed his fly rod and a case of beer in his car, and headed south.

In Orlando, Florida, the Old Swede found the position that would occupy him for the next thirty-two years—building missiles for Lockheed Martin (then called Martin Marietta.) More importantly, he found his wife, Brenda. He's had a couple of health problems, but he says that his physicians and Brenda pulled him through each time. He retired from Lockheed in 1993, and fit and feisty, he enjoys life in Orlando and remains more fun to talk with than anybody.

Chesty Puller. By the time he left Korea, Chesty Puller was no longer simply a Marine Corps cult figure. He had become a general officer, and a national military hero as well. His outspoken comments were covered in the press, because the press learned he could be counted on for a quote. He never failed. I got a strong sense of his celebrity in the summer of 1952, when the First Marine Division reunion was held over a weekend in Washington, D.C. at the Mayflower Hotel.

I was stationed then at the Navy Yard in Washington, and because I had the duty on Saturday, I went over to the Mayflower on Friday afternoon when the Marines were checking in.

In the famous Mayflower Ballroom, I found the crowd, a long receiving line of reunion Marines stretching around the ballroom and growing larger by the minute. I joined at the end of the line and, in time, found myself before the personage described in one of the newspapers of that time as "the blunt, wonderfully profane, barrel-chested little man . . . recognized as the toughest and among the bravest of all Marines."

Chesty Puller was friendly, and his greeting fairly glowed with warmth. It was a singular moment for me as I suppose it was for others like me who'd had little contact with him before and just wanted to shake his hand. This was certainly a bigger event for us than it was for him, but it was obvious that he was enjoying it too.

The next day, Saturday, I was on duty, and that night—actually about 0200 Sunday morning—I'd made the rounds of guard posts and turned in. I was in the sack in the officer of the day's office at the Navy Yard's main gate when the phone rang. When I answered, I heard a voice that sounded like it was coming out of the bottom of a gravel pit.

"Are you the officer of the day?"

"Yes, sir."

"This is General Puller. I'm calling from the Mayflower Hotel. We're having a dinner over here, and some of the boys have had a few drinks and may have gotten a little loud."

"Yes, sir."

"Well somebody here was dumb enough to call the goddamn Armed Services Police Detachment. The ASPD is here now, just outside the door. And somehow the dumb sons-a-bitches sent *Air Force* policemen! I'm just afraid that when these Marines see the *Air Force* here to quiet them down, this place'll blow! They'll have a riot on their hands! Can you get some *Marines* together and get over here to take care of this?"

"General, I wish I could. We'll do anything we can to help you. But all the Marines I have are on post right now. I can't pull them off."

I guess he understood that. He didn't press. He may have gone back to the ballroom and quelled the riot himself, as he certainly could have.

That brief, fragmentary call was my last contact with General Puller, an unforgettable voice in the night, asking for something I couldn't deliver.

In the summer of 1956, General Puller returned to Parris Island to testify for the defense in the court martial of S/Sgt. Mathew McKeon. The sergeant, a drill instructor, had taken a platoon of recruits on an unscheduled march into the surrounding marshes on a Sunday evening, and six recruits had drowned in a backwater called Ribbon Creek. The court martial was serious for the Marine Corps, as it was for McKeon. His defense was that Marine training has to be tough and realistic to train young Marines for the rigors of combat. And it was clear that Chesty Puller was the perfect spokesman for that point of view. Puller relished the opportunity. And he had no objection to coverage in the national press.

The *New York Times* story the day after his appearance rang out like a bugle call:

> "A living legend came back to Parris Island today. He is Lieut. Gen. Lewis B. (Chesty) Puller, retired, the most decorated and revered of living Marines . . . . General Puller said the night march the sergeant had led into a tidal stream had been good military tactics, and not oppression . . . .
>
> The appearance of the stubby, tenacious man with the face of an English bulldog and the chest of a pouter pigeon brought the largest crowd yet to the schoolhouse where the sergeant is on trial.
>
> Ramrod-straight, his uniform blouse ablaze with fifty ribbons, the general sat in the witness chair and testified in a drill field voice."

McKeon, had been charged with manslaughter, but he was convicted only of two alcohol-related charges and negligence resulting in death of six recruits. He was reduced to private, served three months in the brig, and left the Marine Corps. That relatively light sentence was the result of the Marine Corps finding itself and swinging around behind the rigorous recruit training policy that General Puller stood for and advocated to the McKeon court.

This was Chesty Puller's last public appearance of note. He returned to his hometown, Saluda, Virginia, where he lived in quiet retirement, visited regularly by an endless procession of Marines from all over the country. His health had declined for several years before his death on October 11, 1971. He was seventy-three.

Joe Reed. Joseph Dues Reed, or Dues as he is sometimes called, returned from Korea when I did, early in 1952. He was stationed for a year at Eighth and Eye, the Marine Corps' top ceremonial post and site of the storied evening parades, Washington's top military ceremony. On his release to inactive duty, Joe was recruited by AT&T for their executive training program. Through the years, he rose through positions of increasing responsibility in New York, Ohio, and finally Chicago where, as vice president of external affairs, he was responsible for all of the company's governmental and community affairs in the ten-state Midwest region.

I got some idea of what Joe was able to do during a crisis in 1972. A Lufthansa airliner with Robert Kennedy's son Joe aboard had been hijacked in India, and I was one of a small group that gathered with his mother, Ethel Kennedy, at Hickory Hill. For what seemed like the longest of days, we were seeking to make contact with Joe Kennedy, or with the plane.

Around noon, the plane put down at Abu Dhabi and was sitting on the tarmac there. We had a lot of resources including John Warner, then secretary of the navy, and U.S. warships in the Persian Gulf, but at the end of the day, we had made no progress in getting through to the plane or the hostages. Then, we learned that all of the hostages had been taken off the plane and were being held there in a waiting room at the airport. From the BP office in Abu Dhabi, we got the number for a telephone in the waiting room, but still we couldn't get through. Finally, we were told that the radio relay through Addis Ababa had gone down for the night, and no calls could be made until the following day.

It was at that point that I called Joe Reed, somewhere in Ohio. While I waited on the line, he called Washington and put me on with an AT&T executive who handled these kinds of special situations. After the executive got the information, he said he'd call back in ten minutes, which he did. He had gotten through to the waiting room at the Abu Dhabi airport, and they were getting Joe Kennedy to the phone. When he came on, he asked to talk with his uncle, and I handed the phone to Ted Kennedy, then standing a few feet away. After the long, frustrating day, making this connection halfway around the world in a few minutes made Joe Reed look like Mandrake the Magician. But he treated it like it was all in a day's work.

In the late 1980s, Joe retired from AT&T, and he and his wife, Marilyn, were headed for Beaver Island, in Lake Michigan, where they'd spent vacations with their family for years. It was at that point that John Sivright, another Basic School classmate of ours and then a Chicago banker, persuaded Joe to take on the reorganization of Chicago's public schools. This was an effort driven by the business and political interests in the city, the same interests that had long respected Joe for integrity and fairness. He became head of an organization called Leadership for Quality Education, and after three years of painstaking effort, they managed to begin the reorganization of the Chicago public schools, generally decentralizing the system and moving the schools to the control of local, elected school boards.

Finally, Joe and Marilyn did get to Beaver Island where they live today, except for a few months in the winter each year in Florida.

Bill Rockey. Together with Joe Reed and me, Bill left Korea on New Year's Eve, 1951, to return to the States on USS *General William Weigel.* We had been among the first in our Basic School class to get to Korea, and we're the first to come back on rotation. Bill was assigned to the tactics section, TBS, Quantico. After that, he commanded the Marine detachment on USS *Salem* and had various commands at Camp Lejeune and at the Naval Academy. During 1967-1968, he commanded a rifle battalion in Vietnam, and he later had further command and staff assignments to the time of his retirement in 1980. After retiring from the Marine Corps, Bill was an overseas representative for various U.S. corporations, serving in Saudi Arabia, in Oman, and in Cairo, Egypt. He and Anna, his wife, have been married since the day after his graduation from the Naval Academy in 1950. They have two daughters and a son and six grandchildren. Bill and Anna now live in Falls Church, Virginia.

David Shoup. Shortly after his tour as CO of The Basic School, Shoup became the fiscal director of the Marine Corps. Known as a hard man with a dollar, he was dedicated to cutting out frills and spending only for battle readiness. Later he commanded each of the three Marine divisions, and he reorganized Marine recruit training after the Ribbon Creek disaster in 1956. These achievements caught the eye of President Eisenhower who reached well down into the ranks of the general officers to tap Shoup, then fifty-four, to be Commandant of the Marine Corps, late in 1959.

As Commandant, General Shoup carried on the independent judgment and blunt, direct style that had stamped him as a service original, and he spoke to the Corps in a series of directives that he wrote out himself in longhand. His first administrative order ended on the subject of swagger sticks, a wholly unnecessary item then carried by many officers and some NCOs. Shoup thought the swagger stick was an affectation, although his directive said that it would remain optional. But he concluded by stating simply that "if you feel the need of it, carry it." Of course, swagger sticks disappeared overnight. By the next morning, there may not have been a dozen left in the Corps.

During the years General Shoup was Commandant, 1960 through 1963, I saw him a couple of times. The first occasion was a Mess Night Reunion of the Seventh Basic Class at Quantico with the Commandant as the guest of honor. This was a silver-candelabra affair, mess dress or black tie, Harry Lee Hall, toasts to Corps and Country, one of the Corps' finest traditions. The twenty or so of us from our class were almost all from the Washington, D.C. area, except for Hal Hayes, then editor of *Esquire*, who came down from New York. As you might expect, the highpoint of the evening came at the end, over Port and cigars. At the head of the long table, dark wood polished and glowing softly in the candlelight, General Shoup rose to say a few words. He talked for maybe an hour and a half, entirely off the cuff without note or the slightest hesitation, ranging widely over topics that included the Marine Corps, military affairs, and world issues. As always, he was candid, earthy, by turns ironic and funny, and, here, marvelously profane. But somehow it all made sense, and it was pure Shoup, a stunning performance. You just didn't want it to end.

The second meeting was two years later when I went to see the general on behalf of a friend who—to his great disappointment—was about to be separated from the Marine Corps Reserve. I thought he had a strong case, and I drafted it in the form of a letter to the Commandant, finishing after 9:00 one evening. Because I had to leave Washington early the next morning, I took a cab directly to the Commandant's house, where I arrived shortly before 10:00. When I rang the bell, the door was opened by a Marine orderly who said that General and Mrs. Shoup had gone out for a walk and invited me in to wait for their return. Then, as now, Eighth and Eye was in a neighborhood where not many couples would go out for a stroll at that time of night, so I was a little surprised at the orderly's statement. But I waited, and the Shoups returned shortly.

The general received my letter and brief comments about the case very cordially. He said he would read the letter that night and have someone contact me about it. I thanked him and left.

Shortly after noon the next day, a two-page response addressed to me and signed by General Shoup was delivered to my office by courier. It stated that the regulation requiring my friend's separation was necessary and that no exceptions were made for regular or reserve officers. Shoup said that he had personally examined the case, and he could find no reason for an exception, although my friend was entitled to a hearing, which he would receive. The hearing didn't work either, so the effort was unsuccessful. But I thought it had been handled by the general with fairness and extraordinary dispatch. That may have been an example of the way he did everything.

General Shoup also became a great favorite of President Kennedy. In late 1963, shortly before his assassination, Kennedy advised Shoup that he intended to name him Director of Central Intelligence when his term as Commandant was up. Later, at Shoup's retirement ceremony in the White House, President Johnson pointedly said that the general should hold himself in readiness for another important assignment—and that there would be more on that later. But there never was. Johnson must have known that Shoup was an early and vocal critic of the war in Vietnam, which he was. He was also a critic of the planning for the Bay of Pigs invasion, albeit after the fact. He had not known about the landing in advance.

General Shoup lived out his years of retirement gracefully in Washington and on his 1,900-acre working farm along the Cacapon River in West Virginia. He died early in 1983 at the age of seventy-eight. His contributions were many, and he'd had a truly extraordinary life, both before and after he was our first commanding officer in the Marine Corps.

John Sivright. From The Basic School, John was ordered to artillery training at Fort Sill, Oklahoma, and he went out to Korea later with the Eleventh Marines. He resigned from the Marine Corps in 1954 to start as a management trainee at the Harris Bank in Chicago, and in the next few years, he completed the Graduate School of Banking at the University of Wisconsin and an MBA at the University of Chicago. He rose rapidly through the ranks at the bank to become an executive vice president in 1980 and senior relationship executive in 1991, before his retirement from the bank in 1994. He was a director of the Maytag Corporation for twenty-five years, an Honorary Trustee of the Shedd Aquarium in Chicago, and an officer or director of many other organizations. John and his wife, Marion, have three children and five grandchildren. They live in Winnetka, Illinois, and Vero Beach, Florida.

Gary Spalding. Gary was our corpsman in the first platoon. He had been scheduled to be discharged from the Navy in November 1950, but when the Korean War started, his enlistment was extended for a year. On November 11, 1950, he landed in Korea and headed up to the Chosin Reservoir with the Marines.

After coming out of Korea, Gary reported to the Navy Base at Bremerton, Washington, where he was discharged on November 20, 1951. Back home, he took a job with the Missouri Highway Department and worked initially on a survey crew. Then he was transferred to the District 5 office in Jefferson City, and he worked there for almost forty years planning highways for the State of Missouri.

Gary and his wife were both at Eagle River, Wisconsin, for the Baker Company reunion in 1986. His wife, a former schoolteacher, died in 1998, and Gary now continues to live at their home in Russellville, Missouri, close to the homes of both of their daughters.

Notes

Page viii "changes that war has made in a man" and "most war memoirs come late in life": Samuel Hynes, *The Soldiers' Tale: Bearing Witness to Modern War* (Viking Penguin, 1997) 4. An excellent read for anyone considering a memoir about combat experience.

Page 3 "no division of a nation": Gregory Henderson, chapter in *Divided Nations in a Divided World*, (David McKay, 1974) 43.

Pages 3 "Asia was a seething cauldron of change": see James Stokesbury, *A Short History of the Korean War* (Quill, 1988) 30.

Page 4 "little strategic interest in maintaining": *History of the JCS III*, 13-14, cited in Clay Blair, *The Forgotten War: America in Korea, 1950-1953* (Times Books, 1987) 40.

Page 4 "Korea is a young country": Don Oberdorfer, *The Two Koreas* (Basic Books, 1997) 17.

Pages 4-5   Our presence in Korea was "untenable," "not of
                 decisive strategic importance" etc.: Blair, *supra*, 41
                 and fn. 24.

Page 6   Korea might be abandoned "whether we want it
                 or not": Senator Tom Connally interview. Blair,
                 supra, 54.

Page 6   "Mr. President, I have very serious news": David
                 McCullough, *Truman* (Simon & Schuster, 1992) 775.

Page 7   "almost unspoken acceptance . . . to meet this
                 aggression": President Harry Truman, *Memoirs II,
                 Years of Trial and Hope* (Doubleday, 1956) 334.

Page 12   "'Til Tarawa": David M. Shoup Papers, Archives,
                 U.S. Marine Corps University, Quantico, VA.

Page 13   "Friends End": *Ibid.*

Page 13   "Ship to Shore at Tarawa" (Bill): *Ibid.*

Page 14   "For him we feel a personal bond": Program, Mess
                 Night Reunion, 7th Basic Class, Harry Lee Hall,
                 Quantico, VA, 12 February 1960.

Page 15   "Your reconnaissances have to be supplemented":
                 Gil Hershey, Mimeographed Notes, TBS,
                 Quantico, VA, 1950.

Page 15   "Those sons-a-bitches won't escape me this
                 time!": Marine Corps lore re Chesty Puller.

Page 17   "It's with reluctance that I leave you men" and
                 "roared down the dusty strip": *The Sentry*, Quantico,
                 March 8, 1951.

Page 23   "We heard God speak here today": William
                   Manchester, *The Glory and the Dream: A Narrative
                   History of the United States, 1932-1972* (Little Brown,
                   1973) 563, and "a reincarnation of St. Paul," *Ibid.*

Page 23   "It's nothing but a bunch of bullshit": Walter
                   Isaacson & Evan Thomas, *The Wise Men: Six Friends
                   and the World They Made* (Simon & Schuster, 1986)
                   550.

Page 23   "the story of a family": Isaacson & Thomas, *supra*,
                   551.

Page 38   "Marines fire well from that position," "don't go
                   see the doctor" etc. More of the colorful
                   phraseology that Marine Corps lore attributes to
                   Chesty Puller.

Page 42   "Sorry, but this one was a full load": Marine Corps
                   lore re Bigfoot Brown.

Page 47   "The Peoples Volunteers blackened the
                   ridgeline": Murphy Memo.

Page 48   "Willie Hammond, a black squad leader from
                   Winona, Miss.": Murphy Memo.

Page 49   "they brought their little son along": LeBaron
                   Memo.

Pages 50-51   "In the last week of May": LeBaron Memo.

Pages 52-54, 55   "The approach march that day": Reed Memo

Pages 76-77, 79-82 "the only hairy part of taking it" and following
                   Chap. 9 quotes: Murphy Memo.

Page 77   "a steep-sided hill": 2nd Bn, 1st Marines Historical Diary for June 1951, 1-2.

Pages 83-85   "About 35 yards to our front" and following Chap. 10 quotes: Rockey Memo.

Pages 86-87   "The slaughter the NK's had earlier wreaked" and following Murphy Chap. 11 quotes: Murphy Memo.

Page 87   "It was a glorious spectacle": Bigfoot Brown ltr., June 8, 1958, cited in *U.S. Marine Operations in Korea, Vol. IV.*, p. 150. More casualties than Chosin: *Id.* 152.

Page 104   "Hill 907, a towering peak": LtGen Charles G. Cooper, *Cheers and Tears: A Marine's Story of Combat in Peace and War* (Trafford Publishing, 2002) 60.

Pages 151-153   "In early September, we moved": LeBaron Memo.

Pages 155-157   "From the bunker we had a good view": Reed Memo.

Page 160   "I sure hope they don't run out" and "the cops in Omaha will be glad": Donald Knox and Albert Coppel, *The Korean War: Uncertain Victory, Concluding Volume* (Harcourt Brace Jovanovich, 1988) 301-302.

Page 162   "Their casualties had been horrific": 2nd Bn, 1st Marines, Historical Diary, September 1951.

Page 164   "If a guy did not have the backing of his squad": Knox and Coppel, *supra*, 263.

Page 183   "the only night helicopter troop lift": See *U.S. Marines Operations in Korea*, Vol. IV, 210-212 and operation reports cited therein.

Page 217   "I really had no desire to leave": E.B. Sledge, *With The Old Breed at Peliliu and Okinawa* (Presidio Press, 1981) 171.

Page 218   "Bob Hope asks Jerry Colonna": Sledge, *supra*, 39.

Page 218   "for want of a nail": *The Oxford Dictionary of Quotations*, 5th Ed. (Oxford University Press, 2001) 600 (41).

Page 219   "Nothing in life is so exhilarating": Winston Churchill, John Bartlett, *Familiar Quotations* (Litte, Brown, 1948) 848.

Page 220   "No man is an Iland [island]": John Donne, Barlett, *supra*, 1039.

Pages 224-225   "A king does not dine": Stephen Pressfield, *Gates of Fire* (Doubleday 1998), cited in program for the Passage of Command U.S. Marine Corps, 13 January 2003.

Page 225   "We feel stronger about our traditions:" Tony Zinni, Tom Clancy and Tony Zinni, *Battle Ready* (G.P. Putnam's Sons, 2004) 142; and

                  "we probably have the greatest tolerance" and "we carry a sense of responsibility": *Ibid*.

Page 243   "A living legend came back": *The New York Times*, August 3, 1956, 1.

Sources

Anyone who compares the text of this book to the sources listed here will notice a striking disparity between the two. The text is a personal account of the Korean War over a period of several months from the perspective of a Marine rifle platoon leader. Sources listed, on the other hand, range widely from the causes of the war, through various aspects of the fighting, to the impact of the war on the world of our time. There is a reason for the disparity.

In approaching the writing of this book, all of the questions I'd not had a chance to answer earlier came back. And I found myself reading widely in an effort to get the bigger picture. In the course of that reading, I did get many answers that satisfied my interest. But the resulting information was well beyond what could be included in the limited focus of this book. I learned, for example, why the war started in June 1950 (Stalin finally agreed to the repeated pleas of Kim Il Sung to okay the invasion and to support it). I also learned why the United States, after repeatedly signaling that Korea was not essential to its defense in the Pacific, immediately moved to defend South Korea (the invasion was a naked power grab so threatening to the Cold War balance of power that it had to be confronted). And I learned something of the profound and varied impacts of the Korean War, not only well beyond the scope of this volume but deserving of separate study in their own right.

With that explanation, the following are books I read or referred to:

Acheson, Dean. *Present at the Creation*. W. W. Norton, 1969.

Ambrose, Stephen. *Eisenhower: Soldier and President*. Simon & Schuster, 1990.

Ambrose, Stephen. *Eisenhower*, Vol. 2 Simon & Schuster, 1984.

Blair, Clay. *The Forgotten War: America in Korea, 1950-1953*. Times Books, 1987.

Bussey, Charles M. *Firefight at Yechon: Courage and Racism in the Korean War*. Brassey's, 1991.

Cooper, Lt. Gen. Charles G. *Cheers and Tears: A Marine's Story of Combat in Peace and War*. Trafford Publishing, 2002.

Cumings, Bruce. *The Origins of the Korean War*, 2 vols. Princeton University Press, 1981, 1990.

Donne, John. *Devotions, XVIII*.

Eisenhower, Dwight. *Mandate for Change*. Doubleday, 1963.

Fehrenbach, T. R. *This Kind of War: A Study of Unpreparedness*. Macmillan, 1963.

Hastings, Max. *The Korean War*. Simon & Schuster, 1987.

Henderson, Gregory. *Divided Nations in a Divided World*. David McKay, 1974.

Hynes, Samuel. *The Soldiers' Tale: Bearing Witness to Modern War*. Viking Penguin, 1997.

Isaacson, Walter, and Evan Thomas. *The Wise Men*. Simon & Schuster, 1986.

Kaufman, Burton I. *The Korean War: Challenges in Crisis, Credibility and Command*. Temple University Press, 1986.

Knox, Donald. *The Korean War: An Oral History, Pusan to Chosin*. Harcourt Brace Jovanovich, 1985.

Knox, Donald, and Alfred Coppel. *The Korean War: The Concluding Volume, Uncertain Victory*. Harcourt Brace Jovanovich, 1988.

Lowe, Peter. *The Origins of the Korean War*. Longman, 1986.

Krushchev, Nikita. *Krushchev Remembers*. Little, Brown, 1970.

MacDonald, Callum. *Korea: The War Before Vietnam*. The Free Press, 1986.

Manchester, William. *The Glory and the Dream: A Narrative History of the United States*. Little Brown, 1973.

Marshall, S. L. A. *The River and the Gauntlet*. Morrow, 1953.

Marshall, S. L. A. *Pork Chop Hill*. Morrow, 1956.

Matray, James I. *Historical Dictionary of the Korean War*. Greenwood Press, 1991.

Meador, Daniel J., and James Monroe. *The Korean War in Retrospect*. University Press of America, 1998.

McCullough, David. *Truman*. Simon & Schuster, 1992.

Merrill, John. *Korea: The Peninsular Origins of the War*. University of Delaware Press, 1989.

Millett, Allan R. *Their War for Korea*. Brassey's Inc., 2002.

Oberdorfer, Don. *The Two Koreas*. Basic Books, 1997.

Pressfield, Stephen. *Gates of Fire*. Doubleday, 1998.

Ridgway, Matthew B. *Soldier: The Memoirs of Matthew B. Ridgway*. Harpers, 1956.

Stokesbury, James. *A Short History of the Korean War*. Morrow, 1988.

Talbott, Strobe. *The Master of the Game*. Alfred A. Knopf, 1988.

The Oxford Dictionary of Quotations, 5th ed. Oxford University Press, 2001.

Toland, John. *In Mortal Combat*. Morrow, 1991.

Truman, Harry S. Truman's Farewell Address. Public Papers of the Presidents, Harry S. Truman, 1945-1953.

Truman, Harry S. *Memoirs I: Years of Trial and Hope*. Doubleday, 1956.

Weathersby, Kathryn. Soviet Survey: On the Korean War. National Security Archive, George Washington University, 1966.

Weathersby, Kathryn. "New Findings on the Korean War," Translation and Commentary. *Cold War International History Project Bulletin 3*, Fall 1993.

The Seventh Basic Class

S eventh Basic was a class of newly commissioned Marine second lieutenants that started The Basic School at Quantico in the summer of 1950, shortly after the Korean War broke out. On a schedule accelerated for war, the class graduated in the spring of 1951, and most served in Korea over the next two years. By the mid-1980s, when the last career Marines were retiring, the class history was nearly complete. And a spectacular record it was, indeed.

Sometimes referred to as "the class the stars fell on," Seventh Basic had clearly rung the bell in producing eleven general officers, some five winners of the Navy Cross or the Distinguished Service Cross, and scores of officers wounded in action or otherwise decorated for their performance under fire. Included were a Commandant of the Marine Corps, P. X. Kelley; an Assistant commandant, J. K. Davis; and Lieutenant Generals Eddie Bronars, Charlie Cooper, and Dave Twomey; Major Generals Wm. Fleming, W. R. Johnson, Joe McLernan, and Hal Vincent; and Brigadier Generals Bain McClintock and A. P. McMillan. The Navy Cross winners were George Morrison, Ray Swigart, Ken Taft and Bill Yates, and Walter Murphy was awarded the DSC.

Pete Armstrong, writing from Hawaii, has suggested the following as his recollections of our time at The Basic School. I thought they succinctly captured the experience. They may be familiar to others as well.

- How self-conscious you felt that first day arriving in Quantico in "summer service A."
- Finding out what you already knew—you weren't really a second lieutenant. You pulled targets in the butts, and Sergeant Red Ebert, who ruled the butts, controlled you and—more importantly, the water supply!
- Cleaning your M-1. It was the first year they had bore cleaner. In the summer of '49, we had hot water, soap, and drying patches.
- "Mighty Mouse" Lindsey—the smallest (and probably the toughest) captain in the Marine Corps. He arrived each day immaculately turned out with a second uniform to change into in the afternoon.
- Dave Shoup and his combat poetry that sort of puzzled me. "I hate you, Bill." But we also took note that he wore the Medal of Honor.
- "Bad chits" awaiting you on your bunk for infractions concerning your bunk area.
- Captain "Quiet, Please" Collins our map reading instructor and how poorly most of us did on the map reading test.
- Master Gunnery Sergeant Bockerman who knew every infantry weapon backward and forward and inside out—and demonstrated his proficiency repeatedly.
- Three instructors with a sense of humor—Brewster, Kelly, and Miller—maybe the only ones in the Basic School. They would pull antics such as walking into the middle of one another's classes with ladders and training aids on a subject totally different from the one being taught.
- Uniform fittings with that strange man from the great city of Quantico—Al "Below the Knees" Bolognese.
- The "Greasy Spoon" for hamburgers when all else failed.
- "Combat in Built up Areas" a.k.a. Hi-Hat Lounge in D.C. a.k.a. "The Body Exchange."
- Tests on small arms. I still remember that the breach lock pin and the accelerator pin on the HMG were interchangeable. Why? Because it always appeared on tests, and I needed all the help I could get.

- Learning stealthy night entry procedures by rubber boat—only trouble was there was a sheet of ice on the Chopawamsic, and the bowman had to break the ice with his paddle. Whomp! Whomp! Whomp!
- How about our bayonet instructor—Casimir Ksycewski—"I love cold steel." Come to find out he had never been out of CONUS. Someone yelled out, "How many footballs do you have on your American Theatre Ribbon, Ski?" Lucky it was dark. The culprit was never found.
- Map exercise in the company in the defense complete with a terrain map and a walk of the position. We screwed that one up except for one guy who aced it. He later admitted that as there was a bit of rain falling; he never got out of the truck and did it all from under canvas.
- Lt. Col. Lew Walt, chief of the Tactics section, walking around observing tactical problems in the field accompanied by a brace of Boxers. One look into his steely blue eyes and you knew you were dealing with a formidable man. I found myself working for him repeatedly.
- "Mrs. General Hart"—a formidable lady. General Hart—He wanted to see that we were prepared for the Korean War, but he also wanted to have the best service football team in America. What with the likes of Eddie LeBaron, Charlie Cooper, Gene Foxworth, Bill Hawkins, Wit Bacauskas, Dave Ridderhoff, and a host of other Seventh Basicers, we fulfilled his wish.
- The Three Day War! Was it you that started the fire?—a mystery never resolved.

The Rosters, Current and In Memoriam

Following is a roster of the two hundred or so remaining from the original Seventh Basic Class in the summer of 2006. It is followed by the In Memoriam list of those no longer with us.

When compiled in former years, those thought to have departed were referred to as Fallen Comrades, and they proved difficult to list accurately. First one, then a second, and finally a third who had made the Fallen Comrades list reported in as alive and well. This led some wag to remark that the best way to ensure longevity was to get on the Fallen Comrades list. Hopefully, the list included here is more accurate.

Those given to counting will find that the numbers here do not add up to the total that started as the Seventh Basic Class. This is largely due to the existence of a third list, The Lost Patrol, those classmates with whom the class has lost contact.

For keeping track of all this, the class is indebted to Dave Hytrek, Leucadia, California, who does a superb job as Class Secretary.

Current Roster

LtCol Charles W. Abbott
Jacksonville, NC

Col James W. Abraham
San Diego, CA

Capt Birney A. Adams
Vashon, WA

Col Ernest O. Agee
Rio Vista, CA

Mr. Frank F. Alagia
North Palm Beach, FL

Mr. Ernest B. Altekruse
Chattanooga, TN

LtCol Art W. Anthony
Pismo Beach, CA

Col Peter F.C. Armstrong
Honolulu, HI

Mr. Edwin H Arnaudin, Jr.
Midlothian, VA

Mr. Harold Arutunian
Playa del Rey, CA

LtCol Howard L. Barrett, Jr.
Bedford, NH

Maj George E. Beattie
Alexandria, VA

Col Lee R. Bendell
Diamond Bar, CA

Col Robert H. Berkshire
Omaha, NE

Mr. Malcolm R. Blakeslee, Jr.
Vista, CA

Mr. F. Anthony Brewster
Madison, WI

Mr. Paul W. Brosman, Jr.
New Orleans, LA

Mr. Frederick F. Brower
Oxford, OH

LtCol Robert G. Brown
Tucson, AZ

Maj Richard K. Buchanan
DeLand, FL

LtCol Clem C. Buckley
Oak Harbor, WA

Col Thomas E. Bulger
Rockport, TX

Mr. F. Kent Burns
Raleigh, NC

LtCol John E. Buynak
Lynnhaven, FL

Mr. Robert E. Byle
Ormond Beach, FL

Mr. Gary I. Carle
Franklyn, TN

Mr. Bruce Chandler
Lake Forest, IL

Mr. Will J. Clardy, Jr.
Renton, WA

LtGen Charles G. Cooper
Falls Church, VA

Col John E. Courtney
Bloomfield Hills, MI

Mr. Randle C. Cox
Birmingham, AL

LtCol Francis C. Cushing, Jr.
San Diego, CA

Gen J. K. Davis
San Clemente, CA

Lt Rodney C. Dench
Ft. Myers, FL

Maj James J. DiNardo
Virginia Beach, VA

Mr. William T. Doughtie
Hillsboro, TX

Col Richard E. Campbell
Owosso, MI

LtCol David I. Carter
Lexington, KY

LtCol Gregory J. Cizek
Springfield, VA

Lt. Col. Harold C. Colvin
Baker City, OR

Mr. Lawrence G. Copeland
Hope Sound, FL

Mr. J. Phil Cowley
Salt Lake City, UT

Mr. James J. Creamer
Indianapolis, IN

Mr. John S. Daggett
Micanopy, FL

Col Claude E. Deering
Durango, CO

Col Birchard B. DeWitt
Oceanside, CA

Col Lawrence R. Dorsa
Oceanside, CA

Mr. William H. Duquette
Ocean City, MD

Mr. William D. Duryea
Hamilton, MA

Mr. Adolf F. Ems
Littleton, CO

Mr. Robert B. Farrell
Anaheim, CA

Mr. Leo J. Fitzpatrick, Jr.
Pittsburgh, PA

Mr. Ernest S. Friesen, Jr.
Silverthorne, CO

Mr. W. Phillip Fuller, Jr.
Columbia, SC

Mr. Hobart C. Gardiner
Southport, CT

Mr. Robert B. Gawne
Beltsville, MD

Col Jesse L. Gibney
San Diego, CA

Mr. William N. Gregory
Richmond, VA

LtCol Lawrence A. Hall
Colorado Springs, CO

Col Elwin B. Hart
Puyallup, WA

Mr. Vernon F. Eisenbraun
Greece, NY

LtCol Jack Erwin
Dallas, TX

Mr. Milton A. Fischer
Gulfport, MS

Mr. Richard D. Freeman
Corona del Mar, CA

Mr. J. Rawles Fulgham, Jr.
Dallas, TX

LtCol Walter A. Gagne, Jr.
Acton, MA

Maj Harry L. Gary
Prescott Valley, AZ

LtCol Johan S. Gestson
Kailua Kona, HI

Col John E. Greenwood
Arlington, VA

Mr. Vernon Grizzard
North Palm Beach, FL

Mr. Orville W. Hampton
Estes Park, CO

Mr. William F. Hawkins
Mount Pleasant, MI

Mr. Stanley A. Herman
Davidsonville, MD

Col William M. Herrin, Jr.
San Diego, CA

Mr. William L. Heuser
Kissimmee, FL:

Mr. Clifford J. Hofmann
Tucson, AZ

Col G. W. Houck
San Diego, CA

Mr. Helge R. Hukari
Atlanta, GA

Col David Hunter
Brevard, NC

Col David J. Hytrek
Leucadia, CA

Mr. Jack F. Ingalls
Providence, RI

Col Kenneth J. Ivanson
Redondo Beach, CA

Mr. Charles V. H. Jarman
Kaysville, UT

Mr. Albert B. Jeffers
Morristown, NJ

Mr. Kenneth C. Johnson
Bend, OR

MajGen Warren R. Johnson
Woodstock, GA

LtCol Richard E. Jones
Inverness, FL

Mr. Ralph C. Joynes
Richmond, VA

Gen Paul X. Kelley
Arlington, VA

Mr. Raymond H. Koch
Upper Saddle River, NJ

Mr. Theodore H. Kruse
Piscataway, NJ

Mr. Richard E. LaFreniere
Raleigh, NC

Col Elliott R. Laine, Jr.
Springfield, VA

Mr. Richard M. Larsen
Racine, WI

Mr. Robert L. Larson
Pepper Pike, OH

Mr. Edward N. LeBaron, Jr.
Fair Oaks, CA

Mr. Richard D. Lindow
Beverly Hills, MI

LtCol Robert A. Lindsley
Barstow, CA

Mr. John L. Lowe
Ormond Beach, FL

Mr. Nolan Lushington
Hartford, CT

Mr. Ralph F. MacDonald, Jr.
Stoneville, NC

Mr. Jimmy Magoulas
Charleston, SC

LtCol Robert B. March
Jackson, TN

Col Jerry F. Mathis
Middleburg, VA

Mr. Paul F. McBain
Alachua, FL

BrigGen Bain McClintock
Sterling, VA

Col Norman B. McCrary
Ogden, UT

Mr. Robert F. McCulloch
Washington, DC

MajGen Joseph McLernan
Panama City, FL

Col Paul G. McMahon
Springfield, VA

BrigGen Alexander F. McMillan
Tampa, FL

Col Richard D. Mickelson
El Cajon, CA

LtCol Donald C. Miller
North Bend, PA

Mr. Eric T. Miller
Bronxville, NY

Mr. Steve Minko
Carson, CA

Col Theodore F. Moellering
Irving, TX

LtCol Robert R. Montgomery
Dallas, TX

Mr. Alan F. Moreno
Buford, GA

Col Rodney B. Moss
Charlotte, NC

Col Ross L. Mulford
McLean, VA

Maj Robert J. Murphy
Newburyport, MA

Col Walter F. Murphy
Albuquerque, NM

Dr. Harvey A. B. Myers, III
Boise, ID

Mr. Hal S. Needham
Vista, CA

Mr. John E. Nolan
Bethesda, MD

Mr. Aloysius E. O'Flaherty, III
Chatsworth, CA

LtCol Robert W. Oliver
Annandale, VA

Mr. Howard B. Olson
Nashville, TN

Mr. Stanley H. Olson
Orlando, FL

Mr. John J. Oltermann
Spring, TX

Mr. Glenn E. Omholt
Oakbrook, IL

Col Peter G. Paraskos
Columbus, OH

Dr. David A. Patriquin
West Dummerston, VT

Col Jack N. Phillips
Greenwood Village, CO

Col Reagan L. Preis
San Antonio, TX

LtCol Robert E. Presson
Enterprise, AL

Mr. Kenneth F. Provost
Coventry, RI

Col H. Judd Redfield, III
Boone, NC

Mr. Joseph D. Reed
Beaver Island, MI

Mr. Grover J. Rees, Jr.
LaFayette, LA

Col Claude L. Reynolds
Roanoke, VA

Mr. James L. Rice
Newbury Park, CA

Mr. Nicholas E. Ries, Jr.
Littleton, CO

Capt Pressley M. Rixey
The Villages, FL

Dr. Edward A. Robbins, Jr.
Ocean City, MD

Col William K. Rockey
Falls Church, VA

LtCol Charles A. Rosenfeld
San Diego, CA

Mr. Donald E. Ross
Township of Washington, NJ

Col Earl F. Roth
Kissimmee, FL

LtCol George V. Ruos, Jr.
Heathrow, FL

Mr. Bryan M. Rust
Columbus, GA

Maj Adolph G. Sadeski
Canal Winchester, OH

Maj Donald B. Saunders
Drexel Hill, PA

Col Byron T. Schenn
Temecula, CA

Mr. Charles B. P. Sellar
Leesburg, FL

Mr. A. Earl Shaw, Jr.
East Greenwich, RI

LtCol Richard W. Scheppe
Owls Head, ME

Col Richard B. Sheridan
Claremont, CA

Mr. John A. Sivright
Winnetka, IL

Mr. Charles A. Sloan, Jr.
Palo Alto, CA

Mr. Erin D. Smith
Ridgecrest CA

Mr. Richard J. Smith
Indian Harbor, FL

Mr. Thomas G. Snipes
Carrolton, TX

Mr. James E. Spangler
Santa Rosa, CA

Mr. David M. Staples
Ventura, CA

Mr. John S. Steel
Harwich Port, MA

Mr. Richard B. Steinmetz, Jr.
New Canaan, CT

LtCol Richard L. Still
Louisville, MS

LtCol Harold E. Stine
Fairfax, VA

Col O. Ivar Svenson, Jr.
Punta Gorda, FL

Maj Lloyd Eugene Tatem
Annandale, VA

Mr. Richard L. Thompson
Merritt Island, FL

Mr. John M. Travis
Alexandria, VA

Dr. Richard E. Tremblay
Olympia, WA

Col George F. Tubley
Lansdowne, VA

LtGen David M. Twomey
Wake Forest, NC

LtCol Edward R. Watson
Long Beach, CA

LtCol Robert E. Wehrle
Mesa, AZ

LtCol Charles K. Whitfield
Davidsonville, MD

Mr. Robert M. Wilkins
Houston, TX

Mr. Joel D. Sugg, Jr.
Katy, TX

Mr. Anthony D. Tall
Cheshire, CT

Mr. Arvin C. Teschner
East Boothbay, ME

Maj Dallas B. Trammell
Cazenovia, NY

LtCol Marshall J. Treado
Gaithersburg, MD

Mr. Thomas G. Troxel, Jr.
Dripping Spring, TX

Mr. Taylor J. Tucker
Houston, TX

MajGen H. W. Vincent
San Juan Capistrano, CA

Maj John N. Webb
Bal Harbour, FL

Col William V. H. White
Nokesville, VA

Mr. David J. Wightman
Greensboro, NC

Mr. David W. Wilkinson
Chicago, IL

Mr. Walter G. Wilson
Greensboro, NC

Mr. Anthony H. Winchell
West Chester, PA

Mr. Edwin W. Wislar
Princeton, NJ

LtCol Fred Woeller
La Mesa, CA

LtCol Henry E. Wold
Darien, CT

Mr. J. Lew Wood
Temecula, CA

Mr. Keith L. Woods
Park Rapids, MN

LtCol Richard B. Wyatt
Grayson, CA

Maj Thomas S. Young
Pasadena, CA

Mr. Kenneth W. Younkman
Miamisburg, OH

Mr. Marvin Zelibor
Plano, TX

In Memoriam

James R. Aichele
Withold J. Bacauskas
Joe M. Barnes
Donald J. Beatty
Garland T. Beyerle
Frank R. Bonner
Alvin R. Bourgeois
James L. Bowman
Edward J. Bronars
Thomas J. Burchell
Richard H. Burnett
James B. Callahan
Donald A. Campbell
Winston D. Chapman
William F. Clarkson Jr.
Eugene T. Corcoran Jr.
William R. Corson
John R. Cowan
William E. Cross Jr.
James P. Cruise
David I. Curtis
Stanley P. Daggett Jr.
Albion C. Deane III
John C. Drenning
John D. Driggers Jr.
Tommie G. Dudley
Robert A. Eccles Jr.
Rex D. Ellison
Philip B. Ezell
William B. Fleming
Marvin J. Fournier
Eugene D. Foxworth Jr.
Harrison G. Frasier
John M. Frease
Wilson A. Frease
Winfield P. Fuller

William J. Gaylon
Joseph J. Gambardella
Walter Gibbs Jr.
Robert N. Good
Carleton D. Goodiel Jr.
Frederic A. Green
Richard T. Guidera
Robert L. Gunter
Joseph R. Gutheinz
Arthur J. Hale
Joseph W. Hall
P. H. H. Harrington
Harold T. P. Hayes
Eugene F. Hertling Jr.
John H. Hews
Sanford P. Holcomb
Winnans D. Holliday
Gilbert H. Holmes
Kenneth D. Hornbacher
Robert E. Hunter Jr.
Troy T. Hysmith
Don L. Keller
Kenneth J. Kilgore
Grover C. Koontz
Laurence D. Krentzlin
Jerod Krohn
Elmer Jenner
Ronald H. Laack
Frederick D. Leder
William Lesser
James S. Levoy
Paul S. Maeder
Thomas F. Manley
James W. Marsh
Henry V. Martin
Darrel L. McCormick

William B. McCurdy
James R. McEnarey
Thomas P. McGeney Jr.
Keith McKee
Audrey McNair
David G. Mehargue
Ira L. (Shine) Morgan
Anthony G. Morrison
Frederick M. Muer
William B. Muir
Stuart A. Munroe Jr.
Philip E. Neff
Murray L. Nelson
Neil H. Ness
Richard E. Packard
Thomas A. Palmer
J. Patrick Plunkett
David J. Pudas
Martin B. Reilly
David M. Ridderhof
Edward J. Rigby
Harvey F. Robbins
Ray C. (Bob) Roberts Jr.
Phillip E. Ruppel
Raymond M. Ryan
Henry F. Schleuter
William G. Schwefel
David E. Schwulst
Walter J. Sharpe
Leslie T. Shelton
Wiliam B. Shields
Newell D. Staley Jr.
Marvin H. Stevens
A. Malcolm Stewart
Samuel T. Stumbo
Oral R. Swigart Jr.

Kenneth E. Taft
Aubrey W. Talbert Jr.
William M. Tatum
Holcomb H. Thomas
Clinton J. Thro
James G. Todd
Andrew F. Toxey
Paul J. Uhlig
Wendell N. Vest
Paul D. Walker Jr.
Walter V. Walsh
Robert D. Whitesell
Alan C. Wilson Jr.
William B. Wilson Jr.
Richard H. Winter
James W. Wood
William T. Woodley
George W. Yates
Albert J. Zlogar
Joe F. Zuccarello

Acknowledgments

I n writing this book, I've had the support and assistance of so many that I'm humbled at the thought of recounting their essential and varied contributions.

Initially, when I talked first with Haynes Johnson and later with Jay Cantor about the possibility of doing a book on the Korean War, they were encouraging at a time when that encouragement was probably essential to my starting. Then, when I got into the actual writing, there were two giants whose continuing counsel showed me the way: Brigadier General Edwin H. Simmons (USMC retired) and Walter Murphy. General Simmons, with whom I had only slight acquaintance before this, read everything in first draft and commented succinctly, forcefully, and almost immediately on whatever I sent him. His sage counsel often opened my eyes to what was possible and held me back from major errors of organization. Walter, a valued friend for more than a half century, sent me a 38-page memo of his Korean experience. The memo was so good that my first thought was to include it in its entirety. Later, as the book developed, he commented on each draft as it was available.

Others, whose Korean experiences as rifle platoon leaders are included here, were invaluable. Charlie Cooper's account of combat on Hill 907 had been published in *Shipmate* and in his own book, but he gave freely of his time in further discussions of the experience. Eddie LeBaron, Joe Reed, and Bill Rockey responded to my inquiries in interviews as well as providing me with written accounts of what happened. Most unfortunately, Jim Marsh had died before I got around to writing, but his exploits in the First Marines were a legend I was familiar with, and Dottie Marsh, Jim's wife, provided me with selections from his letters home and the letters of George O'Connor, whom I later talked with, and additional letters from Clarence Ricker, Pfc. Scarlott, and others who served with Jim.

Beyond that, I was able to talk again with Marines in my platoon, including Howard Allmain, Bob Bradford, Marvin Burnett, Bernie Hletko, Bob Mueller, Gary Spalding, and, of course, Vic Heins, still indispensable after all these years. Joann Landry, widow of E. J. Landry, and R.J. Gustafson were considerate enough to respond in writing to my inquiries.

Over time, I'd had extensive discussions with Dick Kitchen, although he'd died before I had gotten to this book, as had Jim Cowan, the earlier Baker Company commander. After Jim's death in early February 2003, I talked with his daughter, Kendall Whitney, and some of the passages about Jim from this book were read by his son-in-law, Greg Whitney, at a memorial service for Jim in Malibu, California. I was also able to talk several times with Tex Lawrence, my fellow platoon leader in Baker Company, and with Tom Parsons, Stan Olson, and Bob Oliver who were in the First Marines during the same period, and John Sivright, who followed us to Korea a short time later.

I'm indebted to John Greenwood for guiding my approach to the Marine Corps Research Center at Quantico, to General Parks for authorizing my research there, and C. L. Grotzky, Sean Dehlinger, and Mike Miller for finding the battalion historical diaries and other records I was looking for. Dave Hytrek, who does a great job in keeping the rolls of the Seventh Basic Class current, was extremely helpful, and Pete Armstrong provided his wry recollections of The Basic School.

Similarly, John Ripley opened the doors for me at the Marine Corps Museum in Washington, D.C., and Lena Kaljot was wonderful in finding the photographs I was looking for and making them available.

Our daughter, Patti McNeill, arranged all of the photos and their captions and rearranged and edited them through a series of changes in the midst of her life already filled with active responsibilities. Then Debra Hare and Kate Sanderson final-finished the photo section. Lu Joyce typed and retyped outlines, drafts, book proposals, and summaries, seemingly without end, from the very beginning and largely resolved our vital copyediting issues. I will always be grateful for their assistance and their talents.

Clare Wolfowitz superbly edited our initial book proposal and several chapters before they were submitted to publishers. First, Robbie Lantz and, later and more extensively, Don Gastwirth, provided support and encouragement in acting as agents for this book. I very much appreciate their efforts and the top quality of their representations.

Finally, anyone who has ever been involved in writing a book knows how important the role of a spouse is. It requires tolerance, understanding, and infinite patience. Joan had all of these qualities and much, much more. While always supportive, she was also direct and candid. And her judgment—especially about personal aspects of the effort—was and is flawless. I could never thank her enough.

Index

Murphy, Walter, 18-19, 24, 47-48, 56, 73, 76-82, 86-88, 94, 219, 223, 235-237, 240

Needham, Hal, 33

Ness, Neil, 29, 33

Nickerson, Herman, 50

No Name Line, 36, 39

Nolan, Joan, 9, 17-19, 126, 209, 230, 239

Nolan, John (significant references): June 9 firefight, 62-72; minefield recovery operation, 110-114; combat patrol to Hill 467, 170-181; return to States, 214; afterward, 237-239

Noren, Wes, 140, 226, 231

O'Brien, Larry, 239

Oliver, Bob, 10, 21, 27-29, 33, 45, 137, 194, 211, 239-240

Olson, Stan, 29, 45, 101, 127, 133, 211, 240-241

Olterman, John, 21, 29, 194

Operation Blackbird, 88, 183

Oran-ni (Murphy's Frog Town), Korea, 56, 77

Pak Yon Kun "Parks," 93, 99, 143, 146-150, 210, 217

Parsons, Tom, 100, 133, 134, 160

Pressfield, Steven, 225

Puller, Lewis Burwell "Chesty," 15-17, 29, 33, 38, 42, 226, 241-243

Punch Bowl, 143, 151, 153, 154, 158-159, 161, 183, 236

Pusan, Korea, vii, 1, 14, 22, 27-31, 105

Raggedy-Ass Marines (song), 52, 131-132

Reed, Joe, 10, 19, 21, 22, 25, 27, 29, 33, 45, 52-55, 94, 100, 126, 127, 128-129, 137, 154-157, 167, 193, 205, 209, 211, 213-214, 222, 243-245

Reed, Marilyn, 19, 212, 214, 244-245

Rhee, Syngman, 4, 5, 150

Ricks, Tom. 224

Ridderhoff, Dave, 21, 261

Ridgway, Matthew (Gen USA), 95-96

Ripley, John, 226

Robatin, Mike, 53

Roberts, Doc (corpsman), 82

Rockey, Bill, 10, 73-75, 82-85, 87-88, 94, 127, 165-166, 183, 214, 219, 223, 236, 245

Rockey, Keller (MajGen), 74

Roll the Gook (a game), 86-87

Roosevelt, Franklin (President), 2

Rozelle, Pete, 234

Rusk, Dean, 2-3

Schmuck, Donald "Buck," 132, 135, 226, 231

Schramm, Tex, 233-234

Scott, Bobby, 126, 128-129

Seintan-ni, Korea, 204

Seventh Basic Class, ix, 10, 13, 21, 29, 48, 88, 235, 246, 259-274

Ship to Shore at Tarawa (Bill), poem, 13

Shoup, David M., 11-14, 16, 226, 245-247

Shula, Don, 234

Silverthorn, Merwin (LtGen), 16

Simmons, Edwin (BGen), 226

Sivright, John, 10, 244, 247-248

Spalding, Gary (corpsman), 68, 248

Stalin, Joseph, 4, 6

Stamm, S/Sgt, 37

Steptoe & Johnson, 237-239